KT-485-683

$14.75

# *Rules for Writers*
## A BRIEF HANDBOOK

# *Diana Hacker*

A BEDFORD BOOK
ST. MARTIN'S PRESS ♦ NEW YORK

For information, write St. Martin's Press, Inc.,
175 Fifth Avenue, New York, NY 10010
*Editorial Offices:* Bedford Books of St. Martin's Press,
29 Commonwealth Avenue, Boston, MA 02116

ISBN: 0–312–69585–3

*Typography:* Claire Seng-Niemoeller

*Cover design:* Richard Emery

## Acknowledgments

Russell Baker, from "From Song to Sound: Bing and Elvis," copyright © 1972
by The New York Times Company, and from "Poor Russell's Almanac," copyright © 1977 by The New York Times Company. Reprinted by permission.

Alan Brinkley, from *Voices of Protest: Huey Long, Father Coughlin, and the
Great Depression.* Copyright © 1982 by Alan Brinkley. Reprinted by permission of Alfred A. Knopf, Inc.

Jane Brody, from *Jane Brody's Nutrition Book.* Copyright © 1981 by Jane E.
Brody. Reprinted by permission of W. W. Norton & Company, Inc.

Bruce Catton, from "Grant and Lee: A Study in Contrasts," *The American
Story,* Earl Schenck Miers, editor. © 1956 by Broadcast Music, Inc. Reprinted
by permission.

Napoleon A. Chagnon, from *Yanomamo: The Fierce People.* Reprinted by permission of Holt, Rinehart and Winston, Publishers.
*(Continued on page 396.)*

# *Preface for Instructors*

When I began writing this book, I had been teaching long enough to know just what I wanted in a handbook. Like many of my colleagues, I teach five classes a semester, each with twenty-five students of varying abilities, so there is all too little time for individualized grammar lessons. I wanted a handbook so clear and accessible that my students could learn from it on their own. I had in mind a book that would give students what they seem to prefer—straightforward, unambiguous rules—but without suggesting that rules are absolutes or that writing well is simply a matter of following the rules.

Further, though I preferred a brief, quick reference, I wanted a handbook comprehensive enough to address the full range of problems that crop up in my students' drafts. And because my students have such a wide range of abilities, I hoped for a book that would be useful for all of them, offering a little help or a lot of help depending on their needs.

Finally, I envisioned a handbook that would support the philosophy of composition that I work so hard to convey in the classroom. Writing is a process, I tell my students, and revision is central to that process. Revision is not a punishment for failing to get things right the first time. Nor is it a perfunctory clean-up exercise. It occurs right on the pages of a rough draft, often messily, with cross-outs and insertions, and it requires an active mind: a mind willing to look at a draft from the point of view of the reader, to spot problems, and to choose solutions.

With these aims in mind, then, I began writing this book. And it was with them in mind that I rewrote it again and again, with each draft edging closer to my vision. Three years later, *Rules for Writers* has emerged from my typewriter for the last time. The book comes as close as I could make it to what I wanted it to be. Here are its principal features.

***Comprehensive coverage and compact format.*** To make *Rules for Writers* brief, I have limited myself within each section to the essentials: straightforward rules backed up by concise explanations, realistic examples, and brief comments on examples. In its coverage, however, the book is complete. It is a guide to the full range of conventions of grammar, punctuation, mechanics, and usage as well as to the writing process, paragraphs, style, diction, logic, the research paper, business letters, and résumés. The chapter on the research paper includes both the new MLA system of parenthetical citations and the traditional system of footnoting.

***Hand-edited sentences.*** Most examples appear as they would in a rough draft, with handwritten revisions made in color over typeset faulty sentences. Unlike the usual technique of printing separate incorrect and corrected versions of a sentence, hand-edited sentences highlight the difference between the two versions and suggest how extensive a change is required. Further, hand-edited sentences mimic the process of revision as it should appear in the students' own drafts.

***An organization reflecting the writing process.*** *Rules for Writers* moves from the whole paper and paragraphs through sentence rhetoric and diction to grammar, punctuation, and mechanics. This organization puts the stages of the writing process in context, thereby showing students when—as well as how—to revise and edit their drafts.

***An emphasis on rules.*** As its title suggests, *Rules for Writers* focuses on rules rather than on grammatical abstractions. Though abstract section headings such as "parallelism" and "agreement" are understandable to instructors, they are not always clear to students. Rules such as "Balance parallel ideas" and "Make subjects and verbs agree" are clearer because they both identify the problem and tell students what to do about it.

Handbooks are by their very nature prescriptive, but that does not mean they must be unbending. Like other modern handbooks, *Rules for Writers* alerts students to levels of formality, rhetorical options, and current standards of usage. It distinguishes between rules intended as rhetorical advice and those that are more strictly matters of right and wrong.

***A problem-solving approach to errors.*** Where relevant, *Rules for Writers* attends to the linguistic and social causes of errors and to the effects of errors on readers. The examples of errors in the text are realistic, most having been drawn from student papers and local newspapers. The text treats these errors as problems to be solved, often in light of rhetorical considerations, not as violations of a moral code. Instead of preaching at students, it shows them why problems occur, how to recognize them, and how to solve them.

***Full explanations for students who need them.*** Because *Rules for Writers* highlights rules and examples, it provides quick answers for students who need nothing more. But students who need more help will find it. Throughout the text, they will find extra help in full explanations following rules and in analytical comments pegged to examples. They will also find it in Part IX, Grammar Basics, which includes fuller-than-usual descriptions of grammatical concepts and terms used elsewhere in the book. This part appears near the end of the book, not at its beginning, because it serves as a reference source within a reference book. Many of the earlier sections of the book are cross-referenced to it.

***A unique section on nonstandard English.*** Part VI, Editing for Standard English, is devoted to written errors caused by the speech patterns of nonstandard English. Students who need help with matters such as omitted -*s* and -*ed* endings will find a detailed description of important differences between standard and nonstandard English. The technique of contrastive analysis pinpoints just where problems are likely to arise, and it helps prevent students from hypercorrecting as they struggle to meet the demands of standard English.

***Extensive exercises, some with answers.*** At least one exercise set accompanies nearly every section of the book. Most sets begin with five lettered sentences whose answers appear at the back of the book so that students may test their understanding independently. The sets then continue with ten numbered sentences whose answers appear only in the Instructor's Manual, so that instructors may use exercises in class or assign them for homework.

***Instructor's manual.*** All exercise sentences not answered in the book are reproduced in the 8½″ × 11″ Instructor's Manual, making it easy for instructors to duplicate them for classwork or assignments. Answers to these exercises are of course included in the manual as well.

## Acknowledgments

In the three years of its making, this book has been reshaped, refined, amended, repaired, smoothed, tightened, and polished—all with the help of a great many professionals to whom I owe more than perfunctory thanks. For helping me to see the book as a whole, to re-envision it again and again, and finally to fine-tune it, thanks go to an unusually perceptive group of reviewers: Richard S. Beal; Elaine Bell, Harcum Jr. College (Bryn Mawr, PA); Mark Branson, Davidson County Community College (Lexington, NC); Peggy Broder, Cleveland State Univ.; Barbara Carson, Univ. of Georgia; Ruth Foreman, South Dakota State Univ.; George Gadda, UCLA; Polly Glover, Univ. of Tennessee–Martin; Gary Hall, North Harris County College (Houston, TX); Malcolm Kiniry, UCLA; Donald A. McQuade, Queens College; Michael Meyer, Univ. of Connecticut; Carol Niederlander, St. Louis Community College–Forest Park; Hephzibah Roskelly, Univ. of Louisville; Robert Schwegler, Univ. of Rhode Island; Judith Stanford, Merrimack College; Warren Westcott, Francis Marion College (Florence, SC); and Kristin Woolever, Northeastern Univ.

Special thanks are due to the people at Bedford Books: to Charles Christensen for his confidence and his wise and expert counsel; to Joan Feinberg for patiently coaching me from draft to draft, always with intelligence, grace, and good humor; to Sue Warne for taking an active interest in all aspects of the book—from its design to its grammar—while guiding it through production; to Karen Henry for helping with the exercises and for a variety of improvements throughout the text; and to Claire Seng-Niemoeller for designing clean, uncluttered pages that highlight the book's hand-edited sentences.

For their assistance with the research paper chapter I would like to thank William Peirce, who drafted it, and Lloyd Shaw and Charmaine S. Yochim, who served as consultants. I am also grateful to Nancy Lyman, Christine Rutigliano, Eileen Shakespear, and Carol Verburg for a variety of contributions; and to copy editor Barbara Flanagan for bringing consistency and grace to the final manuscript.

Finally, a note of thanks goes to my parents and to Joseph and Marian Hacker, Robert Hacker, Tom Henderson, Robbie Nichols, Paul O'Connell, Greg Tarvin, and the Dougherty family for their support and encouragement; and to the many students over the years who have taught me that errors, a natural by-product of the writing process, are simply problems waiting to be solved.

D.H.
*Prince Georges Community College*

# Introduction
# to Students

Though it is small enough to hold in your hand or to tuck into a hip pocket, *Rules for Writers* will answer just about all of your questions about the rules of English. It is brief only because it limits itself to the essentials: straightforward rules, concise explanations, and clear examples.

## The plan of the book

As a glance at the table of contents will show you, *Rules for Writers* is organized to reflect the writing process. Advice about the whole paper and paragraphs comes first, followed by strategies for revising and editing sentences.

In Part I, Writing and Revising the Whole Paper, you will find advice about generating ideas, sketching a plan, roughing out an initial draft, and making major revisions. After this overview of the writing process, the book turns in Part II to paragraphs, showing how to focus them, how to develop them, and how to link sentences to one another to create a smooth flow.

Part III, Revising Sentences, and Part IV, Changing Words, discuss flaws in style or readability that frequently occur in a rough draft. There you will discover how to identify and revise away such problems as dangling modifiers, distracting shifts, and wordy sentences.

The next two parts move on to matters of grammar and standard English. Part V, Editing for Grammar, treats the grammatical errors that can mar a rough draft—errors such as sentence fragments, comma splices, and faulty subject and verb agreement. Part VI, Editing for Standard English, deals with a special category of grammatical errors: problems such as omitted *-s* and *-ed* endings that are caused by the speech patterns of nonstandard English.

Part VII, Editing for Punctuation, covers all of the basic comma rules, along with the major uses of the other marks of punctuation. Part VIII, Editing for Mechanics, treats problems with abbreviations, numbers, italics, spelling, the hyphen, and capital letters. Also included is a section explaining how to prepare a manuscript.

Part IX, Grammar Basics, is a short course in grammatical concepts and terminology. If you are already familiar with subjects, verbs, direct objects, subordinate clauses, and so on, you can safely ignore these pages except when the meaning of a term used elsewhere in the book is unclear. If your background in grammar is weak, however, these should be among the first pages you turn to. You'll be able to use the rest of this handbook more quickly and accurately once you are familiar with the basics.

Part X is devoted to special types of writing. There you will find a full section describing the steps involved in writing a research paper, along with a sample paper; a section on logic in argumentative essays; and a practical guide to business letters and résumés.

At the end of the book is a Glossary of Usage, which lists alphabetically many common problems in word choice. The choices given are those generally preferred by educated speakers and writers of English.

Throughout this handbook you will find exercises that provide practice in revising and editing sentences. Most exercise sets begin with five sentences lettered from *a* to *e* and conclude with ten sentences numbered from *1* to *10*. Answers to the five lettered sentences appear in an appendix at the end of the book, allowing you to test your understanding of the material.

## How to find information

When you are revising a paper that has been marked by an instructor, tracking down information is simple. If your instructor marks problems with a number such as *16* or a number and letter such as *12c*, you can turn directly to the appropriate section of the handbook. Just flip through the colored tabs on the upper corners of the pages until you find the number in question. The number *16*, for example, leads you to the rule "Tighten wordy sentences," and 12c takes you to the subrule "Repair dangling modifiers." If your instructor uses an abbreviation such as *w* or *dng* instead of a number, consult the list of abbreviations and symbols inside the back cover of the book, where you will find the name of the problem (wordy, dangling modifier) and the number of the section to consult.

When consulting the handbook on your own, you may find information in several ways. The alphabetical index at the back is usually the fastest and most reliable way to find what you're looking for. As you become familiar with the overall plan of the book, however, you can also make use of the full table of contents at the beginning of the book or of the brief table of contents inside the front cover. And as you become accustomed to the headings at the tops of the pages next to the colored tabs, you may be able to find information simply by flipping.

Many sections of the handbook contain cross-references to other sections of the book. Most of these will lead you to specific sections in Part IX, Grammar Basics, where you will find a discussion of grammatical concepts and terminology necessary for understanding many of the rules in the rest of the book. Whenever the book uses a grammatical term that you don't fully understand, you can also track down its meaning by consulting the list of grammatical terms inside the back cover.

## The process of revision

*Rules for Writers* shows you how to improve sentences the way practicing writers do it—by working directly on a rough draft version of the paper. Instead of making corrections as you recopy sentences and paragraphs, try marking up your drafts with cross-outs and insertions. This technique gives you better control over your sentences, and it saves you time as well. To see what a marked-up draft looks like, turn to the sample paper on pages 29–32 or flip through the central sections of this book, which are illustrated with sentences that look just like those in a carefully revised draft.

# Contents

## *Part II*

## *Part III*

# *Part IV*

# *Part V*

## Part VI

# *Part VII*

## *Part VIII*

## Part IX

## Part X

# Writing and Revising the Whole Paper

Since it's not possible to think about everything all at once, most experienced writers take a paper through drafts. They begin by generating ideas mentally, on scratch paper, or through nonstop, uncensored writing. When they feel ready to attempt an initial draft, they rough it out imperfectly, concentrating more on content than on style, grammar, and punctuation. If possible, they then get away from the draft for a while.

For the experienced writer, revising is rarely a one-step process. The larger elements of writing generally receive attention first — the focus, supporting material, organization, paragraphing, point of view, and overall tone. Improvements in sentence structure, word choice, grammar, punctuation, and mechanics come later.

Of course the writing process does not always occur quite as simply as just described. While revising, for example, the writer may find it necessary to generate more ideas and draft new material. The process, in other words, is recursive: It moves from stage to stage but circles back to earlier stages whenever the need arises.

# 1

## Generate ideas and sketch a plan.

Try putting some ideas on paper before even attempting a first draft. Those ideas might be suggested by the writing task itself, such as a specific college assignment or a technical report required on the job. Or they might come from your own interests, experiences, values, and insights on topics you choose for yourself.

**1a**  Work from a list of specifics.

To avoid getting stuck somewhere in the middle of a draft wondering what to write next, first jot down a list of specifics. Many writers use questions — such as the journalists' Who? What? When? Where? Why? — to help them generate such lists.

For example, after asking herself, "What steps can the average homeowner take to conserve energy?" one writer jotted this list:

> install storm windows
> blow insulation into the attic and walls
> caulk and weatherstrip
> purchase insulated draperies or shades
> lower the thermostat at night
> set the hot water heater at a moderate temperature
> run the dishwasher only when full
> use the cold water cycle of the washing machine
> install glass doors on fireplaces

The suggestions appear here in the order in which they first occurred to the writer. When she began drafting the actual paper, she felt free to rearrange them, to cluster them into more general categories, to drop some, and to add others. In other words, she treated her list of specifics as a source of ideas and a springboard to new ideas, not as a formal outline.

**1b**  Experiment with ways of clustering specifics.

For a short paper, a simple list of specifics can serve as a rough outline, but for essays of any length it is best to cluster specifics into more general categories. If more than one method of organizing the information is possible, consider the options. For example, the woman who jotted ideas on conserving energy could cluster them into categories labeled "inexpensive," "moderately expensive," and "expensive." Or she might decide to use the house itself as a principle of organization or to group her suggestions according to the amount of labor they involve. Once she has thought about these various options, the writer can then make an informed choice.

Groups of specifics can become a preliminary sketch of the design of a paper. Here, for example, is one writer's early blueprint for a paper on the limitation and disposal of nuclear waste.

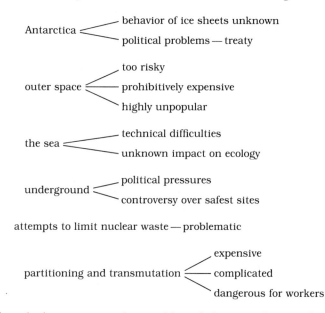

where to dispose of nuclear waste — no locations look good

Antarctica
- behavior of ice sheets unknown
- political problems — treaty

outer space
- too risky
- prohibitively expensive
- highly unpopular

the sea
- technical difficulties
- unknown impact on ecology

underground
- political pressures
- controversy over safest sites

attempts to limit nuclear waste — problematic

partitioning and transmutation
- expensive
- complicated
- dangerous for workers

Though this tentative plan could easily be turned into a formal outline, such outlines are rarely necessary early in the writing process. Formal outlining is more likely to be helpful later, when the writer is ready to make relatively firm decisions about the arrangement of a paper's parts. (See 1d.)

## 1c Settle on a tentative focus.

The focus of an essay is its central idea. For many types of writing, the central idea can be summed up in one sentence, a generalization covering all of the specifics that will be brought up in the paper. Such a sentence, which ordinarily appears in the paper itself, most likely in its opening paragraph, is called a *thesis.* A successful thesis — like those below, all taken from articles in *Smithsonian* — points both the writer and the reader in a definite direction:

> Though the Soviet leadership has decided to write off Andrei Sakharov as "cuckoo," they cannot erase his remarkable scientific achievements.

> Much maligned and the subject of unwarranted fears, most bats are harmless and highly beneficial.

> Geometric forms known as fractals may have a profound effect on how we view the world, not only in art and film but in many branches of science and technology, from astronomy to economics to predicting the weather.

> Aside from his more famous identities as colonel of the Rough Riders and President of the United States, Theodore Roosevelt was a lifelong professional man of letters.

The thesis sentence usually contains a key word or controlling idea that limits its focus. The sentences above, for example, will lead into paragraphs that focus on Sakharov's *scientific* achievements, the *beneficial* aspects of bats, the *effect* of fractals on how we view the world, and Roosevelt's identity as a writer or a *man of letters.*

It is a good idea to formulate a thesis early in the writing process, perhaps by jotting it on scratch paper, by putting it at the head of a rough outline, or by attempting an introductory paragraph. But be prepared to reformulate the thesis later, if necessary, as your drafts evolve. As you do so, keep in mind that a thesis should be

1. more general than the material supporting it,
2. limited enough to be supported in the space allowed, and
3. an accurate summary of the true thrust of the paper.

For some types of writing, it may be difficult or impossible to express the central idea in a thesis sentence; or it may be unwise to put such a sentence in the paper itself. A personal narrative, for example, may have a focus too subtle to be capsulized in a single sentence, and such a sentence could well ruin the story. Strictly informative writing, too, such as that found in many business memos, may be difficult to summarize in a thesis. In such instances, do not try to force the central idea into a thesis sentence. Instead, think in terms of an overriding purpose, which may or may not be articulated in the paper itself.

## 1d Settle on a tentative plan.

Once you have listed specifics, clustered them informally, and formulated a tentative thesis, you may want to construct an outline. The outline might be informal, consisting perhaps of the thesis written at the top of a list of clustered specifics, but for complex writing tasks a formal outline will provide a clearer blueprint.

The following outline, based on the writer's earlier rough sketch (see 1b), brought order to the complexities of a difficult subject, the various methods for limiting and disposing of nuclear waste.

Thesis: Although various methods for limiting or disposing of nuclear wastes have been proposed, each has serious drawbacks.

I. Limiting nuclear waste: partitioning and transmutation
   A. The process is complex and costly.
   B. Radiation exposure to nuclear workers would increase.

II. Antarctic ice sheet disposal
   A. Our understanding of the behavior of ice sheets is too limited.
   B. An international treaty prohibits disposal in Antarctica.

III. Space disposal
   A. The risk of an accident and resulting worldwide disaster is great.
   B. The cost is prohibitive.
   C. The method would be unpopular at home and abroad.

IV. Seabed disposal
   A. Scientists have not yet solved technical difficulties.
   B. We do not fully understand the impact of such disposal on the ocean's ecology.

V. Deep underground disposal
   A. There is much political pressure against the plan from citizens who do not want their states to become nuclear dumps.
   B. Geologists disagree about the safest disposal sites.

In constructing an outline, keep the following guidelines in mind:

1. Put the thesis at the top.
2. Make items on the same level of generality as parallel as possible.

   In the sample outline, all of the Roman numerals state methods of limiting or disposing of nuclear waste, and all of the capital letters state drawbacks. *Caution:* If your material cannot honestly be presented in such perfectly parallel fashion, do not force it.

3. Use sentences unless phrases are clear.

In the sample outline, phrases were clear enough for the major categories, but the writer felt that sentences were necessary in stating the drawbacks of each method.

4. Use the conventional system of numbers and letters for the levels of generality.

I.
   A.
   B.
      1.
      2.
         a.
         b.
            (1)
            (2)
               (a)
               (b)
II.

5. Always use at least two subdivisions for a category.

If a subject is divided, logically it must have at least two parts. When you are tempted to use a 1 without a 2 or an *a* without a *b*, either incorporate the idea into the level of generality immediately above it or omit it from the outline.

6. Limit the number of major sections in the outline.

If the list of Roman numerals grows too long, find some way of clustering the items into more general categories. In the sample outline, for example, the writer might have decided to treat the two methods for limiting nuclear wastes separately, in which case he could have reduced the major sections to two:

I. Limiting nuclear wastes
   A. Partitioning
   B. Transmutation
II. Disposing of nuclear wastes
   A. Antarctic ice sheet disposal
   B. Space disposal
   C. Seabed disposal
   D. Deep underground disposal

7. Be flexible.

   Do not feel that if you have two points under Roman numeral I you must have an equal number of points beneath the other Roman numerals. Also, do not assume that every bit of material that will come up in the paper itself must be specifically covered in the outline. In the sample outline, for example, the writer does not attempt to describe the various methods of disposing of nuclear wastes, though such descriptions will certainly appear in the paper.

## 1e Explore your purpose and audience.

Your general purpose will often be dictated by the specific task that faces you. Perhaps you have been asked to take minutes for a club meeting, to draft a letter requesting payment from a client, or to describe the results of an experiment in biology. Even though your overall purpose is fairly obvious in such situations, exploring that purpose can deepen your insights. How detailed should these minutes be, for example? Is your purpose to summarize the meeting, or is it to establish a careful record of discussion in case future controversies arise? How firm should the letter requesting payment be? Do you need the money at all costs, or do you hope to get it without risking loss of the client's business? How detailed and how technical is the biology report expected to be?

In writing situations less structured than those just mentioned, exploring your purpose becomes even more important. In unstructured situations, such as those you may face in a composition class, part of the challenge of writing is discovering a purpose. Though no precise guidelines will lead you to a purpose for putting words on paper, you might begin by asking whether you hope to inform readers, to persuade them, to entertain them, or to call them to action. And such questions will bring you to another important question: Just who are those readers?

On the whole, it is easier to write for a specific and known group of readers such as colleagues at the office than for a general and unknown audience such as readers of a national newspaper. To explore a known audience, you can ask yourself some fairly specific questions. What values, for example, do your readers hold? What interests do they share with you? How close a relationship with them can you safely assume?

The less known your readers are, the more important it is to explore any unconscious assumptions you may be making about them. The choices you make as a writer will reveal your sense of audience — how educated you assume them to be, for example — so it is best to make conscious decisions at the outset. The following questions will help you make such decisions.

How well informed are these readers about the subject?

How interested and attentive are they likely to be?

Will they resist any ideas in the essay?

How sophisticated are they as readers? Do they have large vocabularies? Can they process long and complex sentences?

Even if your audience is so unknown that you can't honestly answer such questions, you must still make decisions about these matters, even if this means creating an audience that is in some sense a fiction.

In college composition classes, you are rarely presented with a real audience. Your instructor will read the paper, of course, but he or she should not be your audience. Essays aimed only at the instructor are cut off from the real world, written in a vacuum. Unless an assignment supplies you with an audience, therefore, you will need to invent one. Decide what group of people might reasonably be informed, persuaded, entertained, or called to action by what you have to say. Then aim the paper in their direction.

### EXERCISE 1 – 1

Generate a list of at least fifteen items for one of the following topics.

1. Violence in music videos
2. Television's approach to the news
3. The disappearance of childhood in the late twentieth century
4. Reinstituting a military draft
5. A bilateral nuclear freeze

### EXERCISE 1 – 2

Review the list you generated in Exercise 1 – 1 and cluster the items into categories.

### EXERCISE 1 – 3

Write a focused thesis statement for two of the following topics.

1. The problem of gentrification in major American cities
2. Failing public school systems
3. Stress and single mothers
4. The emphasis on competition in education
5. The arms race in space (space wars)

## EXERCISE 1–4

Organize the following list of items into two rough outlines, each with a different thesis. If some items do not support the thesis, eliminate them; if you can think of other items that do, add them.

Topic: The growing influence of computers on our daily lives

Automatic banks
Personal computers installed in every dorm room in colleges
Computers in grade schools
Computer literacy as a job requirement in many fields
Computers in scholarship
Computer games
Isolation of many "hackers"
Mechanization of society
Fear of computers
Robots
Liberal arts education made obsolete by computers
Computer cash registers in stores
Robot actors at Epcot Center and Disneyworld
Revenge of computers as the subject for science fiction films
Computer dating
Computers eliminating jobs
Computers eliminating tedious work

## EXERCISE 1–5

Revise the following outline. Make items on the same level of generality parallel wherever possible; if a category is subdivided, make sure that there are at least two subdivisions; rearrange items to ensure a coherent, logical development from one point to the next.

Thesis: Government should do whatever possible to relieve the inordinate amount of stress placed on single mothers in America.

I. Economic hardships
   A. Women earn $.59 for every $1.00 men earn in comparable jobs.
   B. Women with small children must pay for day care in order to work.

   C. A mother's emotional relationship with her children is often fraught with tension because of stress.

II. Physical stress
   A. Job, child care, and housework combined demand too much energy day after day.

III. Emotional hardships
   A. Most single mothers do not have enough time to develop significant relationships with friends and possible mates.
   B. Single mothers do not have enough time to devote to careers or to education, so there is often no hope of advancement to better-paying jobs.

IV. Response of single mothers to their situation
   A. All single mothers interviewed for this study agree that they live with too much stress.
   B. By the year 2000, 99 percent of those living at or below the poverty level will be women (most of them single mothers) and their children.

V. Possible solutions to the problem
   1. Exercise programs for single mothers (to relieve tension)
   2. Federally or state-funded health, car, life, and homeowner's insurance programs to protect single mothers and their children
   3. A constitutional amendment passed and enforced to ensure equal pay for equal work regardless of gender
   4. Private, state, or federal funding (or a combination of all three) of day care for the children of women who work
   5. Federal or state funding for educational and job-training programs for single mothers

# 2

## Rough out an initial draft.

As long as you treat an initial draft as a rough draft, you can focus your attention on important matters, knowing that problems with sentence structure and word choice can always be dealt with later. Your major concerns for most writing tasks will be your audience and your subject.

## 2a Keep your audience in mind.

As they head into a draft, writers too frequently forget their audience. Consider, for example, one dentist's postcard reminder to his patients, sent out twice yearly:

> It is the custom of this office to notify patients on record, for periodical examination of the mouth. This service is rendered to safeguard previous work and to ensure future good health and appearance. May I suggest you call.

Not surprisingly, the dentist got a better response when he decided to address his audience directly:

> Things to do today:
> 1. Floss.
> 2. Call your dentist.
> It's time again for your regular dental checkup, so please call today for an appointment.

The new version, simple and clear, is easier to read. And it has a human voice behind it, one that speaks out directly, person to person, in a tone appropriate to the dentist's audience.

Keeping your audience in mind, then, will help you adopt an appropriate tone. It will also help you make a variety of other choices. Assume, for example, that you are writing an instruction booklet for machinists at Caterpillar Tractor Company. You are considering two ways of structuring a sentence, both of which are perfectly grammatical. In light of your audience, however, which one do you choose?

Move the control lever to the reverse position after the machine stops.

After the machine stops, move the control lever to the reverse position.

Once you've envisioned machinists with the control lever in front of them, ready to pull it, you'll choose the second version because it is safer. Not everyone reads instructions all the way through before putting them into action, so some readers of the first version will move the lever while the machine is still running. The second version ensures that machinists will stop the machine first.

One last example: If you were posting a notice in a community clubhouse, which of the following two announcements would you decide to pin on the bulletin board?

We have had many requests from our residents for information on the HMO medical plan. This plan provides
1. free medical care
2. eyeglasses
3. certain dental work
4. free prescriptions.
Arrangements have been made for one of the plan's representatives to give us full details at our clubhouse at 7:00 P.M. on Wednesday, August 10. A question-and-answer period will follow.

Due to the many requests from our residents seeking more information about the HMO medical plan which we have heard so much about lately, whereby you receive free medical care plus eyeglasses, certain dental work and free prescriptions, your board of directors has contacted the HMO medical center located at 1200 W. Maple Street, Oshkosh, and made arrangements with them to have one of their representatives come to the clubhouse at 7:00 P.M. on Wednesday, August 10, to give us full details of the plan. There will be a question-and-answer period at which time you should feel free to ask any questions pertaining to the above.

There is no question about it: The first version wins the prize. The reader's eye is drawn to the important information, which may be scanned. Only a committed reader will work through the other version, which opens with a sentence eighty-three words long. If there are competing interests in the club-house, such as a pool table or a card game or a political discussion group, the second announcement will be overlooked.

In addition to considering your specific audience, keep in mind the needs of readers in general. Most readers appreciate a writer who

respects their intelligence,

gives them real content,

presents the message as simply as the subject allows,

refuses to waste their time, and

provides a touch of human interest wherever possible.

## 2b  Keep the facts in mind.

If you do not have in mind a rich assortment of specific facts, examples, and details, you will almost certainly get stuck in the middle of a draft. Or you will find yourself simply repeating generalizations, moving forward without really advancing. Whether your facts come from personal experience, from direct observation, from interviews, or from written sources, you'll be better able to keep them in mind if you have first jotted them down. (See 1a and 1b.) Keep any notes close at hand as you begin writing.

Having the facts at hand will make a great difference in the quality of the draft you produce. Consider, for example, the following two sentences, taken from drafts written by different students. You'll have no difficulty deciding which student had the facts at hand.

First and foremost, the hamburgers that are sold in the cafeteria's machines are dry in texture and cold to the taste.

When I turned to the machine, I decided to try a sizzling hamburger, lean and juicy. Instead out came a small dry patty so cold that the fat was congealed in tiny globs on top of the meat.

The second writer is reporting specific and vivid facts. The first writer needs to head back to the cafeteria for another look, perhaps another taste, this time with a notebook in hand.

EXERCISE 2–1

Write the first draft of an essay of approximately 500 words, perhaps using one of the topics in the exercises in section 1.

# 3

**Make major revisions: Think big.**

Revising is not just a matter of moving words around and correcting the grammar. It involves much larger changes, ones made in response to questions like these:

> Is the main point clear?
>
> Can readers follow the structure?
>
> Does the paragraphing make sense?
>
> Is the supporting material persuasive?
>
> Are the parts proportioned sensibly?
>
> Is the point of view consistent and appropriate?
>
> Is the overall tone appropriate?

Changes made in response to such questions are likely to be dramatic. Whole paragraphs might be dropped, others added.

Material once stretched over two or three paragraphs might be condensed into one. Entire sections could be rearranged. Even the content may change dramatically, for the process of rewriting stimulates thought.

Major revising can be difficult, sometimes even painful. You might discover, for example, that an essay's first three pages are nothing but padding, that its central argument tilts the wrong way, and that you sound like a stuffed shirt throughout. But the sheer fact that you can see such problems in your writing is a sign of hope. Those opening pages can be dropped, the argument's slant realigned, the voice made more human.

## 3a  Improve the unity, organization, and development.

A draft is unified when it focuses on a clear main point and does not stray from that point. To check for unity, compare the paper's introduction, particularly its thesis sentence, with the body of the paper. Do they match? If not, one or the other must be adjusted. Either rebuild the introduction to fit the body of the paper or keep the introduction and delete any sentences or paragraphs that stray from its point.

To review the organization of a draft, scan the thesis sentence and the topic sentences of the paragraphs in the body of the paper. (Topic sentences, as you probably know, express the main idea of a paragraph.) Are the divisions logical? Are the paragraphs arranged in the most effective order?

Restructuring a paper can be as simple as moving a few sentences from one paragraph to another or switching the order of paragraphs. Often, however, the process is more complex. Topic sentences may require major revision, and whole sections of the paper may need to be torn apart and rebuilt. If such major restructuring becomes necessary, it is a good idea to revise the preliminary outline or to construct a new one. Divisions in the outline can become topic sentences in the restructured paper. (See topic sentences, 5a.)

In reviewing the development of a draft, consider whether any material should be deleted or added. Look first for sentences and paragraphs that can be cut — those that are off the point or simply repeat generalizations or give undue emphasis to minor ideas. Cuts may also be necessitated by any word limits within which you may be working, such as those imposed by a college assignment or by the realities of the business world, where readers are often pressed for time.

If any paragraphs or sections of the paper are too skimpily developed, you will need to add material. This necessity will take you back to the beginning of the writing process: listing specifics, perhaps clustering them, and then roughing out new sentences and paragraphs. Many writers deliberately overwrite a first draft, filling it out with more details than they will probably need, to prevent their having to produce new material later. Cutting and rearranging is almost always easier than beginning again from scratch.

## **3b** If necessary, adjust the point of view.

If the point of view of a draft shifts confusingly or if it seems not quite appropriate, given your purpose, audience, and subject matter, consider adjusting it.

There are three basic points of view to choose from: the first person (*I* or *we*), the second person (*you*), and the third person (*he/she/it/one* or *they*). Each point of view is appropriate in at least some contexts, and you may need to experiment before discovering which one best suits your needs.

### The third-person point of view

Much academic and professional writing is best presented from the third-person point of view (*he/she/it/one* or *they*), which puts the subject in the foreground. The "I" point of view is usually inappropriate in such contexts because, by focusing attention on the writer, it pushes the subject into the background. Consider, for example, one student's first-draft description of the behavior of a species of frog that he had observed in the field:

> Each frog that *I* was able to locate in trees remained in its given tree during the entirety of *my* observation period. However, *I* noticed that there was considerable movement within the home tree.

Here the "I" point of view is distracting, as the student himself noticed when he began to revise his report. His revision focuses more on the frogs, less on himself:

> Each frog located in a tree remained in that tree throughout the observation period. The frogs moved about considerably, however, within their home trees.

Just as the first-person pronoun *I* can draw too much attention to the writer, the second-person pronoun *you* can focus unnecessarily on the reader. One biology manual, for example, in an exercise meant to focus on the skeletal system, shifts the attention instead to the reader:

> Give at least two reasons for the purpose of the backbone from *your* reading.

This exercise would be clearer and more direct if presented without the distraction of the "you" point of view:

> What are two functions of the backbone?

Although the third-person point of view is often a better choice than the "I" or "you" point of view, it is by no means trouble-free. Writers who choose it can run into problems when they want to use singular pronouns in an indefinite sense. For example, when Miss Piggy says that a reason for jogging is "to improve *one's* emotional health and make *one* feel better about *oneself*," one wishes she wouldn't use quite so many *one*'s, doesn't one? The trouble is that American English, unlike British English, does not allow this pronoun to echo unselfconsciously throughout a sentence. The repetitions sound stuffy.

Some years ago Americans would have said "to improve one's emotional health and make *him* feel better about *himself*," with the understanding that *him* really meant *him* or *her*. Today, however, this use of *him* is offensive to enough readers that it is best avoided. On the other hand, "to make *him or her* feel better about *himself or herself*" is distinctly awkward. So what is poor Miss Piggy to say?

Her only hope, it turns out, is a flexible and inventive mind. She might switch to the plural: *Joggers run to improve their emotional health and make them feel better about themselves.* Or she could restructure the sentence altogether: *Jogging improves a person's emotional health and self-image.* (See 22a.)

### The second-person point of view

The "you" point of view, which puts the reader in the foreground, is appropriate if the writer is advising readers directly, as in tips on raising children or instructions on flower arranging. All imperative sentences, such as rules for writers in this book, are written from the "you" point of view, although the word itself is frequently omitted and understood. "Generate ideas" means "*You* should generate ideas," and everyone knows this, so the "you" is not necessary.

In the course of giving advice or instructions, the actual word *you* may be necessary. In advising gardeners on walkways, for example, columnist Henry Mitchell feels free to use the words *you* and *your* as the need arises:

> If *your* main walk is less than four feet wide, and if it is white concrete, then widen it, no matter what has to be sacrificed . . . and resurface it with brick, stone, or something less glaring and dull. Three flowers against a good-looking pavement will do more for *you* than thirty flowers against white concrete. [Italics added]

Mitchell might have written this passage from the third-person point of view instead ("If *the gardener's* walk is less than four feet wide . . ."), but the effect would have seemed oddly indirect. Even at the risk of seeming a bit bossy, Mitchell has wisely selected the imperative stance instead.

Notice that Mitchell's *you* means "you, the reader." It does not mean "you, anyone in general." Indefinite uses of *you,* such as those below, are nearly always inappropriate, especially in formal writing:

> Young Japanese women wired together electronic products on a piece-rate system: The more *you* wired, the more *you* were paid.

Here the writer should have stayed with the third-person point of view instead:

> The more *they* wired, the more *they* were paid.

### The first-person point of view

If much of a writer's material comes from personal experience, the "I" point of view will prove most natural. It is difficult to imagine, for example, how James Thurber could have avoided the word *I* in describing his early university days:

> *I* passed all the other courses that *I* took at my university, but *I* could never pass botany. This was because all botany students had to spend several hours a week in a laboratory looking through a microscope at plant cells, and *I* could never see through a microscope. *I* never once saw a cell through a microscope. This used to enrage my instructor. [Italics added]
> —*My Life and Hard Times,* 1933

Thurber's "I" point of view puts the writer in the foreground, and since the writer is in fact the subject, this makes sense.

Writers who are aware that the first-person point of view

is often inappropriate in academic writing sometimes over-generalize the rule. Concluding that the word *I* is never appropriate, they go to extreme lengths to avoid it.

> Mama read with such color and detail that *one* could fancy *oneself* as the hero of the story.

Since the paper in which this sentence appeared was a personal reminiscence, the entire paper sounded more natural once the writer allowed himself to use the word *I:*

> Mama read with such color and detail that *I* could fancy *myself* as the hero of the story.

## 3c   If necessary, modify the tone.

The tone of a draft expresses the writer's feelings about the subject and audience, so it is important to get it right. If the tone seems too flippant — or too stuffy, bossy, patronizing, or hostile — obviously it should be modified.

Any piece of writing drafted in anger or frustration will almost certainly need to be toned down. The following rough draft, for example, was written by a secretary in response to criticisms of a newsletter sent out by the organization for which she worked:

> Dear Mr. Martin:
>
> I know our newsletter is crudely laid out, the reason being that I type it from rough drafts under a tight enough deadline that only major errors of judgment get retyped. Perhaps we'd do better if we had a word processor.
>
> I think you were wrong to dismiss the offending story as bragging about *Nuclear War: What's in It for You?* The book was nominated for the prize, a fact worthy of mention despite the fact that it did not win.

In any case, I am glad to hear that you liked the open letter to the President. Would that the *Philadelphia Inquirer* had liked it as well.

Sincerely,

Robbie Nichols

As she reached the last paragraph of the rough draft, the writer saw the need to be more diplomatic. Later, in a calmer mood, she revised the letter like this:

Dear Mr. Martin:

We are glad to hear that you liked Roger Molander's "An Open Letter to the President." Would that the *Philadelphia Inquirer* had liked it as well.

I do think you were wrong to dismiss the sentence about *Nuclear War: What's in It for You?* as "bragging." It is a fairly direct sentence, and there may well be those among the faithful who wouldn't otherwise have known about its nomination for the prize.

Your comments about the physical layout of the story were, in fact, echoed by the staff here. The layout could not be changed, however, because it was typed under a tight deadline that allowed retyping only in cases of major errors of judgment.

Thank you for writing. Even though our newsletter has a limited circulation, we hope that Roger's open letter will elicit serious thought about the President's March 23 address on the Soviet Union and weapons in space.

Sincerely,

Robbie Nichols

## EXERCISE 3 – 1

Revise the draft you wrote in Exercise 2 – 1, thinking especially about unity, organization, and development. Are your point of view and tone appropriate?

# 4

## Revise and edit sentences.

If a rough draft needs a major overhaul, it makes little sense
to tinker with its sentences, some of which will be thrown
out anyway. The time for fine-tuning is later, when you can
afford to devote your full attention to such matters.

Most of the rest of this book offers advice on revising
sentences for style and clarity and editing them for grammar,
punctuation, and mechanics. The process of revising and editing sentences should ordinarily occur right on the pages of
an earlier draft, like this:

> Finally ~~we decided~~ *deciding* that perhaps our dream needed
>
> ~~some~~ prompting, ~~and~~ we visited a fertility doctor and
>
> began the expensive, time-consuming round of procedures
>
> that held out ~~the~~ *some* promise of ~~fulfilling our dream.~~ *our dream's fulfillment. Our efforts,*
>
> ~~All this was~~ *however, were* to no avail, ~~and as~~ *As* we approached the
>
> sixth year of our marriage, we ~~had reached the point~~ *could no longer*
>
> ~~where we couldn't~~ even discuss our childlessness with-
>
> out becoming very depressed. We questioned why this
>
> had happened to us~~.~~?. Why had we been singled out for
>
> ~~this~~ *such a* major disappointment?

The original paragraph was flawed by wordiness and an
excessive reliance on structures connected with *and*. Such
problems can be addressed through any number of acceptable

revisions. The first sentence, for example, could have been changed like this:

> Finally we decided that perhaps our dream needed
> ~~some~~ prompting$_\wedge$ ^After visiting^ ~~and we visited~~ a fertility doctor$_\wedge$ ~~and~~ ^we^
> began the expensive, time-consuming round of procedures
> that ^promised hope^ ~~held out the promise~~ of fulfilling our dream.

Though some writers might argue about the effectiveness of these improvements compared with the previous revision, most would agree that both new versions are better than the original.

Some of the paragraph's improvements involve less choice and are not so open to debate. The hyphen in *time-consuming* is necessary; a noun must be substituted for the pronoun *this*, which was being used more loosely than grammar allows; and the question mark in the next-to-last sentence must be changed to a period.

As it details the various rules for revising and editing sentences, this handbook will suggest when an improvement is simply one among several possibilities and when it is more strictly a matter of right and wrong.

## EXERCISE 4 – 1

Revise the draft of your essay from Exercise 3 – 1, looking carefully at your words and sentences for clarity and style. Check for errors in grammar, punctuation, and mechanics, consulting this handbook when necessary.

## SAMPLE ESSAY

The following outline and essay were written by Gary Laporte for an English class assignment. Laporte thought about the assignment for several days, but he was unable to come up with a topic. He was still wondering what subject to choose when he watched the national basketball playoffs on television. Besides interviewing the stars of each team, the sportscaster spoke with a ten-year-old fan whose ambition was to become a famous athlete. Why famous? thought Laporte. Why not a *good* athlete? Don't people who see games on TV understand that winning depends on teamwork, not on competing with each other for the camera?

Laporte decided that televised sports might make a good essay topic. It was a subject he felt strongly about, and it would not require much research. He jotted down ideas during breaks in the game and came up with the following list:

Cooperation should be focus, not competition

TV creates stars — cameras follow them, commentators interview them

TV doesn't show whole game, only most dramatic shots, slow-motion replays

More people admire sports stars than admire the President of U.S.

Sports stars make more money than President, also do commercials for money

Money becomes purpose of sport

Sports should represent American values — teamwork, shared enthusiasm — easier to see in live games where spectators participate

Cheering, choosing what to watch, buying beer & hot dogs, catching fly balls

Later, Laporte reread his list and concluded that his topic was the effect of television on both athletes and spectators. With this general topic in mind, he revised his list into an outline:

*Effects of TV on Sports*

  I. Television's convenience
    A. No need to travel and spend money
    B. Ability to see more games

  II. Distance between the sport and the spectator
    A. No way to choose what we see
    B. Can't see and hear the game

  III. Distance between athletes and their teams
    A. TV's focus on individual achievements
    B. TV exposure more important than cooperation

On the basis of this outline, Laporte formulated a thesis statement: *TV makes sports more accessible, but it also creates a distance between the sport and the spectator as well as between athletes and their teams.* He then used his thesis statement and outline to write the first draft of his essay. In doing so, he reworded his thesis slightly to fit better in his opening paragraph.

When he finished his draft, Laporte went back over his manuscript carefully. The basic structure was sound, but his use of pronouns was inconsistent and the essay needed to be more clearly focused. So he tightened up several sections that were unnecessarily wordy, took out material that did not relate directly to his thesis, changed pronouns where appropriate, and made a few additions to strengthen his essay's theme. He also rephrased some negative comments that he felt were exaggerated or unjustified. Finally, he corrected a number of typographical errors and mistakes in grammar and sentence structure.

Here is a copy of Laporte's first draft with his handwritten revisions.

Televised
^Sports ~~on TV~~--A Win or A Loss?

Team sports, ~~are~~ as much a part of American life

as Mom and apple pie, ~~and they have a good tendency~~
                        tend                      cooperation among
to bring ~~people~~ us together.  They encourage^ team members
and
~~to cooperate with each other.  They also create~~ shared
^
enthusiasm among fans.  Because of television, this

togetherness now seems available at the flick of a
Although television does make sports more accessible, it
switch.  But is this really the case?^ ~~It~~ also creates
                                      spectator
a distance between the sport and the ~~fan~~ and between
              their
athletes and ~~the~~ teams. ~~they play for.~~ ^
The advantage of television is that it provides sports fans
~~It is necessary to look at the differences between~~
with greater convenience.
~~live and televised sports.~~  We do not have to buy

tickets/ and travel to a stadium/ to see the World

Series or the Superbowl, ~~these games are on television.~~
but
~~We~~ can enjoy the game s in the comfort of our own living
^      s
room.  ~~During the commercials we can get popcorn,~~
    ^
~~beer, and hot dogs from the kitchen.~~  We can see more

games than if we had to attend each one in person,
                       a      variety
and we can follow^ greater ~~varieties~~ of sports.

     The price paid for this convenience, however,

is high.  Television changes the role of the fans
                          making their participation
who watch the game/, ~~It makes people participate in~~
              ^

*more*

a passive and distant ~~way instead of directly~~. Tele-

vision spectators see only what the camera shows.

*Yes,* ~~Even though~~ we *do* get a clearer look at important plays,

and if we miss a detail we can fall back on the commen-

tator's description or the instant replay/. ~~sometimes~~

~~in slow motion so you can see exactly what happened.~~

But we have no choice about what to watch. If we

would rather follow someone in the backfield than

the quarterback or watch a pitcher warming up instead

of a commercial, we can't. ~~A vital linkage between~~

~~live viewers and the players and also each other is~~

~~created by our seeing and hearing in person.~~ When

a fly ball comes soaring over the fence, *we* ~~you~~ cannot

try to catch it. The roar of cheers after a touchdown

is less exciting from the living room sofa than *from* ~~when~~

~~you are sitting in~~ the bleachers. *We* ~~You~~ may feel silly

cheering at all, since there is no chance those tiny

figures on the screen will hear *us* ~~you~~.

¶ *Besides creating a distance between viewers and players, television has*

TV ~~creates~~ a gap between athletes and their teams. *created*

~~in addition.~~ Traditionally, sports *have* ~~has~~ been viewed

as arenas where teamwork is essential, and the goals

of the group overshadow personal ambition. ~~Stars~~ *TV cameras,* are, however, ~~sexier than teamwork, and so TV cameras~~ *find it more dramatic and more convenient to* focus on individuals instead of *on* the team.   Interviews with ~~big~~ *sports* stars are often part of a televised game. *A successful athlete makes* ~~Athletes make~~ more money than the President of the ~~U.S., he~~ *United States,* appears in the media more often, and *is* more ~~people admire him.~~ *universally admired.*   In addition, sports stars have the extra ~~added~~ benefit of endorsing products on TV commercials for large bonus payments.   ~~The President can't go on TV and endorse razor blades because it would be bad for his image.~~

This high visibility encourages players to make themselves look good *rather than to cooperate with* ~~at the expense of~~ the team.   For example, a basketball player might take a difficult shot instead of passing the ball to a teammate left *unguarded* ~~ungarded~~ and closer to the basket.   At the same time, the team itself encourages the star system, since it needs the attention of the TV cameras to maximize it's exposure.   ~~Before showing a game,~~ Television stations have to choose among many games to show at any given time and naturally choose games that viewers will watch.   TV viewers usually like teams that win. They also like to see star players.

Team sports are a major part of American life/,
All the more so since television has brought them
into most of our homes.  The challenge for sports
fans is to su*p*port their favorite teams in ways ~~to~~ *that*
encourage the best values represented by sports.  One
way is *to* continue to attend live*s* games, even though
*they are* ~~it is~~ less convenient and more expensive than watching
television. / Live games benefit the fans, the players,
and the sport.
A live game provides viewers with a sense of
collaboration and participation that TV, in spite of
its accessibility, will never be able to reproduce.

# Writing and Revising Paragraphs

Except for special-purpose paragraphs, such as introductions or conclusions, paragraphs are clusters of information in support of an essay's main point. They correspond, at least roughly, to the divisions or subdivisions of an outline.

Ideally, paragraphs reflect the organization of the essay: one paragraph per point in short essays, a group of paragraphs per point in longer ones. Some ideas require more development than others, however, so it is best to be flexible. If an idea stretches to a length unreasonable for a paragraph, it should be divided, even if similar points in the essay have been presented in single paragraphs.

Most readers feel comfortable with paragraphs ranging between 100 and 200 words. Shorter paragraphs force too much starting and stopping, and longer ones strain the reader's attention span. There are exceptions to this general rule, however. Paragraphs longer than 200 words frequently appear in scholarly writing, where they suggest seriousness and depth. Paragraphs shorter than 100 words occur in newspapers because of narrow columns; in informal essays to quicken the pace; and in business letters, where information is routinely scanned.

# 5

**Focus on a main point.**

A paragraph should be unified around a main point. The point should be clear to readers, and all sentences in the paragraph must relate to it.

## 5a State the main point in a topic sentence.

As readers move into a paragraph, they need to know where they are—in relation to the whole essay—and what to expect in the sentences to come. A good topic sentence, a one-sentence summary of the paragraph's main point, acts as a signpost pointing in two directions: backward toward the thesis of the essay and forward toward the body of the paragraph.

Like a thesis statement, a topic sentence is more general than the material supporting it. Usually the topic sentence comes first:

> *Nearly all living creatures manage some form of communication.* The dance patterns of bees in their hive help to point the way to distant flower fields or announce successful foraging. Male stickleback fish regularly swim upside-down to indicate outrage in a courtship contest. Male deer and lemurs mark territorial ownership by rubbing their own body secretions on boundary stones or trees. Everyone has seen a frightened dog put his tail between his legs and run in panic. We, too, use gestures, expressions, postures, and movement to give our words point. [Italics added]
> — Olivia Vlahos, *Human Beginnings*

Frequently the topic sentence is introduced by a transitional sentence linking it to earlier material. In the following paragraph, the topic sentence (italicized) has been delayed to allow for a transition.

> But flowers are not the only source of spectacle in the wilderness. *An opportunity for late color is provided by the berries of wildflowers, shrubs, and trees.* Baneberry presents its tiny white flowers in spring but in late summer bursts forth with clusters of red berries. Bunchberry, a ground-cover plant, puts out red berries in the fall, and the red berries of wintergreen last from autumn well into winter. In California, the bright red, fist-sized clusters of Christmas berries can be seen growing beside highways for up to six months of the year. [Italics added]
> — James Crockett et al., *Wildflower Gardening*

Occasionally the topic sentence may be withheld until the end of the paragraph — but only if the earlier sentences hang together so well that the reader perceives their direction, if not their exact point. The opening sentences of the following paragraph state facts, making them supporting material rather than topic sentences, but they strongly suggest a central idea. The topic sentence at the end is hardly a surprise.

> Tobacco chewing starts as soon as people begin stirring. Those who have fresh supplies soak the new leaves in water and add ashes from the hearth to the wad. Men, women, and children chew tobacco and all are addicted to it. Once there was a shortage of tobacco in Kaobawa's village and I was plagued for a week by early morning visitors who requested permission to collect my cigarette butts in order to make a wad of chewing tobacco. Normally, if anyone is short of tobacco, he can request a share of someone else's already chewed wad, or simply borrow the entire wad when its owner puts it down somewhere. *Tobacco is so important to them that their word for "poverty" translates as "being without tobacco."* [Italics added]
> — Napoleon A. Chagnon, *Yanomamo: The Fierce People*

If a topic sentence appears in the middle of a paragraph (a rare occurrence), its function will be twofold: to pull together what went before and to prepare for the sentences to come. In the following paragraph, the writer begins with an anecdote, sums up its point in a topic sentence, and then turns to examples:

> I used to scatter arsenical bait among the seedlings to save them from slugs, but I am not doing that anymore. One year we had a terrible scare with a grandchild who dropped his pacifier into a row of lettuce where bait had been put down. The baited area had been covered with wire for safety, but the mesh was not small enough to keep out the pacifier or his fingers. We saw the episode from the arbor and hurried across the grass. But the child, seeing a group of adults rushing toward him, was alarmed. To reassure himself, he immediately popped the tainted pacifier into his mouth. All turned out well, but the episode taught me a lesson. *There are simpler baits*

*which are equally attractive to slugs and no danger to
children or pets.* I have already mentioned that beer and
halves of squeezed oranges, placed squeezed-side-down on the
ground between the rows, also attract these pests. The garden
may look mildly squalid with this type of preventative strewn
around, but a little squalor is far less hard on the nervous
system than a hurried call to the poison center. [Italics added]
— Thalassa Cruso, *Making Things Grow Outdoors*

Although it is generally wise to use topic sentences, at
times they are unnecessary. A topic sentence is not needed if
a paragraph continues developing an idea clearly introduced
in a previous paragraph, if the details of the paragraph un-
mistakably suggest its main point, or if the paragraph appears in a narrative of events where generalizations might
interrupt the flow of the story.

## **5b**  Do not stray from the point.

Sentences that do not support the topic sentence destroy the
unity of a paragraph. If the paragraph is otherwise well focused, such offending sentences may simply be deleted or
perhaps moved elsewhere. In the following paragraph describing the inadequate facilities in a high school, the information
about the typing instructor (in italics) is clearly off the point.
The student who wrote the paragraph was able to work this
material into a later paragraph in her essay.

As the result of tax cuts, the educational facilities of
Martin Luther King High School have reached an all-time low.
Some of the books date back to 1965 and have long since shed
their covers. The lack of lab equipment makes it necessary for
four to five students to work at one table, with most watching
rather than performing experiments. The few typewriters in
working order have not been cleaned in so long they spatter
ink all over the page. There is only one self-correcting

typewriter and no prospect of the school's acquiring a word processor or computer any time soon. *Also, when the typing instructor left to have a baby at the beginning of the semester, a permanent substitute was not hired, so it has been even harder for students to learn how to type.* As for the furniture, many of the upright chairs have become recliners, and the desk legs are so unbalanced they play seesaw on the floor.

Sometimes the cure for a disunified paragraph is not as simple as deleting or moving material. Writers often wander into uncharted territory because they cannot think of enough evidence to support a topic sentence. Feeling that it is too soon to break into a new paragraph, they move on to new ideas for which the reader has not been prepared. When this happens, the writer is faced with a choice: Either find more evidence to support the topic sentence or adjust the topic sentence to mesh with the evidence that is available.

### EXERCISE 5 – 1

Write two paragraphs, one with its topic sentence at the beginning and one with its topic sentence at the end. Possible subjects: the Olympic games, subliminal suggestions in advertising, the changing value of a college education, the effect of TV violence.

### EXERCISE 5 – 2

The following topic sentences are too broad to allow for a well-focused paragraph. Revise the sentences to make the topic more specific.

1. Life in a large city has many advantages.
2. Economists have proposed a number of solutions for inflation.
3. Capital punishment is a controversial issue.
4. Contemporary horror films are different from horror film classics of years ago.
5. Going to college creates new responsibilities for a student.

## EXERCISE 5 – 3

Choose one of the topic sentences you revised in Exercise 5 – 2 and develop a unified paragraph from it.

## EXERCISE 5 – 4

Underline the topic sentence in the following paragraph and eliminate any material that does not clarify or develop the central idea.

A recent plan of the mayor's threatens to destroy one of the oldest and most successfully integrated neighborhoods in our city, replacing it with luxury condominiums and a shopping mall. This neighborhood, Thompson's Fields, was settled by a mixture of immigrants from Ireland, Italy, Poland, and Austria in the early part of the twentieth century. Over the years Black and Hispanic families have also moved in and have become part of the community. When the mayor designated a five-block area along the neighborhood's main street as the location for a redevelopment program, the community decided to take the mayor to court. The mayor has hired the best urban planners and architects in the country to design and build three large skyscrapers along with parking facilities for the area. One woman has even moved to the city from California to work on the project. If the court accepts the case, the lawyer for the residents will be Ann Tyson, who grew up in Thompson's Fields. The residents have seen a great deal of change over the years, but they refuse to stand by while their homes are razed for some gentrification project that they will never enjoy.

# 6

## Develop the main point.

Topic sentences are generalizations in need of support, so once you have written a topic sentence, ask yourself, "How do I know that this is true?" Your answer will suggest how to develop the paragraph.

## **6a**  Flesh out skimpy paragraphs.

Though an occasional short paragraph is fine, particularly if it functions as a transition or serves to emphasize a point, a series of brief paragraphs suggests inadequate development. How much development is enough? That varies, depending on the writer's purpose and audience.

For example, when she wrote a paragraph attempting to convince readers that it is impossible to lose fat quickly, health columnist Jane Brody knew that she would have to present a great deal of evidence because many dieters want to believe the opposite. She did *not* write:

> When you think about it, it's impossible to lose — as many diets suggest — 10 pounds of *fat* in ten days, even on a total fast. Even a moderately active person cannot lose so much weight so fast. A less active person hasn't a prayer.

This three-sentence paragraph is too skimpy to be convincing. But the paragraph that Brody in fact wrote contains enough evidence to convince even skeptical readers:

> When you think about it, it's impossible to lose — as many diets suggest — 10 pounds of *fat* in ten days, even on a total fast. A pound of body fat represents 3,500 calories. To lose 1 pound of fat, you must expend 3,500 more calories than you consume. Let's say you weigh 170 pounds and, as a moderately active person, you burn 2,500 calories a day. If your diet contains only 1,500 calories, you'd have an energy deficit of 1,000 calories a day. In a week's time that would add up to a 7,000-calorie deficit, or 2 pounds of real fat. In ten days, the accumulated deficit would represent nearly 3 pounds of lost body fat. Even if you ate nothing at all for ten days and maintained your usual level of activity, your caloric deficit would add up to 25,000 calories. . . . At 3,500 calories per pound of fat, that's still only 7 pounds of lost fat.
>
> — Jane Brody, *Jane Brody's Nutrition Book*

**6b** Choose a suitable pattern of development.

Though paragraphs may be patterned in an almost infinite number of ways, certain patterns of development occur frequently, either alone or in combination: examples and illustrations, process, comparison and contrast, analogy, cause and effect, classification, and definition. There is nothing magical about these methods of development. They simply reflect the natural ways in which we tend to think.

### Examples and illustrations

Examples, perhaps the most common pattern, are appropriate whenever the reader is tempted to ask, "For example?" Though examples are just selected instances, not a complete catalog, they are enough to suggest the truth of many topic sentences, as in the following paragraph.

> A passenger list of the early years of the Orient Express would read like a *Who's Who of the World*, from art to politics. Sarah Bernhardt and her Italian counterpart Eleonora Duse used the train to thrill the stages of Europe. For musicians there were Toscanini and Mahler. Dancers Nijinsky and Pavlova were there, while lesser performers like Harry Houdini and the girls of the Ziegfeld Follies also rode the rails. Violinists were allowed to practice on the train, and occasionally one might see trapeze artists hanging like bats from the baggage racks.
> — Barnaby Conrad III, "Train of Kings"

Illustrations are extended examples, frequently presented in story form. Because they require several sentences apiece, they tend to be used more sparingly than examples. When well selected, however, they can be a vivid and readable means of developing a point. The writer of the following paragraph uses illustrations to demonstrate that Harriet Tubman, famous conductor on the underground railway for escaping slaves, was a master at knowing how and when to retreat.

Part of Harriet Tubman's strategy of conducting was, as in all battle-field operations, the knowledge of how and when to retreat. Numerous allusions have been made to her moves when she suspected that she was in danger. When she feared the party was closely pursued, she would take it for a time on a train southward bound. No one seeing Negroes going in this direction would for an instant suppose them to be fugitives. Once on her return she was at a railway station. She saw some men reading a poster and she heard one of them reading it aloud. It was a description of her, offering a reward for her capture. She took a southbound train to avert suspicion. At another time when Harriet heard men talking about her, she pretended to read a book which she carried. One man remarked, "This cannot be the woman. The one we want can't read or write." Harriet devoutly hoped the book was right side up.                                    — Earl Conrad, *Harriet Tubman*

### Process

A process paragraph is patterned in time order, usually chronologically. A writer may choose this pattern either to describe a process or to show readers how to follow a process. The following paragraph, taken from a biography of Thomas Jefferson, describes the process of electing a president during the early years of the United States.

A presidential election in those days was neither simple nor direct. In each State the Electoral College voted for both offices, without designating which of the candidates was to get first place (the Presidency) and which second (the Vice-Presidency). The votes were then sent to the national capital to be counted. The candidate who had the highest number of votes was declared President and the next highest, Vice-President. If the two leading candidates had an equal number of votes, the election was to be decided in the House of Representatives, wherein each State cast one vote. Communication being slow and uncertain, it took several weeks for all the votes to come in from States so far apart as Georgia and Massachusetts.          — Saul K. Padover, *Jefferson*

*Comparison and contrast*

To compare two subjects is to draw attention to their similarities, although the word *compare* also has a broader meaning that includes a consideration of differences. To contrast is to focus only on differences.

Whether a paragraph stresses similarities or differences, it may be patterned in one of two ways. The two subjects may be presented one at a time, block style, as in the following paragraph of contrast.

> So Grant and Lee were in complete contrast, representing two diametrically opposed elements in American life. Grant was the modern man emerging; beyond him, ready to come on the stage, was the great age of steel and machinery, of crowded cities and a restless burgeoning vitality. Lee might have ridden down from the old age of chivalry, lance in hand, silken banner fluttering over his head. Each man was the perfect champion of his cause, drawing both his strengths and weaknesses from the people he led.
> — Bruce Catton, "Grant and Lee: A Study in Contrasts"

Or a paragraph may proceed point by point, treating two subjects together, as in this paragraph comparing Bing Crosby and Elvis Presley:

> There were similarities that ought to tell us something. Both came from obscurity to national recognition while quite young and became very rich. Both lacked formal musical education and went on to movie careers despite lack of acting skills. Both developed distinctive musical styles which were originally scorned by critics and subsequently studied as pioneer developments in the art of popular song.
> — Russell Baker, "From Song to Sound: Bing and Elvis"

The comparison and contrast methods of development sometimes occur together. Usually the comparison is made first, with the contrasts following:

Wilson brought qualities as unusual as those of Theodore Roosevelt to American politics. The two men had much in common: cultivation, knowledge, literary skill, personal magnetism, relentless drive. But, where Roosevelt was unbuttoned and expansive, Wilson was reserved and cool; no one known to history ever called him "Woody" or "W.W." Both were lay preachers, but where Roosevelt was a revivalist, bullying his listeners to hit the sawdust trail, Wilson had the severe eloquence of a Calvinist divine. Roosevelt's egotism overflowed his personality; Wilson's was a hard concentrate within. Roosevelt's power lay in what he did, Wilson's in what he held in reserve.

—Arthur M. Schlesinger, Jr., *The Age of Roosevelt:*
*The Crisis of the Old Order*

### Analogy

Analogies draw comparisons between items that appear to have little in common. They are used to make the unfamiliar seem familiar, to provide a concrete understanding of abstract topics, or to provoke fresh thoughts about a subject. In the following paragraph, physician Lewis Thomas draws an analogy between the behavior of ants and humans.

Ants are so much like human beings as to be an embarrassment. They farm fungi, raise aphids as livestock, launch armies into wars, use chemical sprays to alarm and confuse enemies, capture slaves. The families of weaver ants engage in child labor, holding their larvae like shuttles to spin out the thread that sews the leaves together for their fungus gardens. They exchange information ceaselessly. They do everything but watch television.

—Lewis Thomas, "On Societies as Organisms"

### Cause and effect

When causes and effects are a matter of argument, they are too complex to be reduced to a simple pattern. However, if a writer wishes merely to describe a cause-and-effect relationship that has already been demonstrated, then the effect may be stated in the topic sentence, with the causes listed in the body of the paragraph:

> The fantastic water clarity of the Mount Gamier sinkholes results from several factors. The holes are fed from aquifers holding rainwater that fell decades — even centuries — ago, and that has been filtered through miles of limestone. The high level of calcium that limestone adds causes the silty detritus from dead plants and animals to cling together and settle quickly to the bottom. Abundant bottom vegetation in the shallow sinkholes also helps bind the silt. And the rapid turnover prohibits stagnation.
>
> — Hillary Hauser, "Exploring a Sunken Realm in Australia"

Or the paragraph may move from cause to effects, as in this paragraph describing the radio's effects on the organizations of radical populists Huey Long and Father Coughlin:

> Yet it was the radio itself that was, in the end, the most important influence upon the character of the Long and Coughlin organizations. It gave both leaders direct, immediate access to millions of men and women; it produced a special bond of intimacy and friendship between the speaker and his audience. But that same ease of access had destructive effects upon the movements Long and Coughlin were creating, producing among their followers a sense of detachment from the organizational process.
>
> — Alan Brinkley, *Voices of Protest*

### Classification

Classification is the grouping of items into categories according to some consistent principle. Philosopher Francis Bacon was using classification when he wrote that "some books are to be tasted, others to be swallowed, and some few to be chewed and digested." Bacon's principle for classifying books is the degree to which they are worthy of our attention, but books of course can be classified according to other principles. For example, an elementary school teacher might classify children's books according to the level of their difficulty, or a librarian might group them by subject matter. The principle of classification that a writer chooses ultimately depends on his or her purpose.

Writers frequently classify people or things for fairly whimsical purposes, as in the following paragraph by humorist Russell Baker.

> Considering the millions and millions of antiques that one sees in London, it is surprising how little variety there is. A fairly careful survey of several London antique markets suggests that there are only eight basic items for sale. These are (1) the broken clock; (2) the old map, usually of a place unlisted in the geographies, called Novum Cloacum; (3) the incomplete set of dining-room chairs (commonly five or seven), one of which has a broken rung; (4) the set of three silver spoons; (5) the cracked demi-tasse with saucer; (6) the dining-room table with (Variation A) no leaves or (Variation B) a dangerous split in one leg; (7) the oil portrait of someone who, though unidentified, might very well be the Electress Sophia of Hanover or King Umberto the First; and (8) the first edition volume of a history of animal husbandry during the year 1703 in the environs of Dumfries.
>
> — Russell Baker, *Poor Russell's Almanac*

### Definition

A definition puts a word or concept into a general class and then provides enough details to distinguish it from others in the same class. For example, in one of its senses the term *grit* applies to the class of things that birds eat, but it is restricted to those items — such as small pebbles, eggshell, and ashes — that help the bird grind food.

Many definitions may be presented in a sentence or two, but abstract or difficult concepts may require a paragraph or even a full essay of definition. Extended definitions frequently make use of other patterns of development, such as examples or comparisons and contrasts. In the following paragraph from an essay on self-respect, novelist Joan Didion uses a number of examples to define both *self-respect* and *character.*

> People with self-respect have the courage of their mistakes. They know the price of things. If they choose to commit adultery, they do not then go running, in an access of bad conscience, to receive absolution from the wronged parties; nor do they complain unduly of the unfairness, the undeserved embarrassment, of being named co-respondent. In brief, people with self-respect exhibit a certain toughness, a kind of moral nerve; they display what was once called *character,* a quality which, although approved in the abstract, sometimes loses ground to other, more instantly negotiable virtues. The measure of its slipping prestige is that one tends to think of it only in connection with homely children and United States senators who have been defeated, preferably in the primary, for reelection. Nonetheless, character — the willingness to accept responsibilities for one's own life — is the source from which self-respect springs.
>
> — Joan Didion, "On Self-Respect"

## EXERCISE 6 – 1

Develop one of the following skimpy paragraphs, using the information in parentheses to support your assertions.

1. Edgar Allan Poe, born in 1809, suffered greatly during his life. He struggled with poverty, failure, and misfortune until he died in 1849.

(Poe was born the son of poor traveling actors. His mother died while he was a child. He was adopted by John Allan of Richmond, Virginia, but was eventually disowned by Allan because of Poe's dissolute living habits. He was expelled from the military academy at West Point after one year. He became editor of the *Southern Literary Messenger* in 1835, but he was fired in 1837 because of his unstable temperament. In 1836 he married a thirteen-year-old cousin, Virginia Clemm, who died of tuberculosis in 1847.)

2. The exposure of cardiologist John Darsee's faked experiments has caused a stir in the scientific community. Although his was not the most notorious case of lab fraud, his punishment was severe, and the institution for which he did his research was also penalized. Institutions and scientific journals are developing tougher guidelines for investigating suspected cases of research fraud.

(Seven years after graduating from medical school, John Darsee had more than 100 publications to his name. In 1981 co-workers at Brigham and Women's Hospital in Boston discovered him labeling a few minutes of cardiac recordings so that they looked like a week's work. The National Institutes of Health investigation revealed that Darsee had falsified nearly all his research at Brigham and Women's. For example, he had recorded blood flow data for dogs that were never injected with the radioactive tracer necessary to make the measurement. The National Institutes of Health ruled that Darsee could not receive federal research funds for ten years. The NIH also asked Brigham and Women's to repay $119,000 spent by Darsee on a research contract. In 1982 the Association of American Medical Colleges developed guidelines for investigating suspected fraud. When there is a suspicion of fraud, all collaborators of the suspected scientist, as well as the agency sponsoring the research, are to be informed immediately. The scientist's other projects must also be reviewed. Eighty percent of U.S. medical schools have now adopted some form of guidelines for investigation. — Information from Susan West, "Crackdown on Lab Fraud," *Science 83* May 1983: 14.)

### EXERCISE 6 – 2

Write a paragraph modeled on one of the patterns discussed in this section. Some possible topics are listed below.

*Examples:* the dangers of nuclear power plants, the strengths and weaknesses of your favorite (or least favorite) political candidate, the advantages (or disadvantages) of a national health care system, the necessity for gun control laws

*Process:* repairing something, meeting someone of the opposite sex, a successful job interviewing style, how to survive in the wilderness, how to refinish furniture

*Comparison and contrast:* two adventure (or science fiction) films, two neighborhoods, two political candidates, two teachers, positive reinforcement versus negative reinforcement as a disciplinary approach

*Analogy:* between a family reunion and a circus, between training for a rigorous sport and boot camp, between settling a children's argument and being a courtroom judge

*Cause and effect:* the effects of water pollution on a particular area, the effects of divorce on children, the effects of switching to a national health care system, the causes of widespread cheating in college courses, the causes of American apathy in politics

*Classification:* types of clothing worn on your college campus, types of people who go to college mixers, types of exercise, types of dieters, types of news sources, types of television weather reports

*Definition:* supply-side economics, success, a student's basic needs, a computer addict, a contemporary family, institutional racism

# 7

## Link sentences to sentences, paragraphs to paragraphs.

When sentences and paragraphs flow from one to another without discernible bumps, gaps, or shifts, they are said to be coherent. Coherence may be improved by strengthening the various ties between old information and new. A number of techniques for strengthening those ties are detailed in this section.

## 7a   Repeat key words.

If too much information seems new, a paragraph will be hard to read. Unless we are already familiar with the soap opera summarized in the following paragraph, for example, we will find it nearly impenetrable:

> In the house Gunther hears intruders and hides Jamie in a closet. During a scuffle Donny falls to his death while Vic manages to escape. Standing Elk decides to drop the lawsuit but Marty does not and plans to find out his true Indian name. Marty remembers that his uncle, Proud Bear, was stationed in Monticello before being shipped out to combat and later being listed as missing in action. On the farm Chris is beginning to realize that she doesn't have a deep physical love for Miles, and Miles realizes the same. Chris fears that her attacker will show up at the farm.

Notice how few repetitions tie these sentences together. We hear about Gunther and Jamie in the first sentence, Donny and Vic in the second, Standing Elk and Marty in the third. Only Marty gets picked up again, at which point we are introduced to yet another key player: Proud Bear.

Repeating key words is an important technique for improving coherence. If Gunther is mentioned in the first sentence, pick him up again in the second. To prevent such repetitions from becoming dull, you can use variations of the key word (*hike, hiker, hiking*), pronouns referring to the word (*gamblers . . . they*), and synonyms (*run, sprint, race, dash*). In the following paragraph describing plots among indentured servants in the seventeenth century, historian Richard Hofstadter binds sentences together by repeating the key word *plots* and echoing it with a variety of synonyms:

> *Plots* hatched by several servants to run away together occurred mostly in the plantation colonies, and the few recorded servant *uprisings* were entirely limited to those colonies. Virginia had been forced from its very earliest years to take stringent steps against *mutinous plots*, and severe punishments for *such behavior* were recorded. Most servant *plots* occurred in the seventeenth century: a contemplated

*uprising* was nipped in the bud in York County in 1661;
apparently led by some left-wing offshoots of the *Great
Rebellion*, servants *plotted* an *insurrection* in Gloucester
County in 1663, and four leaders were condemned and
executed; some discontented servants apparently joined
*Bacon's Rebellion* in the 1670's. In the 1680's the planters
became newly apprehensive of discontent among the servants
"owing to their great necessities and want of clothes," and it
was feared that they would *rise up* and *plunder* the
storehouses and ships; in 1682 there were plant-cutting *riots*
in which servants and laborers, as well as some planters, took
part. [Italics added]

—Richard Hofstadter, *America at 1750*

## 7b Use parallel structures for parallel ideas.

When parallel ideas are not expressed in parallel grammatical
form, the effect is jarring.

> **NOT PARALLEL**    The system also has other capabilities such
> as communicating with other computers,
> processing records, and mathematical
> capabilities.

The sentence flows much more smoothly once the three examples are made parallel.

> **PARALLEL**    The system also has other capabilities such
> as communicating with other computers,
> processing records, and performing
> mathematical functions.

Parallel structures may be used to bind together a series
of sentences expressing similar information. In the following
passage describing folk beliefs, Margaret Mead patterns her
examples in a parallel structure.

Actually, almost every day, even in the most sophisticated home, something is likely to happen that evokes the memory of some old folk belief. The salt spills. A knife falls to the floor. Your nose tickles. Then perhaps, with a slightly embarrassed smile, the person who spilled the salt tosses a pinch over his left shoulder. Or someone recites the old rhyme, "Knife falls, gentleman calls." Or as you rub your nose you think, That means a letter. I wonder who's writing?

—Margaret Mead, "New Superstitions for Old"

A less skilled writer might have varied the structure, perhaps like this: *The salt spills. Mother drops a knife on the floor. Someone's nose is tickling.* But these sentences are less effective; the parallel structures help tie the paragraph together.

## 7c    Provide transitions.

Certain words and phrases signal connections between ideas, connections that might otherwise be missed. The coordinating conjunctions *and, but, or, nor, for, so,* and *yet* are common signals, as are the many transitional expressions in the lists below.

**TO SHOW ADDITION**
and, also, besides, further, furthermore, in addition, moreover, next, too, first, second

**TO GIVE EXAMPLES**
for example, for instance, to illustrate, in fact, specifically

**TO COMPARE**
also, in the same manner, similarly, likewise

**TO CONTRAST**
but, however, on the other hand, in contrast, nevertheless, still, even though, on the contrary, yet, although

**TO SUMMARIZE OR CONCLUDE**
in other words, in short, in summary, in conclusion, to sum
up, that is, therefore

**TO SHOW TIME**
after, before, next, during, later, finally, meanwhile, then,
when, while, immediately

**TO SHOW PLACE OR DIRECTION**
above, below, beyond, farther on, nearby, opposite, close, to
the left

**TO INDICATE LOGICAL RELATIONSHIP**
so, therefore, consequently, thus, as a result, for this reason,
since

Skilled writers use transitional expressions with care,
making sure, for example, not to use a *consequently* when
an *also* would be more precise. They are also careful to select
transitions with an appropriate tone, perhaps preferring a *so*
to a *thus* in an informal piece, an *in summary* to an *in short*
for a scholarly essay.

In the paragraph below, taken from an argument that
dinosaurs had the " 'right-sized' brains for reptiles of their
body size," biologist Stephen Jay Gould uses transitions (italicized) with skill:

> I don't wish to deny that the flattened, minuscule head of
> the large bodied "Stegosaurus" houses little brain from our
> subjective, top-heavy perspective, *but* I do wish to assert that
> we should not expect more of the beast. *First of all,* large
> animals have relatively smaller brains than related, small
> animals. The correlation of brain size with body size among
> kindred animals (all reptiles, all mammals, *for example*) is
> remarkably regular. *As* we move from small to large animals,
> from mice to elephants *or* small lizards to Komodo dragons,
> brain size increases, *but* not so fast as body size. *In other*
> *words,* bodies grow faster than brains, *and* large animals have
> low ratios of brain weight to body weight. *In fact,* brains grow

only about two-thirds as fast as bodies. *Since* we have no
reason to believe that large animals are consistently stupider
than their smaller relatives, we must conclude that large
animals require relatively less brain to do as well as smaller
animals. *If* we do not recognize this relationship, we are likely
to underestimate the mental power of very large animals,
dinosaurs in particular. [Italics added]

— Stephen Jay Gould, "Were Dinosaurs Dumb?"

## EXERCISE 7 – 1

Write a coherent paragraph opening with the following topic sentence
and developed with the examples and details provided. The topic sentence and supporting information are from a paragraph in Robert
Nisbet's book *Prejudices*.

Topic sentence: To be a hero requires the desire to liberate the world
from dogma and superstition.

Example: Darwin. His purpose was to present a revolutionary scientific theory, thereby contradicting the Bible's story of the creation
of the species.

Example: Marx. His purpose was to free the world from tyranny and
exploitation.

Example: Freud. His purpose was to free the world from the conflict
between the id and the superego by examining the subconscious.

# PART III

# *Revising Sentences*

# 8

## Highlight major ideas.

To highlight major ideas, put them in subjects, verbs, and objects or complements of independent clauses — the elements that receive most attention from readers. Tuck minor ideas into structures that demand less attention — modifying phrases or subordinate clauses. (See 49.)

```
      SUBORDINATE
┌────────CLAUSE────────┐              S    ┌─V─┐ OBJ
If you were born lucky, even your rooster will lay eggs.
```

Deciding which ideas to highlight is not a simple matter of right and wrong. If your purpose, for example, were to stress your grandmother's acute hearing rather than her blindness, you would write:

As she lost her sight, Grandmother's *hearing sharpened.*

To focus on her growing blindness, you would structure the sentence differently:

Though her hearing grew more acute, *Grandmother* gradually *lost* her *sight.*

The writer, then, must decide what ideas are worth highlighting. The only error is trying to emphasize everything at once, for readers have only so much attention to give. Once you stretch their attention span to the breaking point, you've lost them.

**8a** Combine choppy sentences.

Short sentences demand attention, so they should be used primarily for emphasis. If an idea is not important enough to deserve a sentence all to itself, try pulling it into a sentence close by. Put less important ideas in subordinate structures such as phrases or subordinate clauses.

Too many short sentences make for a choppy style.

> **CHOPPY** The huts vary in height. They measure from ten to fifteen feet in diameter. They contain no modern conveniences.

> **IMPROVED** Varying in height and measuring from ten to fifteen feet in diameter, the huts contain no modern conveniences.

Three sentences have become one, with minor ideas expressed in an introductory phrase.

▶ Agnes, ~~was~~ another student I worked with, ~~She~~ was a hyperactive child.

The revision emphasizes that Agnes was a hyperactive child and de-emphasizes the rest of the information, which appears in an appositive phrase.

▶ *Although the* ~~The~~ Market Inn, is located at 2nd and E Streets, ~~It~~ doesn't look very impressive from the outside, ~~The~~ food, ~~however,~~ is excellent.

Three sentences have become one, with minor ideas expressed in a subordinate clause (*Although . . . outside*), which in turn contains a phrase (*located . . . Streets*).

Though subordination is ordinarily the most effective technique for combining short, choppy sentences, coordination is appropriate when the ideas are equal in importance. To coordinate two or more word groups, connect them with *and, but, or, nor, for, so,* or *yet.* The structure containing the coordinate word groups is said to be compound.

▶ The hospital decides when patients will sleep and wake, It
  dictates what and when they will eat, It tells them when they
  may be with family and friends.

Three sentences have become one, with ideas expressed in a compound predicate. A predicate is a verb plus its objects, complements, and modifiers.

## 8b Restructure strung-together compounds.

Compound structures (those connected with *and, but, or, nor, for, so,* or *yet*) are appropriate only when you intend to draw the reader's attention equally to two ideas: *Schwegler praises loudly, and he criticizes softly.* If one of the ideas is more important than the other, the lesser idea should be subordinated.

Compounds that are simply strung together, like beads on a string, create a monotonous style.

|  |  |
|---|---|
| **INEFFECTIVE** | Alan walked over to his car, and he noticed a few unusual dark spots all over it. |
| **IMPROVED** | When Alan walked over to his car, he noticed a few unusual dark spots all over it. |

The revision subordinates the less important idea by putting it in a subordinate clause (*when Alan walked over to his car*). Notice that the subordinating conjunction *when* signals the relation between the ideas better than the coordinating conjunction *and* does.

▶ *On Death and Dying*, ~~was written~~ by Dr. Elisabeth Kübler-
        ∧
Ross, ~~and it~~ describes the experiences of terminally ill

patients.

The minor idea has become a prepositional phrase.

                *noticing*
▶ My uncle ~~noticed~~ the frightened look on my face, ~~and~~ told me
        ∧                                    ∧
that Grandma had to feel my face because she was blind.

The less important idea has become a participial phrase modifying the noun *uncle*.

## EXERCISE 8–1

Combine short sentences by putting minor ideas in subordinate structures or by putting ideas of equal importance in compound structures. Restructure strung-together compounds by subordinating minor ideas. You must decide which ideas are minor because the sentences are given out of context. Example:

The team rowed until their strength nearly gave out and
                    *where they*                          *to*
finally returned to shore, ~~and~~ had a party on the beach ~~and~~
*celebrate*                  ∧                                ∧
~~celebrated~~ the start of the season.

a. A couple of minutes went by, and the teacher walked in smiling.
b. The secretary decided not to cooperate with Sue, and she sat all day and allowed her work to pile up.
c. Mary will graduate from high school in June. She has not yet decided on a college.

d. Some major companies dictate where their employees must live. They determine where their children should go to school. They decide who their employees' friends should be. These companies exert an overwhelming influence on their employees.

e. We arrived at the Capital Center, and to my dismay we had to pay $2.00 for parking.

1. The American crocodile could once be found in abundance in southern Florida. It is now being threatened with extinction.

2. Robyn was a tall, thin, athletic girl, and she had always appeared to be very healthy.

3. We bought nothing but snacks. The total cost for food was twenty-five dollars.

4. Thurmont, which means "gateway to the mountains," is minutes from the Blue Ridge Mountains. It's also minutes from the Catoctin Zoo and from Catoctin itself, which is a historic site.

5. Sandy wrote letters to the supervisors and told them that she had been forced to resign because a white woman had refused to work under her.

6. The aides help the younger children with reading and math. These are the children's weakest subjects.

7. The concert began exactly at noon. The first act was Patrice Rushen. She performed for about forty-five minutes.

8. We met every Monday morning in the home of one of the members. These meetings would last about three hours.

9. Patsy was a tomboy and she liked to play with boys and she wasn't afraid of anyone.

10. Angry journalists decided to protest, and they wrote the publisher letters condemning his sensational approach to the news.

11. He walked up to the pitcher's mound. He dug his toe into the ground. He swung his arm around backward and forward. Then he threw the ball and struck the batter out.

12. I felt confident that God would hear my prayers. I felt he would keep my brother safe.

13. Four hours went by, and a rescue truck finally arrived.

14. Shore houses were flooded up to the first floor. Beaches were washed away. Brandt's Lighthouse was swallowed up by the sea.

15. Marta was her father's favorite, and she felt free to do whatever she wanted.

## 8c  Do not subordinate major ideas.

If a sentence buries its major idea in a subordinate construction, readers are not likely to give it enough attention. Express the main idea in an independent clause and subordinate all minor ideas.

▶ His starting salary, is roughly $15,000, ~~which~~ will increase by
   $\wedge$
   10 to 15 percent yearly until it reaches $25,000.

> Though the writer had wanted to focus on the future increase, the original sentence highlighted the starting salary and subordinated the future increase. The revision improves the emphasis by expressing the future increase in the independent clause and putting the starting salary in an appositive phrase.

   *As*
▶ I was driving home from my new job, heading down New
   $\wedge$
   York Avenue, ~~when~~ my car started overheating.

> The writer wanted to emphasize that the car was overheating, not the fact of driving home. The revision expresses the main idea in an independent clause, the less important idea in a subordinate clause.

## 8d  Do not subordinate excessively.

In attempting to avoid short, choppy sentences, writers sometimes move to the opposite extreme, putting more subordinate ideas into a sentence than its structure can bear. If a sentence collapses of its own weight, occasionally it can be restructured. More often, however, such sentences must be divided.

▶ Our job is to stay between the stacker and the tie machine
watching to see if the newspapers jam/*If they do,* ~~in which case~~ we pull
the bundles off and stack them on a skid, because otherwise
they would back up in the stacker and the press would have
to be turned off.

## EXERCISE 8-2

In each of the following sentences, the idea that the writer wished to emphasize is buried in a subordinate construction. Restructure each sentence so that the independent clause expresses the main idea and lesser ideas are subordinated. Example:

*Though*
Catherine has weathered many hardships, ~~though~~ she has

rarely become discouraged. [*Emphasize the fact that Catherine has rarely become discouraged.*]

a. This highly specialized medical training is called a "residency," which usually takes four years to complete. [*Emphasize the length of time.*]
b. Lanie, who now walks with the help of braces, had polio at a young age. [*Emphasize how Lanie now walks.*]
c. I presented the idea of job sharing to my supervisors, who to my surprise were delighted with the idea. [*Emphasize the supervisors' response to the idea.*]

1. Manuel worked many odd jobs before finally securing a position in a restaurant, where he was paid twelve pesos a month. [*Emphasize the fact that Manuel secured a position.*]
2. The building housed a school, a grocery store, an auto repair shop, and three families on the top floor when it burned to the ground last week. [*Emphasize the fact that the building burned down.*]

3. The principal lived on Latches Lane, where parents and teachers met to discuss the suspension of several students for misconduct. [*Emphasize the meeting.*]
4. We were traveling down I-96 when we were hit in the rear by a speeding Oldsmobile. [*Emphasize the accident.*]
5. Cecelia, who graduated first in her class, stood last in line. [*Emphasize Cecelia's graduating first in her class.*]

# 9

## Balance parallel ideas.

If two or more ideas are parallel, they should be expressed in parallel grammatical form. Single words should be balanced with single words, phrases with phrases, clauses with clauses.

> A kiss can be a comma, a question mark, or an exclamation point.
> —Mistinguett

> This novel is not to be tossed lightly aside, but to be hurled with great force.
> —Dorothy Parker

> In matters of principle, stand like a rock; in matters of taste, swim with the current.
> —Thomas Jefferson

## 9a  Use parallelism with coordinating conjunctions.

Coordinating conjunctions (*and, but, or, nor, for, so, yet*) are used to connect a pair or a series of items. Those items should be expressed in parallel grammatical form.

| NOT PARALLEL | Theft, vandalism, and cheating can result in *suspension* or even *being expelled* from school. |
|---|---|
| PARALLEL | Theft, vandalism, and cheating can result in *suspension* or even *expulsion* from school. |

The coordinating conjunction *or* links a pair of items. Expressing one of those items as a noun and the other as a gerund phrase is awkward. The revision balances the noun *expulsion* with the noun *suspension*.

▶ As the judge reviewed her case, Mary told him that she had

been pulled out of a line of fast-moving traffic and ~~of her~~ *that she had a*

perfect driving record.

A *that* clause should not be paired with an *of* phrase. One way to correct the problem is to turn the *of* phrase into a *that* clause. Another is to restructure the sentence by adding another verb: *As the judge reviewed her case, Mary argued that she had been pulled out of a line of fast-moving traffic and told him of her perfect driving record.*

▶ David is responsible for stocking merchandise, ~~all in-store items in the store, repairs~~, writing orders for delivery, and ~~sales of~~ mini- and *repairing* *selling* microcomputers.

The items in the series must be made parallel: *stocking, repairing, writing,* and *selling.*

**NOTE:** Clauses beginning with *and who* or *and which* should be balanced with an earlier *who* or *which*, or the conjunction *and* should be dropped.

▶ Austin is a young man of many talents ~~and~~ who promises to

be a successful artist.

Deleting *and* is the best way to revise this sentence, for repeating *who* leads to unnecessary words: *Austin is a young man who has many talents and who promises to be a successful artist.*

## **9b** Use parallelism with correlative conjunctions.

Correlative conjunctions come in pairs: *either . . . or, neither . . . nor, not only . . . but also, both . . . and, whether . . . or.* Make sure that the grammatical structure following the first half of the pair is the same as that following the second half.

▶ The shutters were not only too long but ~~were~~ also too wide.

The words *too long* follow *not only,* so *too wide* should follow *but also.* Repeating *were* creates an unbalanced effect.

                                     *to*
▶ I was advised either to change my flight or ∧ take the train.

*To change my flight,* which follows *either,* should be balanced with *to take the train,* which follows *or.*

## **9c** Repeat function words to clarify parallels.

Function words such as prepositions and subordinating conjunctions signal the grammatical nature of the word groups to follow. Though they can sometimes be omitted, include them whenever they signal parallel structures that might otherwise be missed by readers.

▶ Many smokers try switching to a brand they find distasteful
  *to*
or ∧ a low tar and nicotine cigarette.

In the original sentence the prepositional phrase was too complex for easy reading. The addition of a second preposition *to* prevents readers from losing their way.

▶ The ophthalmologist told me that Julie was extremely
              *that*
farsighted but corrective lenses would help considerably.
           ∧

A second subordinating conjunction helps readers sort out the
two parallel ideas: *that* Julie was extremely farsighted and *that*
corrective lenses would help.

## EXERCISE 9–1

Edit the following sentences to correct faulty parallelism. Example:

    Karen was a friend of many years ~~and~~ who helped us

    through some rough times.

a. The board reported that their investments had done well in the
first quarter but they had since dropped in value.
b. The personnel officer told me that I would answer the phone,
welcome visitors, distribute mail, and some typing.
c. We couldn't decide whether to go to the movie or the concert
would be better.
d. The instructor taught us how to breathe, float, the elementary
backstroke, the crawl, and the dog paddle.
e. Nancy not only called the post office but she checked with the
neighbors to see if the package had come.

1. Many states are reducing property taxes for homeowners as well
as extend financial aid in the form of tax credits to renters.
2. Arch-ups are done on the floor face down, with arms extended
over the head, toes pointed, and knees stay straight.
3. Sue and Terry are completing their math homework, Tom is
giving Jim directions to his apartment, Steve is catching up on
some sleep, and the rest of the class can be seen daydreaming.
4. Basic training was the most humiliating period of my life. I was
not only told what to do but also what to think.
5. The Food and Drug Administration has admitted that sodium
nitrite can be poisonous to small children, can deform the fe-

tuses of pregnant women, and it can cause serious harm to anemic persons.

6. I will do my best in cleaning up this neighborhood and restore law and order.

7. The baseball commissioner warned me that the girls were between the ages of eight and ten years old and most had never played softball before.

8. Your adviser familiarizes you with the school and exactly what you'll be doing for the next four to five months.

9. The jury decided that he had lied, stolen, and he had resisted arrest.

10. The eyewitness reported that he had seen a woman running and the burning of the store.

# 10

## Add needed words.

Do not omit words necessary for grammatical or logical completeness. Readers need to see at a glance how the parts of a sentence are connected.

## 10a Add words needed to complete compound structures.

In compound structures, words are often omitted for economy: *The first half of our life is ruined by our parents,* [*and*] *the second half* [*is ruined*] *by our children.* Such omissions are perfectly acceptable as long as the omitted words are common to both parts of the compound structure.

If the shorter version defies grammar or idiom because an omitted word is not common to both parts of the compound structure, the word must be put back in.

► Some of the regulars are acquaintances whom we see at

work or live in our community.
*who*
∧

The word *who* must be included because *whom live in our community* is not grammatically correct.

*accepted*
► I never have and never will accept a bribe.
∧

*Have . . . accept* is not grammatically correct, so *accepted* must be inserted to complete *have.*

*in*
► Many of these tribes still believe and live by ancient laws.
∧

*Believe . . . by* is not idiomatic in English, so the appropriate preposition must be inserted: *believe in.*

**10b** Add the word *that* if there is any danger of misreading without it.

If there is no danger of misreading, the subordinating conjunction *that* may be deleted: *The value of a principle is the number of things [that] it will explain.* Occasionally, however, a sentence might be misread without *that.*

*that*
► As Joe began to prepare dinner, he discovered the oven
∧

wasn't working properly.

Joe didn't discover *the oven;* he discovered *that the oven wasn't working properly.*

*that*
► Many civilians believe the Air Force has a vigorous exercise
∧

program.

The subordinating conjunction tells readers to expect a clause, not just *the Air Force*, as the direct object of *believe*.

## 10c  Add words needed to make comparisons logical and complete.

Comparisons should be made between like items. To compare unlike items is illogical and distracting.

▶ Agnes had an attention span longer than ^*that of* most of her

classmates.

It is illogical to compare an attention span to classmates. Since repeating the words *attention span* would be awkward, insert *that of* to correct the problem.

▶ My current life is not as exciting as ^*the lives of* some of my friends.

Lives must be compared with lives, not with friends.

Sometimes the word *other* must be inserted to make a comparison logical.

▶ Chicago is larger than any ^*other* city in Illinois.

Since Chicago is not larger than itself, the original comparison was not logical. The word *other* corrects the problem.

In addition to being logical, comparisons should be complete enough to ensure clarity.

| | |
|---|---|
| **INCOMPLETE** | The soil was too acidic. |
| **COMPLETE** | The soil was too acidic for peonies. |

| | |
|---|---|
| **UNCLEAR** | Mr. Kelly was able to help me more than my roommate. |
| **CLEAR** | Mr. Kelly was able to help me more than he was able to help my roommate. |
| **CLEAR** | Mr. Kelly was able to help me more than my roommate was. |

## EXERCISE 10–1

Add any words needed for grammatical or logical completeness in the following sentences. Example:

> **Some say Ella Fitzgerald's renditions of Cole Porter's songs**
> *those of other*
> **are better than any singer.**
> ∧ ∧

a. For many years Americans had trust and affection for Walter Cronkite.

b. My brother's car was bigger than any of his friends.

c. SETI (the Search for Extraterrestrial Intelligence) has and will continue to excite interest among space buffs.

d. Many people believe the government is wasting money by monitoring outer space for signs of intelligent life.

e. The author uses the Sanchez family to provide an inside view of family life and what it means to grow up in a one-room apartment in Mexico City.

1. We were glad to see the State House was being restored.

2. More plants fail from improper watering than any other cause.

3. I quit Weight Watchers not because I didn't want to go but my friend stopped going with me.

4. Our graduates are more skilled and have an absentee rate lower than the rest of the work force.

5. She worked at the Department of Agriculture for five years and Brook Foundation for six months.

6. The doctor informed us that Toni had a tumor the size of a small grapefruit and cancerous cells were raging throughout her body.

7. Uncle John's car resembled other bootleggers; it had a smoke screen device useful in case he was pursued by the constable.
8. Gunther Gebel-Williams, whom we watched today and is a star of the Ringling Brothers and Barnum & Bailey Circus, is well known for his training of circus animals.
9. Thomas finally decided to join the army and been in it ever since.
10. My story isn't much different from thousands of other young people who decided to join the navy and see the world.

# 11

## Untangle mixed constructions.

A mixed construction contains parts that do not sensibly fit together. The mismatch may be a matter of grammar or of logic.

## 11a Untangle the grammatical structure.

Once you head into a sentence, your choices are limited by the range of grammatical patterns in English. You cannot begin with one pattern and end with another.

| | |
|---|---|
| **MIXED** | The more experienced men in the system Zeke assigned two aircraft to them. |
| **REVISED** | The more experienced men in the system were assigned two aircraft by Zeke. |
| **REVISED** | Zeke assigned two aircraft to the more experienced men in the system. |

If the original sentence is to begin with *The more experienced men in the system*, it must end in the passive voice: *were assigned two aircraft.* The writer who prefers to emphasize Zeke needs to head into the sentence another way: *Zeke assigned two aircraft. . . .*

▶ ~~By~~ ͟Loosening the soil around your jade plant will help the air and nutrients penetrate to the roots.

The writer began with a long prepositional phrase that was destined to be a modifier but then tried to press it into service as the subject of the sentence. This cannot be done. Deleting *by* corrects the problem since the gerund phrase *loosening the soil around your jade plant* can be the subject.

▶ ~~In~~ ͟The whole-word method children ~~learn~~ *teaches* to recognize entire words;~~rather than by~~ the phonics method ~~in which they~~ *teaches them* ~~learn~~ to sound out letters and groups of letters.

Occasionally a mixed construction is so tangled that it defies grammatical analysis. When this happens, back away from the sentence, rethink what you want to say, and then say it again as clearly as you can.

## 11b Straighten out logical connections.

The subject and the verb should make sense together. When they don't, the error is known as *faulty predication.*

> **FAULTY** The growth in the number of applications is increasing rapidly.

> **REVISED** The number of applications is increasing rapidly.

It is not the growth that is increasing, but the number of applications.

▶ On the third day ~~my name and~~ a man named Barnes were

*and I* (inserted above "my name and")

∧ (caret below "were")

called to go with the First Infantry Division.

Two men were called, not a name and a man.

## EXERCISE 11 – 1

Edit the following sentences to untangle mixed constructions. Example:

**I brought a problem into the house that my mother wasn't**

**sure how to handle ~~it~~.**

a. My instant reaction was filled with anger and disappointment.
b. The three who came in together I gave the books to first.
c. For people who are incapacitated or bedridden they may have their meals delivered by a service known as "meals on wheels."
d. When one is promoted without warning can be alarming.
e. By encouraging the players to excel may help them learn to overcome obstacles later in life.

1. By winning all the primaries in the western part of the country helped the senator from Wyoming claim the final victory.
2. In unfair supervising, workers often feel resentment against the whole company, not just against the managers at fault.
3. The change in the quality of students has worsened each year.
4. In pushing the button for the insert mode opens the computer memory.
5. This entails giving the bartender two dollars and he gives you a mug that may be filled with as much beer as you want throughout the tournament.
6. Visitors to Chewonki have commented on their observations that campers seem busy and challenged.
7. The tax accountant can be a very lucrative field.
8. You will know that the customer has written a bad check when you enter the account number, found on the bottom of the check, and a two-digit number will appear on the screen.

9. First the attitude of the parent is disappointment toward the child, then anger, and reaches the point of abusing the child.

10. The little time we have together we try to use it wisely.

# 12

## Repair misplaced and dangling modifiers.

Modifiers, whether they are single words, phrases, or clauses, should point clearly to the words they modify.

**12a** Put limiting modifiers next to the words they modify.

Limiting modifiers such as *only*, *even*, *almost*, *nearly*, and *just* should appear in front of a verb only if they modify the verb. If they limit the meaning of some other word in the sentence, they should be positioned next to that word.

▶ You will ~~only~~ need to plant <sub>∧</sub>*only* one package of seeds.

Our team didn't ~~even~~ score *even* once.

Bob ~~almost~~ *almost* ate the whole chicken.

*Only* limits the meaning of *one*, not *need. Even* modifies *once*, not *score; almost* modifies *the whole chicken*, not *ate*.

**12b** Position phrases and clauses so that readers can see at a glance what they modify.

When whole phrases or clauses have been positioned oddly, absurd misreadings can result.

| | |
|---|---|
| **MISPLACED** | The king returned to the clinic where he underwent heart surgery in 1972 in a limousine sent by the White House. |
| **REVISED** | Traveling in a limousine sent by the White House, the king returned to the clinic where he underwent heart surgery in 1972. |

The king did not undergo heart surgery in a limousine. The revision corrects this false impression.

*on the walls*

▶ ~~There~~ are many pictures of comedians ~~on the walls~~ who have
  ∧

performed at Gavin's.

The walls didn't perform at Gavin's; the comedians did. The writer at first revised the sentence like this: *There are many pictures of comedians who have performed at Gavin's on the walls.* But this creates another absurd effect. Surely the comedians weren't performing on the walls.

*by the media*

▶ The Secret Service was falsely accused of mishandling the
  ∧

attempted assassination ~~by the media.~~
  ∧

The media did not attempt an assassination. The phrase *by the media* should be moved closer to the verb it modifies, *was accused.*

Occasionally the placement of a modifier leads to an ambiguity, in which case two revisions will be possible, depending on the writer's intended meaning.

| | |
|---|---|
| **AMBIGUOUS** | We promised when the play was over we would take Charles to an ice cream parlor. |
| **CLEAR** | When the play was over, we promised Charles that we would take him to an ice cream parlor. |
| **CLEAR** | We promised Charles that we would take him to an ice cream parlor when the play was over. |

The first revision suggests that the promising occurred when the play was over, the second that the taking would occur when the play was over.

EXERCISE 12–1

Edit the following sentences to correct misplaced modifiers. Example:

*in a telephone survey*
**Answering questions can be annoying.~~in a telephone survey.~~**
                  ∧                    ∧

a. Marie almost played the whole game, but she was taken out in the last ten minutes.
b. He only wanted to buy a single rose, not a dozen.
c. Our interest in the British royal family is sparked in the opinion of the press by royal weddings and births, but not by royal politics.
d. He promised never to remarry at her deathbed.
e. Each state would set a program into motion of recycling all reusable products.

1. We will inherit the library of a professor of exceptional quality.
2. Sarah said she could handle the diet because she only had to stay on it for a week.
3. Eric took a course at a university that represents a new low in education.
4. In late 1973, the major oil producers put an embargo on crude oil sent to the United States that shocked the nation.
5. Within the next few years, orthodontists will be using the technique Kurtz developed as standard practice.

**12c**  Repair dangling modifiers.

When a sentence opens with a modifier that suggests an action but lacks a subject, the modifier's "understood" subject should be the same word as the subject of the sentence. If the subject of the sentence cannot serve logically as the understood subject of the modifier, the modifier is said to dangle.

**DANGLING** *Reaching the heart,* a bypass is performed by the surgeon on the severely blocked arteries. [*participial phrase*]

**DANGLING** *After swimming across the lake,* the lifeguard scolded me for risking my life. [*preposition followed by a gerund phrase*]

**DANGLING** *To please the children,* some fireworks were set off a day early. [*infinitive phrase*]

**DANGLING** *Though only sixteen,* UCLA accepted Martha as a freshman. [*elliptical clause with an understood subject and verb*]

These dangling modifiers falsely suggest that the bypass reached the heart, that the lifeguard swam across the lake, that the fireworks intended to please the children, and that UCLA is only sixteen years old.

To repair a dangling modifier, you must restructure the sentence in one of two ways: (1) change the subject of the sentence so that it expresses the logical understood subject of the phrase or (2) turn the modifier into a word group containing a subject.

**DANGLING** After swimming across the lake, the lifeguard scolded me for risking my life.

**REPAIRED** After swimming across the lake, I was scolded by the lifeguard for risking my life.

**REPAIRED** After I swam across the lake, the lifeguard scolded me for risking my life.

Modifiers can also dangle when they appear at the end of a sentence, so you cannot repair a dangling modifier simply by moving it: *The lifeguard scolded me for risking my life after swimming across the lake.* The understood subject of *swimming* is still the subject of the sentence, *lifeguard*, so the meaning continues to be illogical.

▶ ~~Thinking~~ *Although Lydia thought* that justice had finally prevailed, ~~Lydia's~~ *her* troubles
were just beginning.

It wasn't the troubles that did the thinking; it was Lydia. The writer corrected the problem by turning the opening participial phrase into an adverb clause, a word group containing a subject.

▶ After completing seminary training, ordination or access to *women have often been denied*
the pulpit ~~has often been denied to women.~~

The subject of the sentence, *ordination or access to the pulpit*, is not the logical understood subject of *completing*. The writer corrected the problem by making *women* the subject of the sentence.

EXERCISE 12–2

Edit the following sentences to correct dangling modifiers. Most sentences can be repaired in more than one way. Example:

*students are required*
To acquire a degree in almost any field, ~~most universities~~
*to complete*
~~require that~~ two science courses ~~be completed.~~

a. By taking good care of myself, the flu never kept me from work this year.
b. To protest arms buildup, bonfires were set throughout the park.
c. Feeling unprepared for the exam, the questions were just as hard as she had expected them to be.
d. While still a beginner at tennis, the coaches recruited the gifted young athlete for the Olympic team.
e. Commercials are especially irritating when watching my favorite series.

1. Opening the window to let out a huge bumblebee, the car accidentally swerved into the lane of oncoming cars.
2. To get the most from walking, Dr. Curtis recommends striding rather than strolling.
3. While waiting in line for gas, the attendant washed my windshield and checked under the hood.
4. Seeing her standing there with suitcase in hand, it dawned on me that this was the moment for which we had been waiting.
5. Shortly after being seated, a waiter approached our table with a smile and a bowl of freshly popped corn.

# 13

## Pull related words together.

**13a** Make the sentence flow from subject to verb to object, without lengthy detours along the way.

Readers can hold fairly long word groups in mind, but they can do so more easily if related words are kept together.

▶ ~~Kilmer,~~ after doctors told him that he would never walk
     *A*
     *Kilmer*
again, initiated on his own an intense program of
         *∧*
rehabilitation.

There is no reason to separate the subject *Kilmer* from the verb *initiated* with a long adverb clause.

▶ ~~Roberto seemed,~~ although he took his responsibilities as a
              *A*

father seriously and professed a deep love for his children,
*Roberto seemed*
  unable to display his affection.
*∧*

The verb *seemed* should not be so distant from its complement, *unable to display his affection.*

## 13b Put helping verbs close to their main verbs.

It is perfectly acceptable to put one or two words between a helping verb and its main verb: *The jury has not yet reached a decision.* However, when longer word groups intervene between the two parts of a verb, the result is awkward.

> ~~Mavis has finally,~~ after weighing the pros and cons of job
> *Mavis has finally*
> sharing, decided to inquire about it.

The helping verb *has* should be closer to its main verb, *decided*.

## 13c Do not split infinitives needlessly.

An infinitive consists of *to* plus a verb: *to think, to breathe, to dance.* When words appear between its two parts, an infinitive is said to be "split": *to carefully balance.* If a split infinitive is obviously awkward, it should be revised.

> *If possible, the*
> ~~The~~ patient should try to, ~~if possible,~~ avoid going up and
> down stairs.

Usage varies when a split infinitive is less awkward than the preceding one. To be on the safe side, however, you should unsplit such infinitives, especially in formal writing.

> *formally*
> The candidate decided to ~~formally~~ launch her campaign.

When a split infinitive is more natural and less awkward than alternative phrasing, most readers find it acceptable:

*We decided to actually enforce the law* is a perfectly natural construction in English. *We decided actually to enforce the law* is not.

## EXERCISE 13 – 1

Edit the following sentences to pull together sentence parts that have been awkwardly separated. Example:

            *A*                             *Nancy*

~~Nancy,~~ after she won the big jackpot in the lottery, went

                                          ∧

**completely crazy.**

  a. She had, before finally becoming fed up with the questions, answered the telephone survey for at least fifteen minutes.
  b. The prospectors found, despite horrid weather, poor equipment, and long odds, gold.
  c. The Piltdown hoax, coming early in this century when evolutionary theory was in its infancy, had a profound effect on paleoanthropologists' thinking.
  d. Jurors are encouraged to carefully and thoroughly sift through the evidence.
  e. The old house, dilapidated but lovely, with a gabled roof, a wide veranda, and a spreading oak in the back yard, was a good buy.

  1. The candidate promised to once and for all lower taxes and raise the standard of living.
  2. Many students have, by the time they reach their senior year, completed all the requirements for their major.
  3. The journal has a circulation, not including copies sent to libraries and schools, of 30,000.
  4. The firefighters finally, after running up the stairs, barging through the door, and shouting to one another from room to room, found a charred and smoking piece of toast in the kitchen sink.
  5. The spacecraft landed, after a few minor mishaps and a brief loss of communication with Mission Control, on the moon.
  6. Oscar Lewis, in researching *The Children of Sanchez,* spent hundreds of hours living with the Sanchez family in a slum in Mexico City.

7. Joe Martin, after trying a number of graduate programs, including English literature and architecture, finally received a master of fine arts degree from the University of California.

8. Our tiny kitten, Muffin, had finally, after suffering many humiliations from twenty-pound Susie, managed to get her revenge.

9. The way to most conveniently purchase the ticket is to give your credit card number over the phone.

10. Eventually John discovered how to more effectively supervise his employees.

# 14

**Eliminate distracting shifts.**

## 14a Make the point of view consistent.

The point of view of a paper is the perspective from which it is written: first person (*I* or *we*), second person (*you*), or third person (*he/she/it/one* or *they*). Writers who are having difficulty settling on an appropriate point of view sometimes shift confusingly from one to another. The solution is to choose a suitable perspective and then stay with it. (See 3b.)

▶ One week our class met in a junkyard to practice rescuing a

victim trapped in a wrecked car. We learned to dismantle the

car with the essential tools. ~~You~~ *We* were graded on ~~your~~ *our* speed

and ~~your~~ *our* skill in extricating the victim.

The writer should have stayed with the "we" point of view. *You* is inappropriate because the writer is not addressing the reader directly. *You* should not be used in a vague sense meaning *anyone*.

▶ *You*
~~Everyone~~ should purchase a lift ticket unless you plan to
∧
spend most of your time walking or crawling up a steep hill.

Here *you* is an appropriate choice, since the writer is giving
advice directly to readers.

**NOTE:** For shifts from singular to plural pronouns, see 22.

## 14b  Make verbs consistent in tense, mood, and voice.

Consistent verb tenses clearly establish the time of the actions being described. When a passage begins in one tense and then shifts without warning and for no reason to another, readers are distracted and confused.

> **CONFUSING**  My hopes *rise* and *fall* as Joseph's heart *started*
> and *stopped*. The doctors *insert* a large tube into
> his chest, and blood *flows* from the incision onto
> the floor. The tube *drained* some blood from his
> lung, but it *was* all in vain. At 8:35 P.M. Joseph
> *was* declared dead.

The writer had tried to make his narrative more vivid by casting it in the present tense, but he found this choice too difficult to sustain. The wisest option, he decided, was to draft the whole narrative in the past tense:

▶ My hopes ~~rise~~ *rose* and ~~fall~~ *fell* as Joseph's heart started and
                ∧         ∧
stopped. The doctors ~~insert~~ *inserted* a large tube into his chest, and
                     ∧      *inserted*
blood ~~flows~~ *flowed* from the incision onto the floor. The tube
      ∧     ∧
drained some blood from his lung, but it was all in vain. At
∧

8:35 P.M. Joseph was declared dead.

Unnecessary shifts in the mood of a verb can be as distracting as needless shifts in tense. There are three moods in English: the indicative, used for facts, opinions, and questions; the imperative, used for orders or advice; and the subjunctive, used for wishes or conditions contrary to fact (see 27).

Most shifts in mood occur between the indicative and the imperative.

> **CONFUSING** The officers advised against allowing access to our homes without proper identification. Also, alert neighbors to vacation schedules.

The first sentence is written in the indicative mood, the second in the imperative. Since the writer's purpose was to report the police officers' advice, both sentences should appear in the indicative.

▶ The officers advised against allowing access to our homes
   *They also suggested that we*
   without proper identification. ~~Also,~~ alert neighbors to
                                 ∧
   vacation schedules.

The voice of a verb may be either active (with the subject doing the action) or passive (with the subject receiving the action). If a writer shifts without warning from one to the other, readers may be left wondering why (see 27f).

> **CONFUSING** When the tickets are ready, the travel agent notifies the client. Each ticket is then listed on a daily register form and a copy of the itinerary is filed.

The passage begins in the active voice, with the travel agent doing the action, and then switches to the passive, with the tickets receiving the action. Because the active voice is nearly always clearer and more direct, the passage should have the travel agent performing all of the actions.

▶ When the tickets are ready, the travel agent notifies the
client, ~~Each ticket is then listed~~ *lists each ticket* on a daily register form, and
a copy of the itinerary. ~~is filed.~~ *files*

## EXERCISE 14–1

Edit the following sentences to eliminate distracting shifts. Example:

For most people it is not easy to quit smoking once ~~you~~ *they* are

hooked.

a. One man collects the tickets and another would search the concert patrons for drugs.
b. Newspapers put the lurid details of an armed robbery on page 1, and the warm, human interest stories are relegated to page G–10.
c. We waited in the emergency room for about an hour. Finally, the nurse comes in and tells us that we are in the wrong place.
d. We drove for eight hours until we reached the South Dakota Badlands. You could hardly believe the eeriness of the landscape at dusk.
e. The most successful weight-loss programs combine dieting with physical exercise. Don't skip meals and expect to lose weight.

1. The chimpanzees gesture playfully to their keeper. The animals had signs requesting food, water, and attention.
2. As we stroll along the canal we notice turtles sunning on old tree trunks emerging from the water. On the bank opposite us someone noticed an unusual bloom and is busy capturing it with a telephoto lens.
3. According to Dr. Winfield, a person who wants to become a doctor must first earn a B.S. degree. After this you must take a medical aptitude test called the MCAT.

4. Caesar came; he saw; the enemy was conquered by him.
5. The highlight of my weekends in Iowa was riding up and down Main Street seeing how much beer you could drink.
6. I began digging through the pile of magazines I had brought out to the porch. All of a sudden a big red Monte Carlo with two teenage boys in it goes by and toots the horn. One of the guys waved at me, and I waved back.
7. Two years were spent in training, and then Palmer worked for four years aboard a nuclear submarine.
8. To get the most from your practice time, a group should practice together, as a band, instead of individually.
9. When the director travels, you will make the hotel and airline reservations and if necessary you will arrange for a rental car. A detailed itinerary must be prepared.
10. With a little self-discipline and a desire to improve oneself, you too can enjoy the benefits that running has to offer.

# 15

---

**Provide some variety.**

---

When a rough draft is filled with too many same-sounding sentences, try injecting some variety — as long as you can do so without sacrificing clarity or ease of reading.

## 15a  Use a variety of sentence openings.

Most sentences in English begin with the subject, move to the verb, and continue along to the object, with modifiers tucked in along the way or put at the end. For the most part, such sentences are fine. Put too many of them in a row, however, and they become monotonous.

Adverbial modifiers, being easily movable, can often be inserted ahead of the subject. Such modifiers might be single words, phrases, or clauses.

▶ *Eventually a*
 ~~A~~ few drops of sap ~~eventually~~ began to trickle into the pail.
 ∧

Like most adverbs, *eventually* does not need to appear close to the verb it modifies (*began*).

▶ *Just as the sun was coming up, a*
 ~~A~~ pair of black ducks flew over the blind.~~just as the sun was~~
 ∧                                            ∧
 ~~coming up.~~

The adverb clause, which modifies the verb *flew*, is as clear at the beginning of the sentence as it is at the end.

Adjectival modifiers can frequently be moved to the head of a sentence, as long as the subject of the sentence names the person or thing being described.

▶ *Dejected and withdrawn,*
 Edward,~~dejected and withdrawn,~~ nearly gave up his search
 ∧

for a job.

The single-word adjectives *dejected* and *withdrawn* can be moved ahead of the subject, *Edward*, which they modify.

▶            *A*                          *John and I*
 ~~John and I,~~ anticipating a peaceful evening, sat down at the
                                         ∧

campfire to brew a cup of coffee.

Many participial phrases can be moved without mishap. *Anticipating a peaceful evening* can open the sentence as long as the subject of the sentence names the persons doing the anticipating. If the words *John and I* were not the subject of the sentence, the modifier would dangle. (See 12c.)

## 15b Use a variety of sentence structures.

A writer should not rely too heavily on simple sentences and compound sentences, for the effect tends to be both monotonous and choppy. (See 8.) Too many complex or compound-complex sentences, however, can be equally monotonous. If your style tends to one or the other extreme, try to achieve a better mix of sentence types.

| | |
|---|---|
| **SIMPLE** | Education should be gentle and stern, not cold and lax.     — Joubert |
| **COMPOUND** | Victory has a hundred fathers, but defeat is an orphan.     — Count Caleazzo Ciano |
| **COMPLEX** | We never fully grasp the import of any true statement until we have a clear notion of what the opposite untrue statement would be.     —William James |
| **COMPOUND-COMPLEX** | Power undirected by high purpose spells calamity, and high purpose by itself is utterly useless if the power to put it into effect is lacking.     — Theodore Roosevelt |

For a fuller discussion of sentence types, see 50.

## 15c Try inverting sentences occasionally.

A sentence is inverted if it does not follow the normal subject-verb-object pattern. Many inversions sound artificial and should be avoided except in the most formal contexts. But if an inversion sounds natural, it can provide a welcome touch of variety.

▶ *Opposite the produce section is a* ^ A refrigofted case of mouth-watering cheeses ~~is opposite~~ ; ^
~~the produce section;~~ a friendly attendant will cut off just the

amount you want.

The revision inverts the normal subject-verb order by moving the verb, *is*, ahead of its subject, *case*.

*Set at the top two corners of the stage were huge*

▶ ~~Huge~~ lavender hearts outlined in bright white lights ~~were set~~
  ∧                                                        ∧

~~at the top two corners of the stage.~~

In the revision the subject, *hearts*, appears after the verb, *were set*. Notice that the two parts of the verb are also inverted — and separated from one another — without any awkwardness or loss of meaning.

## EXERCISE 15–1

Edit the following paragraph to increase variety in sentence structure.

I have spent thirty years of my life on a tobacco farm, and I cannot understand why people smoke. The whole process of raising tobacco involves deadly chemicals. The ground is treated for mold and chemically fertilized before the tobacco seed is ever planted. The seed is planted and begins to grow, and then the bed is treated with weed killer. The plant is then transferred to the field. It is sprayed with poison to kill worms about two months later. Then the time for harvest approaches, and the plant is sprayed once more with a chemical to retard the growth of suckers. The tobacco is harvested and hung in a barn to dry. These barns are havens for birds. The birds defecate all over the leaves. After drying, these leaves are divided by color, and no feces are removed. They are then sold to the tobacco companies. I do not know what the tobacco companies do after they receive the tobacco. I do not need to know. They cannot remove what I know is in the leaf and on the leaf. I don't want any of it to pass through my mouth.

# PART IV

# *Changing Words*

# 16

## Tighten wordy sentences.

In a rough draft we are rarely economical: We repeat ourselves, we belabor the obvious, we cushion our thoughts in verbiage. As a general rule, advises writer Sidney Smith, "run a pen through every other word you have written; you have no idea what vigor it will give your style."

Long sentences are not necessarily wordy, nor are short sentences always concise. A sentence is wordy if it can be tightened without loss of meaning.

### 16a Eliminate redundancies.

Writers often repeat themselves unnecessarily. Afraid, perhaps, that they won't be heard the first time, they insist that a teacup is small *in size* or yellow *in color,* that married people should cooperate *together,* that a fact is not just a fact but a *true* fact. Such redundancies may seem at first to add emphasis. In reality they do just the opposite, for they divide the reader's attention.

▶ Black slaves were ~~called or~~ stereotyped as lazy even though they were the main labor force of the South.

Standing before us was Stevie Wonder, an entertainer whom

I idolize.~~and for whom I have the deepest admiration.~~
⋀

Each sentence is stronger if its key idea is expressed only once. In the first sentence, *stereotyped* expresses the idea most precisely, so *called or* should be dropped. In the second sentence, the writer should drop either *whom I idolize* or *for whom I have the deepest admiration.*

Though modifiers ordinarily add meaning to the words they modify, occasionally they are redundant.

▶ Sylvia ~~very hurriedly~~ scribbled her name, address, and phone number on the back of a greasy napkin.

Joel was determined ~~in his mind~~ to lose weight.

The words *scribbled* and *determined* already contain the notions suggested by the modifiers *very hurriedly* and *in his mind.*

## 16b Avoid unnecessary repetition.

Though words may be repeated deliberately, for effect, repetitions will seem awkward if they are clearly unnecessary. When a more concise version is possible, choose it.

▶ Our fifth patient, in room six, is ~~a~~ mentally ill~~,patient.~~

▶ The best teachers help each student to ~~become a better student~~ *grow* both academically and emotionally.

## 16c Cut empty or inflated phrases.

An empty phrase can be cut with little or no loss of meaning. Common examples are introductory word groups that apologize or hedge: *in my opinion, I think that, it seems that, one must admit that,* and so on.

▶ ~~In my opinion, our~~ _Our_ current policy in Central America is

misguided on several counts.

▶ ~~It seems that~~ Metro's fare collection system could be

simplified if only area jurisdictions would agree on a flat

rate.

Readers understand without being told that they are hearing the
writer's opinion or educated guess.

Inflated phrases can be reduced to a word or two without
loss of meaning.

| INFLATED | CONCISE |
|---|---|
| along the lines of | like |
| at this point in time | now |
| by means of | by |
| due to the fact that | because |
| for the purpose of | for |
| for the reason that | because |
| in order to | to |
| in spite of the fact that | although (though) |
| in the event that | if |
| in the final analysis | finally |
| in the neighborhood of | about |
| until such time as | until |

▶ We will file the appropriate papers ~~in the event tha~~t _if_ we are

unable to meet the deadline.

▶ _Because_ ~~Due to the fact that~~ the guest of honor is ill, the party is

being postponed until next Saturday.

## 16d Simplify the structure.

If the structure of a sentence is needlessly indirect, try simplifying it. Look for opportunities to strengthen the verb.

▶ Rarely should the doctor ~~give a patient an~~ estimate ~~of~~ how
    *a patient*
many months or years ~~he or she~~ will live.
                   ∧

The verb *estimate* is more vigorous and more concise than *give a patient an estimate of*.

The colorless verbs *is*, *are*, *was*, and *were* frequently generate excess words.

                           *monitors and balances*
▶ The administrative secretary ~~is responsible for monitoring~~
                           ∧

~~and balancing~~ the budgets for travel and contract services.

The revision is more direct and concise. Actions originally appearing in subordinate structures have become verbs replacing *is*.

The constructions *there is* and *there are* (or *there was* and *there were*) also generate excess words.

        *A*
▶ ~~There is~~ another module ~~that~~ tells the story of Charles

Darwin and introduces the theory of evolution.

## 16e Reduce clauses to phrases, phrases to single words.

Word groups functioning as modifiers can often be made more compact. Look for any opportunities to reduce clauses to phrases or phrases to single words.

▶ Thermography, ~~which is~~ a new method of breast cancer detection, records heat patterns on black and white or color-coded film.

A subordinate clause has been reduced to an appositive phrase.

▶ Susan's stylish *leather* jeans, ~~made of leather,~~ were too warm for our climate.

A verbal phrase has become a single word.

## EXERCISE 16 – 1

Edit the following sentences for wordiness. Example:

~~The thing~~ *D* ~~d~~ata sets are used for ~~is~~ communicating with other computers.

a. When visitors come to visit her, she just stares at the wall.
b. The colors of the reproductions were precisely exact.
c. In my opinion, the race for the Democratic nomination is a futile exercise.
d. The town of New Harmony, located in Indiana, was founded as a utopian community.
e. In Biology 10A you will be assigned a faculty tutor who will be available to assign you eight taped modules and help you clarify any information on the tapes.

1. Seeing the barrels, the driver immediately slammed on his brakes.
2. Even the placement of ten terry cloth bath towels stuffed under the door did nothing to stop the flow.
3. Dr. J loves to work with the young people of today.
4. Though orange in color, the letters on the sign were still too dim to be seen and read clearly at night.

5. You will be the contact person for arranging interviews between the institute and the office of personnel.
6. There are two required training classes for all new employees.
7. If there are any new fares, then they must be reported by message to all of our transportation offices.
8. He moved into the house in spite of the fact that the back door was only ten feet away from the train tracks.
9. The institute was established by Congress to develop and provide training for federal, state, and local highway agency employees.
10. Life in early American settlements, which were established under severe conditions, was often brief and bleak.

## EXERCISE 16–2

Edit the following paragraph for wordiness.

We examined the old house from top to bottom. In fact, we started in the attic, which was hot and dusty, and made our way down two flights of stairs, and down one more descent, which was a spiral staircase, into the basement. On our way back up, we thought we heard the eerie noise, the one that had startled us from our sound sleep in the first place. This time the noise was at the top of the staircase that led to the second-floor hallway. We froze and stood quietly at exactly the same moment, listening very intently. Finally, after a few moments, someone said, "Why don't we all go in together and see what it is?" Cautiously, with great care, we stepped over the threshold into the dark hallway, which disappeared into darkness in front of us. There was an unearthly emanating light shining from underneath the door that led into the kitchen. All at once we jumped when we heard a loud crashing sound from behind that door. Before we could rush into the kitchen at high speed, the light went out suddenly, and instantly we were in total pitch black darkness. I thought I heard someone's teeth chattering; then I realized with a shock that it was my own teeth I heard chattering. Without saying a word, we backed silently away from the kitchen door — no one wanted to go in now. Then it was as if someone had shot off a gun, because before we realized what we were doing, we tore up the stairs as fast as we could, and each of us dove into our beds and pulled the covers up and over us to shut out any more frightening sounds and thoughts.

# 17

## Choose appropriate language.

Words are appropriate when they suit your subject, conform to the needs of your audience, and blend naturally with your own style.

## 17a Stay away from jargon.

Jargon is specialized language used among members of a trade, profession, or group. Use jargon only when readers will be familiar with it; even then, use it only when plain English will not do as well.

Sentences filled with jargon are likely to be long and lumpy. To revise such sentences, you must rewrite them, usually in fewer words.

▶ ~~The culturally different student~~ *Minority students* should be ~~subject to meet~~ *evaluated with*  ∧ *the same standards* ~~the same criteria of performance as the majority of the~~ *used for others.* ~~culture.~~

Though a psychologist or sociologist might feel comfortable with the original version, jargon such as *culturally different* and *criteria of performance* is unnecessarily complicated for ordinary readers.

Broadly defined, jargon includes puffed-up language designed more to impress readers than to inform them. Common examples in business, government, higher education, and the military are listed below, with plain English translations in parentheses.

| | |
|---|---|
| ameliorate (improve) | indicator (sign) |
| commence (begin) | optimal (best, most favorable) |
| components (parts) | parameters (boundaries, limits) |
| endeavor (try) | peruse (read, look over) |
| exit (leave) | prior to (before) |
| facilitate (help) | utilize (use) |
| factor (consideration, cause) | viable (workable) |
| impact on (affect) | |

▶ ~~In order that I may increase my expertise in the area of~~

~~delivery of services to clients, I feel that participation in this~~
*This*   *train me to serve our clients better.*
ᴧ conference will ~~be beneficial.~~ ᴧ

*At first the writer tinkered with this sentence — changing* in order that I may *to* to, the area of delivery of *to* delivering, *and so on. The sentence was improved, but it still sounded unnatural. A better solution, this writer discovered, was to rethink what he wanted to say and then rewrite the sentence. Notice that only three words of the original have been preserved.*

## 17b Avoid pretentious language and most euphemisms.

Hoping to sound profound or poetic, some writers embroider their thoughts with large words and flowery phrases, language that in fact sounds pretentious. Pretentious language is so ornate and often so wordy that it obscures the thought that lies beneath.

> When our ~~progenitors reach their silver-haired and golden~~ *parents become old,*
> ~~years,~~ we too frequently ~~ensepulcher~~ *entomb* them in ~~homes for~~ *old-age homes*
> ~~senescent beings~~ as if they were already among the
> ~~deceased.~~ *dead.*

The writer of the original sentence had turned to a thesaurus (a dictionary of synonyms and antonyms) in an attempt to sound educated. When such a writer gains enough confidence to speak in his or her own voice, pretentious language disappears.

Related to pretentious language are euphemisms, nice-sounding words or phrases substituted for words thought to sound harsh or ugly. Like pretentious language, euphemisms are wordy and indirect. Unlike pretentious language, they are sometimes appropriate. It is our social custom, for example, to use euphemisms when speaking or writing about death (*Her sister passed on*), excretion (*I have to go to the bathroom*), sexual intercourse (*They did not sleep together until they were married*), and the like. We may also use euphemisms out of concern for someone's feelings. Telling parents, for example, that their daughter is "unmotivated" is more sensitive than saying she's lazy. Tact or politeness, then, can justify an occasional euphemism.

Most euphemisms, however, are needlessly evasive or even deceitful. Like pretentious language, they obscure the intended meaning.

| EUPHEMISM | PLAIN ENGLISH |
|---|---|
| adult entertainment | pornographic film |
| preowned automobile | used car |
| economically deprived | poor |
| selected out | fired |
| negative savings | debts |
| the Peacekeeper | a nuclear missile |
| strategic withdrawal | retreat or defeat |

## 17c   Avoid obsolete, archaic, or invented words.

Obsolete words are words found in the writing of the past that have dropped out of use entirely. Archaic words are old words that are still used, but only in special contexts such as literature or advertising. Although dictionaries list obsolete words such as *recomfort* and *reechy* and archaic words such as *anon* and *betwixt*, these words are not appropriate for current use.

Invented words (also called *neologisms*) are words too recently created to be part of standard English. Many invented words fade out of use without becoming standard. *Build-down, throughput, parenting,* and *palimony* are neologisms that may not last. *Scuba, disco, sexist, software,* and *spinoff* are no longer neologisms; they have become standard English. Avoid using invented words in your writing unless they are given in the dictionary as standard.

## 17d   Avoid slang, regional expressions, and nonstandard English.

Slang is a vocabulary used by a group such as teenagers, rock musicians, or football fans; it is subject to more rapid change than standard English. For example, the slang teenagers use to express approval changes every few years; *cool, groovy, neat, wicked,* and *awesome* have replaced one another within the last three decades. Sometimes slang shifts its meaning and becomes accepted as standard vocabulary. *Jazz,* for example, started out as slang and is now a generally accepted word describing a style of music.

Slang is a code that not everyone understands, and it is very informal. For these reasons, it is not appropriate for formal writing.

▶ I would like to know ~~where you are coming from emotionally.~~ *the reasons for your mood and your behavior,*

Regional expressions are common to a group in a geographical area. *Let's talk with the bark off* (for *Let's speak frankly*) is an expression in the southern United States, for example. Regional expressions have the same limitations as slang and are not appropriate for formal writing.

> ▶ When I saw black fur by the side of the road, I ~~reckoned~~ the *concluded that* ∧
>
> cat was dead.

Standard English is the language used by educated people in all academic, business, and professional fields. Nonstandard English is spoken by people with a common regional or social heritage. Treating irregular verbs as if they were regular (*It costed $200 to fly there*), omitting necessary verbs (*I been to Texas*), and using double negatives (*Her family don't visit Missouri no more*) are nonstandard. Nonstandard English may be appropriate within a close group, but it is not appropriate in formal writing. See Part VI, Editing for Standard English, for further discussion.

## 17e Choose an appropriate level of formality.

In deciding on a level of formality, consider both your subject and your audience. Does the subject demand a dignified treatment, or is a relaxed tone more suitable? Will the audience be put off if you assume too close a relationship with them, or might you alienate them by seeming too distant?

Formal writing emphasizes the importance of its subject and the exactness of its information. It assumes a distant relationship between writer and audience. An impersonal point of view, a sophisticated vocabulary, and complex sentence structures are typical of formal writing. Contractions (*don't, he'll*) and colloquial words such as *kids* or *buddy* are out of place.

For most college and professional writing, some degree of formality is appropriate. In a letter applying for a job, for example, it is a mistake to sound too breezy and informal.

**TOO INFORMAL**   I'd like to get that receptionist's job you've got in the paper.

**MORE FORMAL**   I would like to apply for the receptionist's position listed in the *Peoria Journal Star.*

Informal writing is appropriate for private letters, articles in popular magazines, and business correspondence between close associates. Like spoken conversation, it allows contractions and colloquial words. Vocabulary and sentence structure are rarely complex.

In choosing a level of formality, above all be consistent. When a writer's voice shifts from one level of formality to another, readers receive mixed messages.

▶ Once a pitcher for the Cincinnati Reds, Bob shared with me
the secrets of his trade. His lesson ~~commenced~~ *began* with his
famous curve ball, ~~implemented~~ *done* by tucking the little finger
behind the ball instead of holding it straight out. Next he
~~elucidated~~ *revealed* the mysteries of the sucker pitch, a slow ball
coming behind a fast windup.

Words such as *commenced* and *elucidated* are inappropriate for the subject matter, and they clash with informal terms such as *sucker pitch* and *fast windup.*

## EXERCISE 17–1

Edit the following sentences to eliminate jargon, pretentious or flowery language, and euphemisms. You may need to make substantial changes in some sentences. Example:

After two weeks in the legal department, Sue has ~~worked~~ *mastered*
~~into~~ the routine ~~of the office~~, *office* and her ~~functional and self~~ *performance has*
~~management skills have~~ exceeded all expectations.

a.  The military plans to defoliate the area with incendiary defense equipment.

b.  Migrations to famed locales of exotica are the diurnal activity of those who have easy access to excess financial resources.

c.  It is a widespread but unproven hypothesis that the parameters of significant personal change for persons in midlife are extremely narrow.

d.  The publicity office believes that the college, through any one of its component members, will be participating in activities that are pregnant with publicity potential. We feel certain that there will be guests and visitors and activities on campus that will be newsworthy. In these instances, we would appreciate any assistance that would alert us to such occurrences.

e.  Dan's early work hours leave him free to utilize afternoons for errands and for helping the children with their homework.

1.  It is your responsibility to impose the regulation standards on the preparation of correspondence. It is also your responsibility to prepare the agenda for each staff meeting with an emphasis on clarification of questions aired during the time lapsed since the last meeting.

2.  When we returned from our evening perambulation, we shrank back in horror as we surmised that our domestic dwelling was being swallowed up in hellish flames.

3.  To facilitate the discussion, Rob began by outlining the factors influencing our decision about whether or not the job training program was viable.

4.  In the vernal season the miraculous reemergence of flora and fauna seems to awaken the human inhabitants of earth from a frigid hibernation.

5.  In my salad days I was under constraints of difficult material circumstances.

## EXERCISE 17 – 2

Edit the following paragraph to eliminate slang and maintain a consistent level of formality.

> The graduation speaker really blew it. He should have discussed the options and challenges facing the graduating class. Instead, he shot his mouth off at us and trashed us for being lazy and pampered. He did make some good points, however. Our profs have certainly babied us by not holding fast to deadlines, by dismissing assignments that the class ragged them about, by ignoring our tardiness, and by handing out easy C's like hotcakes. Still, we resented this speech as the final word from the college establishment. It should have been the orientation speech for us when we entered as freshmen.

# 18

## Find the exact words.

Whatever you want to say, claimed French writer Gustave Flaubert, "there is but one word to express it, one verb to give it movement, one adjective to qualify it; you must seek until you find this noun, this verb, this adjective." Even if you are not reaching for such perfection in your writing, you will sometimes find yourself wishing for better words. The dictionary is the obvious first place to turn, a thesaurus the second.

A good desk dictionary—such as *The American Heritage Dictionary, The Random House College Dictionary,* or *Webster's New Collegiate* or *New World Dictionary of the American Language* — lists synonyms and antonyms for many words, with helpful comments on various shades of meaning.

Under *fertile*, for example, *Webster's New World Dictionary* carefully distinguishes the meanings of *fertile*, *fecund*, *fruitful*, and *prolific:*

> SYN. —*fertile* implies a producing, or power of producing, fruit or offspring, and may be used figuratively of the mind; *fecund* implies the abundant production of offspring or fruit, or, figuratively, of creations of the mind; *fruitful* specifically suggests the bearing of much fruit, but it is also used to imply fertility (of soil), favorable results, profitableness, etc.; *prolific*, a close synonym for *fecund*, more often carries derogatory connotations of overly rapid production or reproduction — ANT. *sterile, barren*

If the dictionary doesn't yield the word for which you are looking, try a sourcebook of synonyms and antonyms such as *Roget's International Thesaurus.* In the back of *Roget's* is an index to the groups of synonyms that make up the bulk of the book. Look up the adjective *still*, for example, and you will find references to lists containing the words *dead*, *motionless*, *silent*, and *tranquil*. If *tranquil* is close to the word you have in mind, turn to its section in the front of the book. There you will find a long list of synonyms, including such words as *quiet*, *quiescent*, *reposeful*, *calm*, *pacific*, *halcyon*, *placid*, and *unruffled*. Unless your vocabulary is better than average, the list will contain words you've never heard or with which you are only vaguely familiar. Whenever you are tempted to use one of these words, look it up in the dictionary first or you may misuse it.

On discovering the thesaurus, many writers use it for the wrong reasons, so a word of caution is in order. Do not turn to a thesaurus in search of exotic, fancy words — such as *halcyon*—with which to embellish your essays. Look instead for words that exactly express your meaning. Most of the time these words will be familiar to both you and your readers. *Tranquil* was probably the word you were looking for all along.

## **18a** Select words with appropriate connotations.

In addition to their strict meanings (or *denotations*), words have *connotations*, emotional colorings that affect how readers respond to them. The word *steely* denotes "made of or resembling commercial iron that contains carbon." But reading the word *steely* calls up a cluster of images associated with steel, such as the sensation of touching it. These associations give the word its connotations — cold, smooth, unbending.

If the connotation of a word does not seem appropriate for your purpose, your audience, or your subject matter, the word should be changed. When a more appropriate synonym does not come quickly to mind, consult a dictionary or thesaurus.

▶ The model was ~~skinny~~ *slender* and fashionable.

The connotation of the word *skinny* was too negative.

▶ As I covered the boats with marsh grass, the ~~perspiration~~ *sweat* I had worked up evaporated in the wind, making the cold

morning air seem even colder.

The term *perspiration* was too dainty for the context, which suggested vigorous exercise.

## **18b** Be as specific and concrete as possible.

Abstract words refer to qualities, properties, and ideas, not to particular objects or sensations: *justice, dignity, democracy, honor, evil, recession, realism.* Concrete words refer to immediate, often sensuous experience and to physical objects: *steeple, asphalt, lilac, stone, garlic, sweet, salty, bitter, cut, embrace, dig, shiver.* Some writers mistakenly use abstract expressions to try to give their writing greater weight and authority. But overuse of abstract writing more often bores or confuses the reader because it offers no particular image and makes the subject difficult to grasp.

> **ABSTRACT** The demonstrators protested against a pattern of oppression that excluded them from society.

> **CONCRETE** Senior citizens, who made up the bulk of the demonstrators, protested against businesses that refused to hire them, developers who pushed them out of their neighborhoods, apartment owners who refused to offer them reasonable rents, and a city administration that cut funds for elderly health care.

General words refer to large classes of things; specific words refer to particular things or groups within a class. For example, if *film* is the general class, *horror film* is a specific item within that class, and *The Birds* is more specific still. *School* is general, whereas *high school* limits the class and *Springfield High School* limits the class even further. Other examples: *team, football team, New York Jets; sound, music, symphony; work, carpentry, cabinetmaking.*

There is a place for generalizations and abstract statements; you cannot write about some subjects without using them. But if a more specific and concrete alternative to a general or abstract word is available, use it.

▶ ~~The senator~~ *Senator Tsongas* spoke about the challenges of the future ⋀ : *problems* ⋀ *of famine, pollution, dwindling resources, and arms control.*

▶ The goalie ~~successfully defended the goal cage.~~ *crouched low, shot out his stick, and hooked the puck away from the mouth of the goal cage.*

General words such as *thing, area, aspect, factor,* and *individual* are especially dull and imprecise.

▶ A career in transportation management offers many ~~things~~.
  ^ *challenges and rewards.*

▶ Try pairing a trainee with an ~~individual with experience~~.
  ^ *experienced employee.*

When precise words elude you, consult a dictionary or a thesaurus.

## 18c Do not misuse words.

If a word is not in your active vocabulary, you may find yourself misusing it, sometimes with embarrassing consequences. Imagine the chagrin of the young woman who wrote that the "aroma of pumpkin pie and sage stuffing acted as an *aphrodisiac*" when she learned that aphrodisiacs are drugs or foods stimulating sexual desire. Blunders like this one are easily prevented: When in doubt, check the dictionary.

▶ The fans were ~~migrating~~ up the bleachers in search of good
  ^ *climbing*

  seats.

▶ Mrs. Johnson tried to fight, but it was to no ~~prevail~~
  ^ *avail.*

▶ Drugs have so diffused our culture that they touch all
  ^ *become* ^ *in*

  segments of our society.

## 18d Use standard idioms.

Idioms are speech forms that follow no easily specified rules. The English say "Maria went *to hospital*," an idiom strange to American ears, which are accustomed to hearing *the* in front of *hospital*. Native speakers of a language seldom have problems with idioms, but prepositions sometimes cause trouble, especially when they follow some verbs and adjectives. When in doubt, consult a good desk dictionary: Look up the word preceding the troublesome preposition.

| UNIDIOMATIC | IDIOMATIC |
|---|---|
| according with | according to |
| abide with (a decision) | abide by (a decision) |
| agree to (an idea) | agree with (an idea) |
| angry at (a person) | angry with (a person) |
| capable to | capable of |
| comply to | comply with |
| desirous to | desirous of |
| different than | different from |
| intend on doing | intend to do |
| off of | off |
| plan on doing | plan to do |
| preferable than | preferable to |
| prior than | prior to |
| superior than | superior to |
| sure and | sure to |
| try and | try to |
| type of a | type of |

## 18e  Avoid worn-out expressions.

The frontiersman who first announced that he had "slept like a log" no doubt amused his companions with a fresh and unlikely comparison. Today, however, that comparison is a cliché, a saying that has lost its dazzle from overuse. No longer can it surprise.

To see just how dully predictable clichés are, put your hand over the right-hand column below, then finish the phrases on the left.

| | |
|---|---|
| cool as a | cucumber |
| beat around | the bush |
| blind as a | bat |

| | |
|---|---|
| busy as a | bee |
| crystal | clear |
| dead as a | doornail |
| from the frying pan | into the fire |
| light as a | feather |
| like a bull | in a china shop |
| playing with | fire |
| nutty as a | fruitcake |
| selling like | hotcakes |
| starting out at the bottom | of the ladder |
| water over the | dam |
| white as a | sheet, ghost |
| avoid clichés like the | plague |

The cure for clichés is frequently simple: Just delete them. When this won't work, try adding some element of surprise. One student, for example, who had written that she had butterflies in her stomach, revised her cliché like this:

> If all of the action in my stomach is caused by butterflies, there must be a hoard of them, with horseshoes on.

The image of butterflies wearing horseshoes is fresh and unlikely, not dully predictable like the original cliché.

## 18f Avoid mixed figures of speech.

A figure of speech is an expression that uses words in an unusual sense to invigorate an idea or make abstract concepts concrete. Most often, figures of speech compare two seemingly unlike things to reveal surprising similarities. For example, Richard Selzer compares an aging surgeon who has lost his touch to an old lion whose claws have become blunted. In a *simile*, the comparison is explicit and is often introduced by *like* or *as* (*hair like spun gold, ruthless as a shark*). In a *metaphor*, *like* or *as* is omitted, and the comparison is implied. The writer describes one object or action in terms of another, revealing the identity between the two (*I sailed through physics, her cavernous eyes*).

Writers often use figures of speech without thinking through the images they evoke. This can lead to mixed figures of speech, the combination of two or more images that don't make sense together.

▶ Crossing Utah's salt flats in his new Corvette, my father flew *at jet speed.* ~~under a full head of steam.~~
  Λ

*Flew* suggests an airplane, while *under a full head of steam* suggests a train. To clarify the image, the writer should stick with one comparison or the other.

▶ Our office had decided to put all controversial issues on a

back burner, ~~in a holding pattern.~~
            Λ

Here the writer is mixing stoves and airplanes. Simply deleting one of the images corrects the problem.


## EXERCISE 18–1

Use a dictionary or thesaurus to find at least four synonyms for each of the following words. Be prepared to explain any slight differences in meaning.

1. decay (verb)
2. difficult (adjective)
3. hurry (verb)
4. pleasure (noun)
5. secret (adjective)
6. talent (noun)


## EXERCISE 18–2

Revise the following paragraph by adding concrete and specific details of your own. Include bits of conversation if you like.

The job interview went fairly well. The interviewer greeted me in a friendly fashion and offered me something to drink as we first sat down. She asked me to tell her about myself, and I did. When she asked me why I was interested in the position, I said that I had always wanted to sell a product that I could believe in. She seemed to be impressed with the answer because she smiled. She asked if I was involved in any extracurricular activities. I didn't know if I should tell her about my peculiar hobby, but I decided to take a chance and explain it to her. She found it fascinating, or so she said. She then explained the company's philosophy to me and asked if I had any questions. I asked just a few. At the end of the interview she told me that I stood a good chance of getting the job.

### EXERCISE 18−3

Edit the following sentences to correct errors in the use of idiomatic expressions. Some sentences are correct. Example:

> We agreed to abide ~~with~~ *by* the decision of the judge.

a. I was so angry at the salesperson that I took his bag of samples and emptied it on the floor in front of him.
b. We plan on doing the plastering a week from Tuesday.
c. Try to come up with the rough outline of a game plan, and we will find someone who can fill in the details.
d. "Your prejudice is no different than mine," she shouted.
e. The parade moved off of the street and onto the beach as the tall ships sailed into the harbor.

1. Be sure and report on the danger of releasing genetically engineered bacteria into the atmosphere.
2. Our painkiller is far superior than any other medicine on the market.
3. According to recent reports, the American public regards arms control as one of the most important issues facing us in the late twentieth century.
4. If we want a license, we have to comply to federal regulations.

5. I intend on writing letters to my representatives in Congress demanding that they do something about the problem of homelessness in this state.

## EXERCISE 18–4

Edit the following sentences to correct misused words, to replace worn-out expressions, and to clarify mixed figures of speech. Example:

**The training required for a ballet dancer is** ~~all-absorbent~~ *all-absorbing.*

a. He stormed into the room like a bull in a china shop.
b. Many of us are not persistence enough to make a change for the better.
c. When he heard about the accident he turned white as a sheet.
d. Hours of long practice often determine an excellent musician from a sloppy one.
e. I told him that he was playing with fire when I learned that he intended to spy on the trustees' meeting.

1. He ironed out the sticky spots in our relationship.
2. Sam Brown began his career as a lawyer, but now he is a real estate mongrel.
3. Alan's plan is to require education and experience to prepare himself for a position as property manager.
4. I could read him like an open book; he had egg all over his face.
5. My roommate was great, but she was as nutty as a fruitcake.
6. Many family relationships have been absolved because of a drug-related incident.
7. When I graduated from high school and started college, I realized that I was leaping from the frying pan into the fire.
8. At the first staff meeting, we realized that we had been saddled with a ship of fools.
9. This patient is isolated to keep him from obtaining our germs.
10. Once he had sunk his teeth into it, he burned through the assignment.

# PART V

# Editing for Grammar

# 19

## Repair sentence fragments.

A sentence fragment is a word group that pretends to be a
sentence. Some sentence fragments are clauses that contain
a subject and a verb but begin with a subordinating word.
Others are phrases that lack a subject, a verb, or both.

You can repair most fragments in two ways. Either pull
the fragment into a nearby sentence, making sure to punctuate the new sentence correctly, or turn the fragment itself
into a sentence.

**19a**  Attach fragmented subordinate clauses or turn
them into sentences.

Subordinate clauses are patterned like sentences, with subjects and verbs, but they begin with a word or words that
mark them as subordinate — words such as *although, because, if, so that, unless, when, who, which,* and *that.* Subordinate clauses function within sentences as adjectives, as
adverbs, or as nouns. It is a mistake, therefore, to separate
them from the sentences in which they function. (See subordinate clauses, 49b.)

Most fragmented clauses beg to be pulled into a sentence
nearby.

▶ Normally the payments consisted of cattle and sheep/,
    *b*
    ~~B~~ecause money had little value to these isolated people.

    *Because* introduces a subordinate clause that modifies the verb
    *consisted.*

▶ When we approached the entrance, the security officer

informed us that visitors would be searched,/~~And~~ that the
　　　　　　　　　　　　　　　　　　*a*

women's purses would be thoroughly inspected.

The subordinate clause has two parts: *that visitors would be searched* and *that the women's purses would be thoroughly inspected.*

If a fragmented clause cannot be attached to a nearby sentence or if you feel that attaching it would be awkward, try rewriting it. The simplest way to turn a subordinate clause into a sentence is to delete the opening word or words that mark it as subordinate.

▶ Violence has produced a great deal of apprehension among
　　　　　　　　　　　　　　　*Self-preservation*
students and teachers. ~~So that self-preservation~~ has become
　　　　　　　　　　　　　　　　　　∧

their primary concern.

For clarity the writer might consider adding a transitional expression: *In fact, self-preservation has become their primary concern.*

## 19b Attach fragmented phrases or turn them into sentences.

Fragmented phrases are usually prepositional or verbal phrases; occasionally they are appositives, words or word groups that rename nouns or pronouns. (See prepositional phrases, 49a; verbal phrases, 49c; appositives, 49d.)

Many fragmented phrases may simply be pulled into nearby sentences.

▶ Ms. Wilson maintained a friendly and supportive

atmosphere*,ᵐ* Making helpful suggestions and respecting the

students' opinions.

*Making helpful suggestions and respecting the students' opin-ions* is a verbal phrase modifying *Ms. Wilson.*

▶ Wednesday morning Phil allowed himself half a grapefruit*,*

*ₜ*The only food he had eaten in two days.

*The only food he had eaten in two days* is an appositive re-naming the noun *grapefruit.*

If a fragmented phrase cannot be pulled into a nearby sentence effectively, turn it into a sentence. You may need to add a subject, a verb, or both.

▶ If Eric doesn't get his way, he goes into a fit of rage. For
                    *he lies*              *opens*
example, ~~lying~~ on the floor screaming or ~~opening~~ the cabinet
                    *slams*
doors and then ~~slamming~~ them shut.

The writer corrected this fragment by adding a subject — *he* — and making the participles *lying, opening,* and *slamming* the verbs of the sentence.

**19c**  Occasionally a fragment may be used deliberately, for effect.

In informal writing, skilled writers occasionally use sentence fragments for emphasis. In the following passage, Richard Rodriguez uses a fragment (italicized) to draw attention to his mother.

Following the dramatic Americanization of their children, even my parents grew more publicly confident. *Especially my mother.* She learned the names of all the people on our block.

—*Hunger of Memory*

## EXERCISE 19–1

Repair any fragment by attaching it to a nearby sentence or by rewriting it as a complete sentence. Some word groups are correct sentences. Example:

I was exhausted/, Having studied for forty-eight hours straight.

a. My favorite athletes are those who combine exceptional physical talent with a tough mental attitude. Like Larry Bird, Martina Navratilova, and Julius Erving.

b. While on a tour of Italy, Maria and Kathleen snuck away from their group to spend some quiet minutes with Leonardo da Vinci's *Last Supper.* A stunning fresco painted in the fifteenth century in a Milan monastery.

c. A tornado is a violent whirling wind. One that produces a funnel-shaped cloud and moves over land in a narrow path of destruction.

d. Relaxing beneath a broad banana leaf, the ancient bearded ape yawned and patted his head. Finally he was content.

e. If the women of these desert tribes showed anger toward their husbands, they would be whipped in front of the whole village. And shunned by the rest of the women.

1. To give my family a comfortable, secure home life. That is the most important goal to me.

2. My brothers are both working for the government in permanent positions. Bill is employed at the Space Center and Alan is with a military agency.

3. I will attack the problem of limited on-campus parking. If I am elected special student adviser.

4. There are several reasons for not eating meat. One reason being that dangerous chemicals are used throughout the various stages of meat production.

5. Sam told us that he would soon be getting out on work release. And that he might be able to come home for a visit on certain weekends.

6. I had pushed these fears into one of those quiet places in my mind. Hoping they would stay there asleep.

7. Working late into the night at the computer terminal, Sylvia finally solved the problem. However, the next day she learned that she had been working on the wrong problem.

8. As he stepped nearer to the edge of the roof. Mario felt the familiar fear moving up through his spine.

9. Underneath all his brashness, Henry is really a thoughtful person. Few of his colleagues realize how sensitive he is.

10. It was surprising to see such a fine dining area in a fast-food restaurant. Carpeted floors, paneled walls, and an outdoor patio with benches. There was even an area sectioned off for non-smokers.

## EXERCISE 19-2

Repair each fragment in this paragraph by attaching it to a sentence nearby or by rewriting it as a complete sentence.

If I brought any good humor with me in the morning, it always gave way to gloom. As soon as I came in sight of the school building. It was a great red brick box squatting in a sea of asphalt. Inside, the walls shed long strips of yellow paint and bits of plaster. Walking up and down the aisles. I would arrange the disordered desks. Then I would spend a little time each day scraping the floor. Which was dotted with hundreds of sticky black blobs. Gum that had been chewed and discarded by several generations of children. All the windows were clouded with grime. Some covered with iron grating or cardboard. Looking through the windows, I could see these words scrawled on an outside wall: "All the kids I think are cool are six feet underground."

# 20

## Revise comma splices and fused sentences.

Comma splices and fused sentences (also known as run-on sentences) contain independent clauses that have been too weakly separated. (An independent clause has at least a subject and a verb and can stand alone as a separate sentence.) When a writer puts no mark of punctuation between independent clauses, the result is a fused sentence.

**FUSED**    ┌─INDEPENDENT CLAUSE─┐ ┌─INDEPENDENT CLAUSE──
Power tends to corrupt absolute power corrupts
absolutely.

A far more common error is the comma splice, which consists of independent clauses separated with only a comma.

**COMMA**    Power tends to corrupt, absolute power corrupts
**SPLICE**    absolutely.

If two independent clauses are to appear in one sentence, they must be firmly separated, either with a comma and a coordinating conjunction (*and, but, or, nor, for, so, yet*) or with a semicolon.

**REVISED**    Power tends to corrupt, and absolute power corrupts absolutely.

**REVISED**    Power tends to corrupt; absolute power corrupts absolutely.

Even if a comma is used with a conjunctive adverb such as *however, nevertheless, moreover,* or *therefore,* the separation is still not firm enough.

**COMMA**   Power tends to corrupt, moreover, absolute power
**SPLICE**    corrupts absolutely.

When a conjunctive adverb is used between independent clauses, it must be preceded by a semicolon.

**REVISED**   Power tends to corrupt; moreover, absolute power
                corrupts absolutely.

To correct a comma splice or a fused sentence, you have four choices:

1. Use a comma and a coordinating conjunction.
2. Use a semicolon.
3. Make the clauses into separate sentences.
4. Restructure the sentence, perhaps by subordinating one of the clauses.

One of these revision techniques will likely work better than the others for a particular sentence. The fourth technique, the one requiring the most extensive revision, is frequently the most effective.

**20a**  Consider separating the clauses with a comma and a coordinating conjunction.

▶ My business is very competitive, ~~therefore~~ *so* I need to continue my education.

I was an excellent worker, ~~however~~ *but* my supervisor was annoyed with me because I was so shy.

*Therefore* and *however* are conjunctive adverbs, not coordinating conjunctions. They cannot be used alone or with only a comma to hook together two independent clauses. One way to correct these sentences is to substitute coordinating conjunctions for the conjunctive adverbs: *so* works in the first sentence, *but* in the second. A comma must also be added in the first sentence because that was a fused sentence, not a comma splice.

## 20b Consider separating the clauses with a semicolon.

▶ Nicklaus is like fine wine, he gets better with time.

Everyone in my outfit had a specific job, as a matter of fact, most of the officers had three or four duties.

Semicolons work well because the relation between the independent clauses is clear without a coordinating conjunction.

## 20c Consider making the clauses into separate sentences.

▶ In one episode viewers saw two people smashed by a boat, one choked, and another shot to death. what purpose does this violence serve?

Since one independent clause is a statement and the other is a question, they should be separate sentences.

▶ I gave the necessary papers to the police officer. then he said I would have to accompany him to the police station, where a counselor would talk with me and call my parents.

Because the second independent clause is quite long, a sensible revision is to use separate sentences.

**20d** Consider restructuring the sentence, perhaps by subordinating one of the clauses.

If one of the independent clauses is less important than the other, turn it into a subordinate clause or phrase. That way, ideas that are logically subordinate will be expressed in grammatically subordinate structures. (For more about subordination, see 8 and 49.)

▶ Lindsey is a top competitor ~~she~~ who has been riding since the age of seven.

Saturday afternoon Julie came running into the house/ ~~she wanted~~ to get permission to go to the park.

Minor ideas in these sentences are now expressed in subordinate clauses or phrases.

## EXERCISE 20–1

Revise any comma splices or fused sentences using the method of revision suggested in brackets. Example:

Because
Orville was obsessed with his weight, he rarely ate anything sweet and delicious. [*Restructure the sentence.*]

a. The city had one public swimming pool, it stayed packed with children all summer long. [*Restructure the sentence.*]
b. Tom Baxter has been irritating me lately, therefore, I avoid him when possible. [*Use a comma and a coordinating conjunction.*]
c. Why should we pay taxes to support public transportation, we prefer to save energy dollars by carpooling. [*Make two sentences.*]
d. The kitchen was ordinarily the hub of activity, in the summer, though, it was nearly always empty. [*Use a semicolon.*]

1. While we were walking down Grover Avenue, Gary told us about his Aunt Elsinia, she was an extraordinary woman. [*Restructure the sentence.*]

2. Most parents want their children to do well in school, however, they don't always know how to help them succeed. [*Restructure the sentence.*]

3. My sister Elaine was awarded the Medal of Honor, however, she was not able to attend the awards ceremony. [*Use a comma and a coordinating conjunction.*]

4. On most days I had only enough money for bus fare, lunch was a luxury I could not afford. [*Use a semicolon.*]

5. The president of Algeria was standing at the podium, he was waiting to be introduced. [*Restructure the sentence.*]

6. I positioned myself next to the smartest girl in class, I wouldn't cheat, of course, but it was comforting to know that the right answer was not far away. [*Make two sentences.*]

7. Our house is still in good shape, it needs only a paint job and some gutter repair. [*Restructure the sentence.*]

8. The experience taught Marianne a lesson, she could not always rely on her parents to bail her out of trouble. [*Restructure the sentence.*]

9. The next time an event is canceled because of bad weather, don't blame the meteorologist, blame nature. [*Make two sentences.*]

10. Most babies come down with a high temperature at some point, mine was no exception. [*Use a comma and a coordinating conjunction.*]

## EXERCISE 20–2

Revise any comma splices or fused sentences using one of the techniques suggested in this section. Some sentences are correct. Example:

**I ran the three blocks as fast as I could, ~~however~~ *but* I still**

**missed the bus.**

a. The trail up Mount Finegold was declared impassable, therefore, we decided to return to our hotel a day early.

b. The duck hunter set out his decoys in the shallow bay and then settled in to wait for the first real bird to alight.

c. Last year's tomatoes were the best we'd ever grown, they were plump, firm, and extraordinarily sweet.

d. Josie had all the equipment necessary for her first parachute jump, however, she forgot the required checklist and had to remain on the ground.

1. Maria gave her mother half of her weekly pay then she used the rest as a down payment on a stereo system at Brown's Sounds.

2. Cross-country skiing is an easy sport to master, that is why it is becoming so popular.

3. Because of their demanding jobs, my brother and sister-in-law sometimes neglect their children.

4. The bridegroom was getting more and more anxious while he waited at the courthouse for the bride to arrive.

5. The A team outfielders shared six pizzas they drowned their sorrows in several pitchers of beer.

6. It was much too late to catch a bus after the party, therefore, four of us pooled our money and called a cab.

7. Pablo had not prepared well for his first overseas assignment, but luck was with him, he performed better than most of the more experienced members of his unit.

8. The volunteers worked hard to clean up and restore calm after the tornado, as a matter of fact, many of them did not sleep for the first three days of the emergency.

9. Taking drugs to keep alert on the job can actually cause a decline in work performance and can lead to severe depression as well.

10. It was obvious that Maria had already been out walking in the woods, her boots were covered with mud and leaves.

# 21

## Make subjects and verbs agree.

In the present tense, verbs agree with their subjects in number (singular or plural) and in person (first, second, or third). The present-tense ending *-s* is used on a verb if its subject is third-person singular; otherwise the verb takes no ending.

Consider, for example, the present-tense forms of the verb *give:*

|  | SINGULAR | PLURAL |
|---|---|---|
| FIRST PERSON | I give | we give |
| SECOND PERSON | you give | you give |
| THIRD PERSON | he/she/it gives | they give |
|  | Alison gives | parents give |

The verb *be* varies from this pattern, and unlike any other verb it has special forms in *both* the present and the past tenses.

| PRESENT TENSE FORMS OF BE | | PAST TENSE FORMS OF BE | |
|---|---|---|---|
| I am | we are | I was | we were |
| you are | you are | you were | you were |
| he/she/it is | they are | he/she/it was | they were |

Speakers of standard English know by ear that *he talks, she has,* and *it doesn't* (not *he talk, she have,* and *it don't*) are the correct forms. For such speakers, problems with subject-verb agreement arise only in certain tricky situations, which are detailed in this section.

If you don't trust your ear, consult 28, which contrasts the present-tense verb systems of standard and nonstandard English. Also see 48a and 48b on subjects and verbs.

**21a**  Make the verb agree with its subject, not with a word that comes between.

Word groups often come between the subject and the verb. Such word groups, usually modifying the subject, may contain a noun that at first appears to be the subject. By mentally stripping away such modifiers, you can isolate the noun that is in fact the subject.

The *tulips* in the pot on the balcony *need* watering.

▶ High levels of air pollution ~~causes~~ damage to the respiratory
   *cause*
   ∧

tract.

A good set of golf clubs ~~cost~~ about three hundred dollars.
   *costs*
   ∧

The nouns *pollution* and *clubs*, which the writers at first treated
as subjects, appear in prepositional phrases. When the writers
mentally stripped away these phrases, they heard the correct
verbs: *levels cause, set costs.*

**NOTE:** Phrases beginning with the prepositions *as well as,
in addition to, accompanied by, together with,* and *along
with* do not make a singular subject plural.

▶ The president as well as his press secretary ~~were~~ shot.
   *was*
   ∧

The writer at first thought the subject was plural because two
people were shot. Grammatically, however, *president* alone is the
subject, because *as well as* begins a prepositional phrase. To
emphasize the fact that two people were shot, the writer can use
*and* instead: *The president and his press secretary were shot.*

**21b** Treat compound subjects connected by *and* as
plural.

A subject with two or more parts is said to be compound. If
the parts are connected by *and,* the subject is nearly always
plural.

*Leon* and *Jan* often *jog* together.

▶ Remember that your safety and welfare ~~is~~ in your own
   *are*
   ∧

hands.

The compound subject *safety and welfare* is plural, requiring the verb *are*.

▶ Jill's natural ability and her desire to help others ~~has~~ led to

*have*

∧

a career in the ministry.

*Ability and desire* is a plural subject, so its verb should be *have*.

**EXCEPTION:** If the two parts of a compound subject are considered as a unit, they are treated as singular.

Bacon and eggs is my favorite breakfast.

**21c** With compound subjects connected by *or* or *nor*, make the verb agree with the part of the subject nearer to the verb.

A driver's *license* or credit *card is* required.

A driver's *license* or two credit *cards are* required.

*is*

▶ If a relative or neighbor ~~are~~ abusing a child, notify the police.

∧

*were*

Neither the instructor nor her students ~~was~~ able to find the

∧

classroom.

*was*

Neither the students nor the instructor ~~were~~ able to find the

∧

classroom.

The verb must be matched with the part of the subject closer to it: *neighbor is* in the first sentence, *students were* in the second, *instructor was* in the third.

**21d** Treat most indefinite pronouns as singular.

Indefinite pronouns are pronouns that do not refer to specific persons or things. *Any, anyone, each, either, everyone, everything, neither, none, no one, someone,* and *something* are common examples. Many of these words appear to have plural meanings, and they are treated as such in casual speech. In formal, written English, however, they are nearly always considered singular.

*Everyone* on the team *supports* the coach.

▶ Each of the ten units ~~are~~ *is* worth fifty points.

Everybody who signed up for the ski trip ~~were~~ *was* taking

lessons.

The subjects are *each* and *everybody.* These indefinite pronouns are singular, so the verbs must be *is* and *was.*

The indefinite pronouns *none* and *neither* are considered singular when used alone.

*None is* immune from this disease.

*Neither is* able to attend.

When these pronouns are followed by prepositional phrases with a plural meaning, however, usage varies. Some experts insist on treating the pronouns as singular, but many writers disagree. It is safest to treat them as singular.

*None* of these trades *requires* a college education.

*Neither* of those pejoratives *fits* Warren Burger.

A few indefinite pronouns (*all, any, some*) may be singular or plural depending on the noun or pronoun they refer to. Such indefinite pronouns cause few problems for native speakers of English.

*Some* of the *lemonade has* disappeared.

*Some* of the *rocks were* slippery.

**21e** Treat collective nouns as singular or plural depending on your meaning.

Collective nouns such as *jury, committee, audience, crowd, class, troop, family,* and *couple* name a class or a group. In American English collective nouns are nearly always treated as singular: They emphasize the group as a unit. Occasionally, when there is some reason to draw attention to the individual members of the group, a collective noun may be treated as plural.

**SINGULAR**   The *class respects* the teacher.

**PLURAL**   The *class are* debating among themselves.

To underscore the notion of individuality in the second sentence, many writers would add a clearly plural noun such as *members:*

**PLURAL**   The class *members are* debating among
          themselves.

                        *meets*
▶ The scout troop ~~meet~~ in our basement on Tuesdays.
                    ∧

The meaning is singular because there is no reason to draw attention to the individual members of the troop. It is the troop as a whole that meets in the basement.

*were*
▶ A young couple ~~was~~ arguing about politics while holding
        ∧
hands.

The meaning is clearly plural. A collective unit doesn't argue and
hold hands. Only individuals can engage in such activities.

**NOTE:** The phrase *the number* is treated as singular, *a number* as plural.

**SINGULAR**   *The number* of school-age children *is* declining.

**PLURAL**     *A number* of children *are* attending the wedding.

**21f**  Make the verb agree with its subject even when the
subject follows the verb.

Verbs ordinarily follow subjects. When this normal order is
reversed, it is easy to become confused. Sentences beginning
with *there is* or *there are* (or *there was* or *there were*) are
inverted; the subject follows the verb.

There *is* an *apple* on the counter.

*are*
▶ There ~~is~~ surprisingly few children in our neighborhood.
      ∧

The subject is *children;* therefore the verb should be *are: children are.*

*were*
▶ There ~~was~~ a social worker and a crew of twenty volunteers.
        ∧

The subject is compound and therefore plural: *worker and crew
were.*

**NOTE:** Occasionally a writer may invert sentences for variety
or effect.

*are*
▶ Behind the fence ~~is~~ a fierce dog and an even fiercer cat.
　　　∧

The subject *dog and cat* is compound, so the verb must be *are*.

## 21g Make the verb agree with its subject, not with a subject complement.

One basic sentence pattern in English consists of a subject, a linking verb, and a subject complement: *Jack is an attorney.* Because the subject complement (*an attorney*) names or describes the subject (*Jack*), it is sometimes mistaken for the subject. (See 48c on subject complements.)

These *problems are* a way to test your skill.

*are*
▶ A tent and a sleeping bag ~~is~~ the required equipment.
　　　　　∧

*Tent and bag* is the subject, not *equipment.*

*is*
▶ A major force in today's economy ~~are~~ women — as earners,
　　　　　　　　　　　　∧

consumers, and investors.

*Force* is the subject, not *women*. If the corrected version seems awkward, make *women* the subject: *Women are a major force in today's economy — as earners, consumers, and investors.*

## 21h Who, *which*, and that take verbs that agree with their antecedents.

Like most pronouns, the relative pronouns *who, which,* and *that* have antecedents, nouns or pronouns to which they refer. Relative pronouns used as subjects of subordinate clauses take verbs that agree with their antecedents.

Take a *suit that travels* well.

▶ Our ability to use language is one of the things that ~~sets~~ us
*set*
∧

apart from animals.

The relative pronoun *that* appears to have two possible antecedents, *one* and *things*. Only by considering the meaning of the
sentence can the writer decide which word is in fact the antecedent. The sentence speaks of language ability as one of a group
of things *all of which* set us apart from animals. Therefore the
antecedent is *things*, and the verb should be *set: things that set*.

▶ The man decided that Frank was the only one of his four
*was*
sons who ~~were~~ responsible enough to handle the estate.
∧

The antecedent of *who* is *one*, not *sons*, since the meaning is
clearly singular: Only *one was* responsible enough.

**21i**  Words such as *athletics*, *economics*, and *news* are
usually singular, despite their plural form.

*is*
▶ Statistics ~~are~~ among the most difficult courses in our
∧

program.

**EXCEPTION:** When the meaning is clearly plural, words ending
in *-ics* are treated as plural: *The statistics are impressive.*

**21j**  Titles of works are singular even if they contain
plural words.

*describes*
▶ *Lost Cities* ~~describe~~ the discoveries of many ancient
∧

civilizations.

## EXERCISE 21–1

Underline the subject (or compound subject) and then select the verb that agrees with it. (If you have difficulty identifying the subject, consult 48a.) Example:

<u>Someone</u> in the audience (has̸/have) volunteered to

participate in the experiment.

a. A tall glass of club soda with a twist of lime (suits/suit) me just fine at the end of a hard tennis match.
b. The old iron gate and the brick wall (makes/make) our courthouse appear older than its fifty years.
c. The dangers of smoking (is/are) well documented.
d. Neither of the police officers (was/were) called to testify.
e. There (is/are) several street people living by the tracks behind the mall.

1. Surprisingly neither my cousin nor his rowdy friends (was/were) accused of the prank.
2. The bed of tulips (is/are) stunning this year.
3. Quilts made by the Amish (commands/command) high prices at antique auctions.
4. Seized in the raid (was/were) $400 in cash, two color televisions, and a set of stereo speakers.
5. Four oranges, one apple, and a banana (goes/go) into the fruit compote.

## EXERCISE 21–2

Edit the following sentences to make subjects agree with verbs. Some sentences are correct. Do not change present-tense verbs to the past tense. Example:

Jack's first few days in the infantry ~~was~~ *were* grueling.

a. High concentrations of carbon monoxide result in headaches, dizziness, unconsciousness, and even death.

b. Each of the furrows have been seeded.
c. At the back of the room is an aquarium and a terrarium.
d. Either Alice or Jan usually work the midnight shift.
e. Crystal chandeliers, polished floors, and a new oil painting has transformed Sandra's apartment.

1. The chances of your being promoted to a higher grade is excellent.
2. Each package of broccoli spears weigh eight ounces.
3. Sitting in the back seat of the car parked in the driveway was John and the class clown, Phillip.
4. The table of contents lists twenty-two feature articles.
5. The main source of income for Trinidad are oil and pitch.
6. The federal government have established a meals-on-wheels program for senior citizens.
7. There's a checkered tablecloth, red candles, and flowers on the table.
8. Zena's family realizes that repaying these debts will not be easy.
9. The key program of Alcoholics Anonymous are the twelve steps to recovery.
10. Our choir knows that all of these problems, one right after another, is God's way of testing our faith.
11. Not until my interview with Dr. Harvey were other possibilities opened to me.
12. All of the witnesses claimed that neither Tom nor his partner Carl were at the scene of the crime.
13. My mother's patience and her internal strength has enabled her to get through the difficult time after the fire.
14. The presence of certain bacteria in our bodies is one of the factors that determines our overall health.
15. Until very recently, economics were not considered a major academic field.
16. The four sacred arrows, often called the "medicine bundle," was among the most sacred Cheyenne relics.
17. Nearly everyone on the panel favors the arms control agreement.
18. After hearing the evidence and the closing arguments, the jury was sequestered.
19. Sheila is the only one of the many applicants who has the ability to step into this position.
20. David Bowie's "Changes" describe an inner struggle.

# 22

---

## Make pronouns and antecedents agree.

---

The antecedent of a pronoun is the word the pronoun refers to. A pronoun and its antecedent agree when they are both singular or both plural.

**SINGULAR**    The *doctor* finished *her* rounds.

**PLURAL**    The *doctors* finished *their* rounds.

**22a**  Do not use plural pronouns to refer to singular antecedents.

Occasionally writers are tempted to use a plural pronoun even though its antecedent is singular, as in this sentence: *No parent wants to see their child miserable.* Some years ago it was acceptable to write *his child*, trusting readers to understand that *his* really meant *his or her*. Today, however, many readers find this use of *his* offensive, so it is dying out. One option is to write *his or her*; another is to write in the plural.

**SINGULAR**    No *parent* wants to see *his or her* child miserable.

**PLURAL**    No *parents* want to see *their* children miserable.

▶ The amount of annual leave a federal worker may accrue
     *his or her*
depends on ~~their~~ length of service.
     ∧

The singular antecedent *worker* demands the singular construction *his or her*. The writer could have changed the antecedent to the plural instead: *The amount of annual leave federal workers may accrue depends on their length of service.*

►  The Navy has much to offer ~~any man or woman~~ who ~~knows~~
    *men and women* ^   *know* ^

what they want.

Here the writer decided to make the antecedent plural to match
the plural pronoun *they*. Notice that the verb *knows* must be
changed to *know: men and women who know.*

## 22b  Treat most indefinite pronouns as singular.

Indefinite pronouns are pronouns that do not refer to specific
persons or things. *Any, anyone, each, either, everyone,
everything, neither, none, no one, someone,* and *something*
are examples. Many of these words appear to have plural
meanings and are treated as such in casual speech. But in
formal English they are nearly always considered singular.

*Someone* has left *her* purse under the desk.

►  At some time in life everyone has had ~~their~~ rights violated.
    *his or her* ^

The writer treated *everyone* as singular when selecting the verb
*has* but as plural when choosing the pronoun *their.* This is inconsistent, but it is fairly common when a writer is trying to
avoid the wordy *his or her* construction. One way to skirt the
problem is to change *everyone* to *we: At some time in life we
have all had our rights violated.*

►  I was taught that no one could escape the fires of purgatory.
    *who wanted to reach heaven* ^
    ^

~~if they wanted to reach heaven.~~

Here the writer, not wanting to change *they* to *he or she,* restructured the sentence. The pronoun *who* applies to persons
of either sex, so no problem of agreement arises.

## **22c** Treat collective nouns as singular or plural depending on your meaning.

Collective nouns such as *jury, committee, audience, crowd, class, troop, family, team,* and *couple* name a class or a group. Ordinarily the group functions as a unit, so the noun should be treated as singular; if the members of the group function as individuals, however, the noun should be treated as plural.

> **AS A UNIT** The *committee* granted *its* permission to build.

> **AS INDIVIDUALS** The *committee* put *their* signatures on the document.

▶ The jury has reached ~~their~~ decision. *its*

There is no reason to draw attention to the individual members of the jury, so *jury* should be treated as singular. Notice also that the writer treated the noun as singular when choosing the verb *has,* so for consistency the pronoun must be *its.*

▶ The audience shouted "Bravo" and stamped ~~its~~ feet. *their*

It is difficult to see how the audience as a unit can stamp *its* feet. The meaning here is clearly plural, requiring *their.*

## **22d** Treat compound antecedents connected by *and* as plural.

*Joanne and John* moved to the mountains, where *they* built a log cabin.

**22e** With compound antecedents connected by *or* or *nor*, make the pronoun agree with the nearer antecedent.

Either *Bruce* or *James* should receive first prize for *his* sculpture.

Neither the *lawyer* nor the *accountants* could trace *their* mistake.

**NOTE:** If one of the antecedents is singular and the other plural, as in the second example, put the plural one last to avoid awkwardness.

EXERCISE 22–1

Edit the following sentences to make pronouns agree with their antecedents. Most of the sentences can be revised in more than one way, so experiment before choosing a solution. Some sentences are correct. Example:

*his or her*
**In this class everyone performs at ~~their~~ own fitness level.**
∧

a. An employee on extended leave may continue their life insurance.
b. The freshman class elects its president tomorrow.
c. The recruiter may tell the truth, but there is much that they choose not to tell.
d. When a person has been drinking or using drugs, they are more likely to abuse their child.
e. David lent his motorcycle to someone who allowed their friend to use it.

1. A runner must follow a rigorous training routine if they want to excel.
2. The audience entered and seated itself in an auditorium facing a uniquely designed map of Gettysburg.

3. No one should be forced to sacrifice their most prized possession — life — for someone else.
4. The troop, hearing gunfire, scattered to their chosen hiding places.
5. I realize now that neither Barbara nor Bianca returned her skis to the rental office on Friday.
6. The pitcher and the catcher agreed about what they had seen.
7. Every applicant wants to know how much they will make.
8. A mountain climber must shift his or her emphasis from self-preservation to group survival. They must learn to rely completely on others.
9. Suddenly the air crackled with machine-gun fire. Everyone hit the ground and scrambled to their foxholes.
10. A year later someone finally admitted their involvement in the kidnapping.

# 23

## Make pronoun references clear.

Pronouns substitute for nouns; they are a kind of shorthand. In a sentence like *After Andrew intercepted the ball, he kicked it as hard as he could,* the pronouns *he* and *it* substitute for the nouns *Andrew* and *ball.* The word a pronoun refers to is called its *antecedent.*

## 23a Avoid ambiguous pronoun reference.

Ambiguous pronoun reference occurs when the pronoun could refer to two possible antecedents.

> *The pitcher broke when Gloria set it*
> ▶ ~~When Gloria set the pitcher~~ on the glass-topped table, it
>   ∧                                                          ∧
>   ~~broke.~~

> The judge gave the mother custody and the father visiting
> *the father*
> rights, but ~~he~~ soon dropped out of sight.
>   ∧

What broke — the table or the pitcher? Who dropped out of sight — the judge or the father? To correct ambiguous pronoun reference, either restructure the sentence (as in the first sentence) or repeat the noun to which the pronoun refers (as in the second sentence).

## **23b** Avoid vague pronoun reference.

Vague reference occurs when a pronoun refers to a word implied but not present in the sentence. Pronouns must refer to nouns or pronouns that have actually been stated.

▶ You may wish to visit the personnel office if you need career
  *The office keeps*
  counseling. ~~They keep~~ a supply of brochures to help
                ∧
  employees seeking advancement.

In the original version *they* appeared to refer to the people in the personnel office, but these people had not been specifically mentioned.

Pronouns must refer to nouns or pronouns, not to words functioning as adjectives.

                    *Euripides*
▶ In ~~Euripides'~~ *Medea,* ~~he~~ explores the plight of a woman
                ∧
  rejected by her husband.

*Euripides'* cannot serve as an antecedent because it is a possessive noun functioning as an adjective.

The pronouns *this, that, which,* and *it* should not be used to refer loosely to earlier word groups.

▶ More and more often, especially in large cities, we are

finding ourselves victims of serious crimes. We learn to
accept ~~this~~ with minor gripes and groans.
$\qquad\ \ \wedge$ *our fate*

## **23c** To refer to persons, use *who* or *that*, not *which.*

In most contexts use *who* (or *whom*) to refer to persons. Though *that* may also be used to refer to persons, it is more frequently used to refer to animals and things. *Which* is reserved only for animals and things, so it is impolite to use it to refer to persons.

▶ When he learned that I had seven children, four of ~~which~~ *whom*

were at home, Gill smiled and said that he loved children.

▶ Fans wondered how an out-of-shape old man ~~which~~ walked *who*

with a limp could play football.

**NOTE:** Occasionally *whose* may be used to refer to animals and things to avoid the awkward *of which* construction.

▶ It is a tree ~~the~~ name ~~of which~~ I have forgotten. *whose*

### EXERCISE 23 – 1

Edit the following sentences to correct errors in pronoun reference. In some cases you will need to decide on an antecedent that the pronoun might logically refer to. Example:

The breakup of AT&T has made buying a telephone a
~~This has~~-led many customers to
<sub>^</sub>
complicated process. *These complications have*

question the wisdom of the breakup.

a. The detective removed the blood-stained shawl from the body and then photographed it.
b. You should take advantage of the company's athletic facilities. They offer squash and tennis courts, a small but adequate track, and several trampolines.
c. Abraham Lincoln was a man the humble origins of which did not prevent him from rising to great prominence.
d. In Camilia's autobiography, she revealed the story behind her short stay in prison.
e. The doctor told Jenny that she was worried about her mother's illness.

1. The thief stole the woman's pocketbook and her car and then destroyed it.
2. The racetrack is well equipped for emergencies. They even have an ambulance at the track on racing days.
3. Uncle John still felt uneasy about taking Mary Jane along, but it was offset by her cheerful chatter and delight in the scenery.
4. Since the instructors are so helpful, it gives us the opportunity to learn more.
5. The transportation specialist reviews the airlines' tariffs to determine if they have added any new fares applicable to government travelers.
6. I don't like waiters which mumble.
7. Tom told James that he had won the lottery.
8. Sometimes a list of ways to save energy is included with the gas bill. For example, they suggest setting a moderate temperature for the hot water heater.
9. Sue braided Ann's hair and put fancy ribbons on them.
10. Prince Georges County is bordered on three sides by the Patuxent, Potomac, and Anacostia rivers. Because this is a likely place for criminals to hide evidence, the police department has created a special search team.

# 24

## Use personal pronouns in the proper case.

The personal pronouns in the following chart change what is known as case form according to their grammatical function in a sentence. Pronouns functioning as subjects (or subject complements) appear in the *subjective* case; those functioning as objects appear in the *objective* case; and those functioning as possessives appear in the *possessive* case.

|  | SUBJECTIVE CASE | OBJECTIVE CASE | POSSESSIVE CASE |
|---|---|---|---|
| **SINGULAR** | I | me | my |
|  | you | you | your |
|  | he/she/it | him/her/it | her/his/its |
| **PLURAL** | we | us | our |
|  | you | you | your |
|  | they | them | their |

Pronouns in the subjective and objective cases are frequently confused. Most of the rules in this section show you when to use one or the other of these cases (*I* or *me, he* or *him,* and so on). Rule 24g details a special use of pronouns in the possessive case.

**24a** Use the subjective case (*I, you, he, she, we,* and *they*) for subjects and subject complements.

When personal pronouns are used as subjects, ordinarily your ear will tell you the correct pronoun. Problems sometimes arise, however, with compound subjects. In such cases, strip away all of the subject except the pronoun in question and your ear will tell you which pronoun to use.

▶ Joel ran away from home because his stepfather and ~~him~~ ^*he*^

had quarreled.

> *His stepfather and he* is the subject of the verb *had quarreled.*
> Strip away all of the subject except the pronoun, and your ear
> will give you the correct case. No native speaker of English, ex-
> cept a young child, would say "him had quarreled."

When a pronoun is used as a subject complement (a word
following a linking verb), your ear may mislead you, since the
correct form is infrequently heard in casual speech. (See subject complement, 48c.)

▶ Sandra confessed that the artist was ~~her~~ ^*she*^.

> The pronoun *she* functions as a subject complement with the
> linking verb *was.* In formal, written English, subject comple-
> ments must be in the subjective case. If your ear rejects *artist
> was she* as too stuffy, try rewriting the sentence: *Sandra con-
> fessed that she was the artist.*

**24b**  Use the objective case (*me, you, him, her, us,
them*) for all objects.

When a personal pronoun is used as a direct object, indirect
object, or object of a preposition, ordinarily your ear will lead
you to the correct pronoun. When an object has two parts,
however, you may occasionally become confused. To hear the
correct form, strip away all of the object except the pronoun
in question.

▶ Father Minnorra gave Dorrie and ~~she~~ ^*her*^ each a white flower.

> *Dorrie and her* is the indirect object of the verb *gave.* Strip away
> the words *Dorrie and* to hear the correct pronoun. No native
> speaker of English would say "gave she a white flower."

> *me*
> Geoffrey went with my family and ~~I~~ to King's Dominion.
> ∧

*Me* is the object of the preposition *with*. No one would say "Geoffrey went with I."

When in doubt about the correct pronoun, some writers try to evade the choice by using a reflexive pronoun such as *myself*. Such evasions are considered nonstandard, despite the fact that they are used by some educated persons. In the following sentence, *me* should be used in place of *myself* since it functions as the object of the preposition *to*.

> My husband's table manners are embarrassing to my
> *me*
> daughter and ~~myself~~.
> ∧

For correct uses of *myself*, see the Glossary of Usage at the back of the book.

**24c**  Put an appositive and the word it refers to in the same case.

Appositives are noun phrases that rename nouns or pronouns. Any pronouns that appear in an appositive are assumed to have the same function (usually subject or object) as the word the appositive refers to.

> *he*
> The winners, Julie and ~~him~~, were unable to attend the
> ∧
> awards ceremony.

The appositive *Julie and he* renames the subject (*winners*), so the pronoun should be in the subjective case.

> The college interviewed only two applicants for the job,
> *me*
> Professor Stevens and ~~I~~.
> ∧

The appositive *Professor Stevens and me* renames the direct object (*applicants*), so the pronoun should be in the objective case.

**24d** In elliptical constructions, choose the pronoun that would be appropriate if the construction were completed.

Elliptical constructions are those in which words are understood or omitted. Sentence parts, usually verbs, are often omitted in comparisons beginning with *than* or *as*. In such cases, finish the sentence mentally and your ear will tell you the correct pronoun.

▶ My husband is six years older than ~~me~~.
                                    *I*
                                    ∧

*I* is the subject of the verb *am*, which is understood: *My husband is six years older than I (am).* If the correct English seems too stuffy, you can always add the verb.

▶ We respected no other candidate as much as ~~she~~.
                                            *her*
                                            ∧

This sentence means that we respected no other candidate as much as (*we respected*) *her. Her* is the direct object of an understood verb.

**24e** When deciding whether *we* or *us* should precede a noun, choose the pronoun that would be appropriate if the noun were omitted.

▶ ~~Us~~ smokers would rather fight than switch.
   *We*
   ∧

*We* is part of the subject and must therefore be in the subjective case. No one would say "Us would rather fight than switch."

*us*
▶ Management is short-changing ~~we~~ tenants.
∧

*Us* is part of the direct object and must therefore be in the objective case. No one would say "Management is short-changing we."

## 24f Use the objective case for subjects of infinitives.

Subjects of infinitives are an exception to the general rule that subjects are in the subjective case. Whenever an infinitive has a subject, it must appear in the objective case. Native speakers of English usually follow this rule without even thinking about it. In the following sentence, *them* is the subject of the infinitive *to be:*

We thought *them* to be innocent.

## 24g Use the possessive case (*my, your, his, her, its, our, their*) to modify a gerund.

A gerund is a verb form ending in *-ing* that functions as a noun. Gerunds frequently appear in phrases, in which case the whole gerund phrase functions as a noun. (See gerund phrases, 49c.) If a pronoun modifies a gerund, the pronoun should appear in the possessive case.

*their*
▶ The missionary disapproved of ~~them~~ dancing.
∧

*Dancing* is a single-word gerund. *Their* modifies the gerund.

*my*
▶ My friend had to pay a fifty-dollar fine for ~~me~~ driving without
∧

a permit.

*Driving without a permit* is a gerund phrase. *My* modifies the gerund *driving.*

## EXERCISE 24–1

Edit the following sentences to correct errors in pronoun case. Some sentences are correct. Example:

> *We*
> ~~Us~~ women really have come a long way.
>   ∧

a. The most traumatic experience for her father and I occurred long after her operation.

b. Tiptoeing up to the locked door, Andrea whispered, "Who's there?" Then I could hear Alfred reply softly that it was he.

c. The supervisor claimed that she was much more experienced than me.

d. At the drama festival, two actors, Christina and me, were selected to do the last scene of *King Lear.*

e. My father always tolerated us whispering after the lights were out.

1. The four candidates — Paul, Erica, Tracy, and I — will participate in tonight's televised debate.

2. Doctors should take more seriously what us patients say about our treatment.

3. Our chief of surgery, Dr. Holmes, chose to ignore two of the interns, Sylvia and he.

4. Grandfather said he would give anything to live nearer to Paulette and I.

5. Even though he is constantly being ridiculed by the other boys, Norman is much better off than them.

6. While diving for pearls, Ikiko and she found a treasure chest full of gold bars.

7. Why won't you give we infielders a little more practice time?

8. Gloria was astounded that the National Endowment Fund gave grants to only two engineers, David Drake and she.

9. Because of last night's fire, we are fed up with him drinking and smoking.

10. The swirling cyclone caused he and his horse to race for shelter.

# 25

## Use *who* and *whom* in the proper case.

*Who* and *whom* are relative pronouns used to introduce subordinate clauses. They are also interrogative pronouns used to open questions.

*Who*, a subjective-case pronoun, can be used only for subjects and subject complements. *Whom*, an objective-case pronoun, can be used only for objects. (For more about pronoun case, see 24.)

**25a** Use the relative pronouns *who* and *whom* in the proper case.

When *who* and *whom* (or *whoever* and *whomever*) appear in subordinate clauses, their case is determined by their function *within the clause*. To choose the correct pronoun, you must isolate the subordinate clause and then look at its internal structure. (See subordinate clauses, 49b.) In the following examples, the relative pronouns function as subjects in the subordinate clauses.

▶ The prize goes to the runner ~~whom~~ *who* collects the most points.

The subordinate clause is *who collects the most points*. The verb of the clause is *collects*, and its subject is *who*.

▶ He tells that story to ~~whomever~~ *whoever* will listen.

The writer selected the pronoun *whomever* thinking that it was the object of the preposition *to*. However, the object of the preposition is the entire noun clause *whoever will listen*. The verb of the clause is *will listen*, and its subject is *whoever*.

When it functions as an object in a subordinate clause, *whom* appears out of order, before both the subject and the verb. To choose the correct pronoun, you must mentally restructure the clause.

> *whom*
> ▶ I saw Gene, a basketball player ~~who~~ I had met after the game.
>                                      ∧

*Whom* is the direct object of *had met*. To find the direct object, read the subject and verb and then ask *what* or *whom: I had met whom?* The answer is an echo—*whom*—but it is the direct object nevertheless.

> *whom*
> ▶ The tutor ~~who~~ I was assigned to was very supportive.
>              ∧

*Whom* is the object of the preposition *to*. That preposition can be moved in front of its object to make smoother reading: *The tutor to whom I was assigned was very supportive.*

**NOTE:** Inserted expressions such as *they know*, *I think*, and *she says* should be ignored in determining the case of a relative pronoun.

> ▶ All of the show-offs, bullies, and tough guys in school want
>                                          *who*
>   to take on a big guy ~~whom~~ they know won't hurt them.
>                          ∧

*Who* is the subject of *won't hurt*, not the object of *know*.

**25b** Use the interrogative pronouns *who* and *whom* in the proper case.

When *who* and *whom* are used to open questions, their case is determined by their function within the question. In the following example, *who* functions as the subject of the question.

*Who*
▶ ~~Whom~~ is responsible for this dastardly deed?
   ∧

*Who* is the subject of the verb *is*. Most writers will use the correct form in this sentence without even thinking about grammar. The writer who selected *whom* was probably overcorrecting, using the form that seemed to be "more correct."

When *whom* appears as an object in a question, it appears out of order, before both the subject and the verb. To choose the correct pronoun, you must mentally restructure the question.

*Whom*
▶ ~~Who~~ did the committee select?
   ∧

*Whom* is the direct object of the verb *did select*. To choose the correct pronoun, restructure the question: *The committee did select whom?*

*Whom*
▶ ~~Who~~ did you enter into the contract with?
   ∧

*Whom* is the object of the preposition *with*, as is clear once the question has been restructured: *You did enter into the contract with whom?*

## EXERCISE 25 – 1

Edit the following sentences to correct errors in the use of *who* and *whom* (or *whoever* and *whomever*). Some sentences are correct. Example:

*whom*
What is the name of the person ~~who~~ you are sponsoring for
                               ∧
membership in the club?

a. Paula yelled that she would date whoever she wanted to date.
b. If asked whom I think was the greatest American writer of the twentieth century, I would have difficulty choosing.

c. In his first production of *Hamlet*, who did Laurence Olivier replace?

d. Who was Martin Luther King's mentor?

e. The elderly woman who I was asked to take care of was a clever, delightful companion.

1. They will become business partners with whomever is willing to contribute to the company's coffers.

2. Who are you going to choose as your successor?

3. Sharon played the stereo loudly, unconcerned for anyone who she might be disturbing.

4. Miller always volunteers information to whomever will listen.

5. Who is Cynthia waiting for?

6. You will practice cutting hair on your mannequin, who will gradually take on the character of a real person.

7. Who conferred with Roosevelt and Stalin at Yalta in 1945?

8. Mr. Barnes is the teacher who I admire most.

9. You will work with our senior industrial engineers, who you will meet later.

10. Datacall allows you to talk to whomever needs you no matter where you are in the building.

# 26

### Choose adjectives and adverbs with care.

The dictionary says that *good* and *bad* are adjectives, that *well* and *badly* are adverbs, and that *fast* can function as either an adjective or an adverb. In general, adverbs are formed by adding *-ly* to adjectives (*formal, formally; smooth, smoothly*). But don't assume that all words ending in *-ly* are adverbs or that all adverbs end in *-ly*. Some adjectives end in *-ly* (*lovely, friendly*), and some adverbs don't (*always, here, there*). When in doubt, consult your dictionary.

**26a** Use adverbs, not adjectives, to modify verbs, adjectives, and adverbs.

When adverbs modify verbs, they nearly always answer the question When? Where? How? Why? Under what conditions? How often? or To what degree? When adverbs modify adjectives or other adverbs, they usually qualify or intensify the meaning of the word they modify. (See adverbs, 47e.)

The incorrect use of adjectives in place of adverbs to modify verbs occurs primarily in casual or nonstandard speech.

▶ The arrangement worked out ~~perfect~~ *perfectly* for everyone.

We discovered that the patients hadn't been bathed ~~regular~~ *regularly*.

*Perfect* and *regular* are adjectives, so they should not be used to modify the verbs *worked* and *had been bathed*.

The incorrect use of the adjective *good* in place of the adverb *well* is especially common in casual and nonstandard speech.

▶ When members of your team perform ~~good~~ *well*, let them know you noticed.

The adjective *good* should not be used to modify the verb *perform*.

Adjectives are sometimes used incorrectly to modify adjectives or adverbs.

▶ We were ~~terrible~~ *terribly* sorry to hear about your uncle's death.

For a man eighty years old, Joe plays golf ~~real~~ *really* well.

Only adverbs can be used to modify adjectives or other adverbs. *Terribly* intensifies the meaning of the adjective *sorry,* and *really* intensifies the meaning of the adverb *well.*

## **26b**  Use adjectives, not adverbs, following linking verbs.

Adjectives ordinarily modify nouns or pronouns, but they can also function as subject complements following linking verbs (see 48c). When a subject complement is an adjective, it describes the subject:

Justice is *blind.*

Problems can arise with verbs such as *smell, taste, look,* and *feel,* which may or may not be linking. If the word following one of these verbs describes the subject, use an adjective; if it modifies the verb, use an adverb.

**ADJECTIVE**    The detective looked *cautious.*

**ADVERB**    The detective looked *cautiously* for fingerprints.

The adjective *cautious* describes the detective; the adverb *cautiously* modifies the verb *looked.*

Linking verbs suggest states of being, not actions. Notice, for example, the different meanings of *looked* in the sentences above. To look cautious suggests the state of being cautious; to look cautiously is to perform an action.

▶ The lilacs in our backyard smell especially ~~sweetly~~ *sweet* this year.

Lori looked ~~well~~ *good* in her new raincoat.

The verbs *smell* and *looked* suggest states of being, not actions. Therefore, they should be followed by adjectives, not adverbs. (Contrast: *We smelled the flowers. Lori looked for her raincoat.*)

**26c** Use the comparative to compare two things, the superlative to compare three or more things.

Most adjectives and adverbs have three forms: the positive, the comparative, and the superlative.

| POSITIVE | COMPARATIVE | SUPERLATIVE |
|---|---|---|
| soft | softer | softest |
| fast | faster | fastest |
| good | better | best |
| careful | more careful | most careful |

Writers occasionally confuse the comparative and superlative forms.

▶ Which of these two brands of toothpaste is the ~~best~~ *better*?

Though Shaw and Jackson are impressive, Hobbs is the ~~more~~ *most* qualified of the three candidates running for mayor.

Since two brands are being compared in the first sentence, the comparative form *better* is appropriate; because three candidates are being compared in the second sentence, the superlative form *most* is appropriate.

**26d** Form comparatives and superlatives according to convention.

To form comparatives and superlatives of most one- and two-syllable adjectives, use the endings *-er* and *-est*: *smooth, smoother, smoothest; easy, easier, easiest.* With longer adjectives, use *more* and *most* (or *less* and *least* for downward comparisons): *exciting, more exciting, most exciting; helpful, less helpful, least helpful.*

Some one-syllable adverbs take the endings *-er* and *-est* (*fast, faster, fastest*), but longer adverbs and all of those ending in *-ly* form the comparative and superlative with *more* and *most* (or *less* and *least*).

The comparative and superlative forms of the following adjectives and adverbs are irregular: *good, better, best; bad, worse, worst; badly, worse, worst.*

▶ The Kirov was the ~~splendidest~~ *most splendid* ballet company we had ever seen.

▶ Lloyd's luck couldn't have been ~~worser~~ *worse* than David's.

**26e**   Do not use double comparatives or superlatives.

If you have added *-er* or *-est* to an adjective or an adverb, do not also use *more* or *most* (or *less* or *least*).

▶ Julia is ~~more~~ happier about the move than her husband and children.

**26f**   Do not use comparatives with absolute concepts such as *unique* or *perfect*.

Avoid expressions such as *more straight, less perfect, very round,* and *most unique.* Either something is *unique* or it isn't. It is illogical to suggest that absolute concepts come in degrees.

▶ That is the most ~~unique~~ *unusual* wedding gown I have ever seen.

▶ John Denver wears ~~very~~ round glasses.

**EXERCISE 26–1**

Edit the following sentences to correct errors in the use of adjectives and adverbs. Some sentences are correct. Example:

> When I watched Carl run the 440 on Saturday, I was amazed
> *well*
> at how ~~good~~ he paced himself.
>       ∧

a. My mechanic showed me exactly where to wrap the wire firm around the muffler.
b. I wanted the bike to be real safe in the truck.
c. Marcia performed very well at her Drama Club audition.
d. My mother thinks that Carmen is the most pleasant of the twins.
e. Paula hissed, "That is the most vilest joke I have ever heard."

1. Mr. Miller visits his doctor regularly for a complete physical.
2. Which restaurant do you think makes a better hamburger: McDonald's, Burger King, or Wendy's?
3. Bill's apple fritters taste real good.
4. Eammon wondered which of his two rivals was the smarter.
5. Phyllis dresses in the most unique style.
6. Though she doesn't earn enough to afford European trips, Sally makes enough to live decent.
7. We all felt badly about her death.
8. Of all the forwards, Ralph is the most agile.
9. Of all of my relatives, Uncle Robert is the most cleverest.
10. The manager must see that the office runs smooth and efficient.

# 27

## Choose verbs in an appropriate tense, mood, and voice.

Native speakers of English usually select verbs in the appropriate tense, mood, and voice. The few problems that arise are treated in this section.

## VERB TENSE

Tenses are classified as present, past, and future, with simple, perfect, and progressive forms for each. See 47c for a chart of these forms and 30 for a discussion and list of common irregular verbs.

**27a**  Use the present tense when writing about literature and when expressing general truths.

Writers occasionally have difficulty choosing between the simple present and the simple past. When writing about a work of literature, for example, one may be tempted to use the past tense. The convention, however, is to narrate fictional events in the present tense (known in this use as the historical present).

▶ In Masuji Ibuse's *Black Rain*, a child ~~reached~~ *reaches* for a
pomegranate in his mother's garden, and a moment later he
~~was~~ *is* dead, killed by the blast of the atomic bomb.

Scientific principles or general truths should not appear in the past tense. Unless such principles have been disproved, they should appear in the present.

▶ Galileo taught that the earth ~~revolved~~ *revolves* around the sun.

Since Galileo's teaching has not been discredited, the verb should be in the present tense. The following sentence, however, is acceptable: *Copernicus taught that the sun revolved around the earth.*

**27b** Use the past perfect tense for an action already completed at the time of another past action.

The past perfect tense consists of a past participle preceded by *had* (*had gone, had worked*).

> *had*
> ▶ A closer look revealed that the fan ͜ ripped into my fuel pump.

The fan's ripping into the fuel pump happened before a closer look revealed the damage.

**27c** Use the appropriate form of infinitives.

An infinitive is the plain form of a verb preceded by *to*. Use the present infinitive to show action at the same time as or later than the action of the verb it follows.

> *raise*
> ▶ The club had hoped to ~~have raised~~ a thousand dollars by
> April 1.

The hoping began before the raising.

Use the perfect form of an infinitive (*to have* followed by a past participle) for an action occurring earlier than that of the verb.

> David would like to have joined the Green Berets, but he did not pass the physical.

The liking occurs in the present; the joining would have occurred in the past.

## MOOD

There are three moods in English: the indicative, used for facts, opinions, and questions; the imperative, used for orders or advice; and the subjunctive, used for wishes or conditions contrary to fact. Of these three moods, only the subjunctive causes problems for native speakers of English.

**27d** In *if* clauses expressing wishes or conditions contrary to fact, use the subjunctive verb form *were.*

The subjunctive verb form *were* replaces *was* in sentences such as the following:

▶ If I ~~was~~ a member of Congress, I would vote for that bill.
   *were*

We could be less cautious if Jake ~~was~~ more trustworthy.
   *were*

Ordinarily *I was* and *he was* are correct, but in the subjunctive mood *were* is the only past-tense form of *be.* The verbs express conditions that do not exist: The writer is not a member of Congress, and Jake is not trustworthy.

**27e** Use the subjunctive in *that* clauses following verbs such as *ask, insist, recommend, request,* and *wish.*

The present-tense subjunctive form is the infinitive, such as *be, drive,* and *employ.* The past-tense subjunctive form of *be* is *were.*

▶ Professor Moore insists that her students ~~are~~ on time.
   *be*

We recommend that Lambert ~~files~~ form 1050 soon.
   *file*

Don't you wish that Janet ~~was~~ *were* here to help us celebrate?

Ordinarily *students are, Lambert files,* and *Janet was* are correct, but in the subjunctive mood verbs do not change form to indicate number and person.


## EXERCISE 27–1

Edit the following sentences to correct errors in verb tense or mood. Some sentences are correct. Example:

The path ~~was~~ *had been* plowed, so we were able to walk through the park.

a. The fire was thought to have been started around nine o'clock.
b. Watson and Crick discovered the mechanism that controlled inheritance in all life: the workings of the DNA molecule.
c. Marion would write more if she wasn't distracted by a house full of children.

1. Sharon told me that she went to the meeting the day before.
2. By the time we arrived, the cake had been eaten.
3. Don Quixote, in Cervantes's novel, was an idealist ill suited for life in the real world.
4. If I were in better health, I would enjoy competing in the dance marathon.
5. They planned to have gone to Canada last summer, but they were unable to coordinate their vacations.


## VOICE

## 27f Prefer the active voice.

Transitive verbs appear in either the active or the passive voice (see 48b). In the active voice, the subject of the sentence does the action; in the passive, the subject receives the action.

Though both voices are grammatically correct, the active voice is usually more effective because it is simpler and more direct.

**ACTIVE**    The committee *reached* a decision.

**PASSIVE**    A decision *was reached* by the committee.

▶ For the opening flag ceremony ~~a dance had been~~ *Mr. Martins had choreographed a dance* ~~choreographed by Mr. Martins~~ to the song "Two Hundred

Years and Still a Baby."

The original version of this sentence, with the receiver of the action (*dance*) as the subject, is needlessly indirect. Notice that the actor — Mr. Martins — appears in a prepositional phrase, where he receives very little emphasis. The revision gives Mr. Martins the emphasis he deserves by making him the subject.

▶ *We have received* ~~Reference is made to~~ your request for installation of a traffic

light at Prospect and Vine.

Very often the actor does not even appear in a passive voice sentence. To turn such sentences into the active voice, you must add a subject, in this case *we*.

The passive voice is appropriate if you wish to emphasize the receiver of the action or to minimize the importance of the doer.

**APPROPRIATE PASSIVE**    Many native Hawaiians *are forced* to leave their beautiful beaches to make room for hotels and condominiums.

**APPROPRIATE PASSIVE**    As the time for harvest approaches, the tobacco plants *are sprayed* with a chemical to retard the growth of suckers.

There is no reason to emphasize the doers of these actions. It would be difficult to pinpoint who or what is forcing the Hawaiians to leave their beaches, and most readers don't care who is spraying the tobacco plants. In each sentence the receiver of the action (*Hawaiians, tobacco plants*) is properly highlighted.

### EXERCISE 27–2

Change the following sentences from the passive to the active voice. You may need to invent an actor. Example:

*The research assistant reported the results.*
~~The results were reported by the research assistant~~
∧

a. Enough discretion is not used by parents in deciding which television programs their children may watch.

b. It was noted right away that the taxi driver had been exposed to Americans because he knew all the latest slang.

c. The buttons were replaced, the hems were lengthened or shortened, and all of the costumes were cleaned and pressed.

1. Two hundred invitations to the opening of the student art show were misplaced by my absentminded friend Joe.

2. No loyalty at all was shown by the dog to his owner, who had mistreated him.

3. The records were played over and over again until the right songs were found.

4. A month before the final production, a guest list was drawn up. Then invitations were designed and mailed.

5. It can be concluded that a college education provides a significant economic advantage.

# PART VI

# *Editing for Standard English*

Many people speak two brands of English — standard English, used in academic and business situations, and a nonstandard dialect, spoken with close acquaintances who share a regional or social heritage. Except when used deliberately, for effect, nonstandard dialects should not appear in written English.

The rules of standard English are based on the speech and writing of educated persons such as journalists, television news commentators, national politicians, poets, novelists, historians, and scholars. The most important of these rules, primarily those involving verbs, are detailed in this section. Other rules appear in the Glossary of Usage.

# 28

**Use the -s form of a verb when standard English requires it.**

In some nonstandard dialects, the present-tense verb system differs from that of standard English. Where standard English requires an -s ending, the dialect may omit it.

> **STANDARD**    Bill *travels* to New York once a year.
>
> **NONSTANDARD**    Bill *travel* to New York once a year.

Where standard English does not require the -s ending, the dialect may add it.

> **STANDARD**    The hedges *need* pruning.
>
> **NONSTANDARD**    The hedges *needs* pruning.

This section explains the general rule for adding the *-s* ending to present-tense verbs. It also highlights the frequently used present-tense *-s* forms *has, does,* and *doesn't,* forms that prove especially troublesome for speakers of nonstandard English.

**28a** Use *-s* endings on present-tense verbs that have third-person singular subjects.

All singular nouns (*hiker, tree*) and the pronouns *he, she,* and *it* are third-person singular. Indefinite pronouns such as *everyone* and *neither* are also third-person singular. When used as subjects, these nouns and pronouns demand present-tense verbs with *-s* endings. (See also 21.)

|  | **SINGULAR** |  | **PLURAL** |  |
|---|---|---|---|---|
| **FIRST PERSON** | I | love | we | love |
| **SECOND PERSON** | you | love | you | love |
| **THIRD PERSON** | he/she/it | loves | they | love |
|  | Rudy | loves | parents | love |
|  | everyone | loves |  |  |

In at least one dialect, the *-s* ending required by standard English is omitted.

> Ellen taught him what he ~~know~~ *knows* about the paperwork in this

agency.

Sulfur dioxide ~~turn~~ *turns* leaves yellow, ~~dissolve~~ *dissolves* marble, and ~~eat~~ *eats*

away iron and steel.

The subjects *he* and *sulfur dioxide* are third-person singular, so the verbs must end in *-s.*

**CAUTION:** Do not add the -s ending to the verb if the subject is not third-person singular.

The writers of the following sentences, knowing they sometimes dropped -s endings from verbs, overcorrected by adding the endings where they don't belong.

▶ I prepares̸ program specifications and machine logic

diagrams.

The writer, unsure of the rules of standard English, mistakenly concluded that the -s ending belongs on verbs used with *all* singular subjects, not just *third-person* singular subjects. The pronoun *I* is first-person singular, so its verb does not require the -s.

▶ The dirt floors requires̸ continual sweeping.

The writer mistakenly thought that the -s ending on the verb indicated plurality. The -s goes on verbs used with third-person *singular* subjects.

## 28b Use *has* (not *have*) with third-person singular subjects.

The present-tense forms of the frequently used verb *have* are listed below.

|  | **SINGULAR** |  | **PLURAL** |  |
|---|---|---|---|---|
| **FIRST PERSON** | I | have | we | have |
| **SECOND PERSON** | you | have | you | have |
| **THIRD PERSON** | he/she/it | has | they | have |

In at least one dialect, *has* does not appear; *have* is used with all subjects.

*has*
► This respected musician almost always ~~have~~ a message to
∧
convey in his work.

*has*
As for the supplemental income program, it ~~have~~ finally been
∧
established.

The subjects *musician* and *it* are third-person singular, so the
verb should be *has* in each case.

**CAUTION:** Do not use *has* if the subject is not third-person
singular. The writers of the following sentences were aware
that they often wrote *have* when standard English requires
*has*. Here they are using what appears to them to be the
"more correct" form, but in an inappropriate context.

*have*
► My business law classes ~~has~~ helped me to understand more
∧
about contracts.

*have*
I ~~has~~ much to be thankful for.
∧
The subjects of these sentences — *classes* and *I* — are third-
person plural and first-person singular, so standard English requires *have*. *Has* is used with third-person singular subjects
only.

**28c**  Use *does* and *doesn't* (not *do* and *don't*) with
third-person singular subjects.

The present-tense forms of the frequently used verb *do* are
listed in the following chart.

**-s**

|  | SINGULAR |  | PLURAL |  |
|---|---|---|---|---|
| **FIRST PERSON** | I | do/don't | we | do/don't |
| **SECOND PERSON** | you | do/don't | you | do/don't |
| **THIRD PERSON** | he/she/it | does/doesn't | they | do/don't |

The use of *don't* instead of the standard English *doesn't* is a feature of many dialects in the United States. Use of *do* for *does* is rarer.

▶ Grandfather really ~~don't~~ *doesn't* have a place to call home.

This ~~don't~~ *doesn't* mean you'll have to pay a higher premium.

~~Do~~ *Does* she know how to get there?

*Grandfather, this,* and *she* are third-person singular, so the verbs should be *doesn't* and *does.*

EXERCISE 28–1

Edit the following sentences to conform to the rules of standard English. Some sentences are correct. Example:

The social worker ~~have~~ *has* so many problems in her own life that she ~~don't~~ *doesn't* know how to advise anyone else.

a. Most psychologists agree that no one performs well under stress.

b. Do he have enough energy to hold down two jobs while going to night school?

c. My days in this department has taught me to do what I'm told without question.

d. Our four older children plays one or two instruments each.

e. Antoinette's skin is blotched and yellowish. She don't look at all healthy.

1. I certainly misses the good times we used to have.
2. Have there ever been a time in your life when you were completely fed up with the world and ready to cash in your chips?
3. The supervisor always answer any questions the employees have.
4. Today a modern school building covers most of the old grounds.
5. Because of his shyness, Jeff rarely ask questions or volunteer answers.

# 29

**Use -ed endings on regular verbs when standard English requires them.**

All verbs have three principal parts: the infinitive, the past-tense form, and the past participle. A verb is regular if both its past-tense and past-participle forms are created by adding -ed or -d to the infinitive.

| INFINITIVE | PAST TENSE | PAST PARTICIPLE |
|------------|------------|-----------------|
| talk | talked | talked |
| smoke | smoked | smoked |
| paint | painted | painted |

A verb is irregular if its past-tense and past-participle forms do not follow the above pattern: *ring, rang, rung; bring, brought, brought; choose, chose, chosen.* (See 30 and 47c.)

Regular verbs cause few problems for native speakers of English. However, people who do not fully pronounce -ed endings may tend to omit them in writing. Failure to pronounce -ed endings is common in many dialects and in informal speech even in standard English. In speech such deletions are most likely to occur when the -ed ending does not add another syllable (*fixed, concerned*), when the infinitive ends in a consonant cluster (*asked, missed*), or when the verb appears before a word whose sound blends into the *-ed* sound (*used to, supposed to*).

**29a** Use an *-ed* or *-d* ending to express the past tense of regular verbs.

The past tense is used when the action occurred entirely in the past.

▶ On the day Ed returned home, Mother ~~fix~~ him a big dinner.
  *fixed*

▶ Last summer my counselor ~~advise~~ me to talk to my
  *advised*

  chemistry instructor.

**29b** Use an *-ed* or *-d* ending on past participles of regular verbs.

Past participles are used in three ways: (1) following *have, has,* or *had* to form one of the perfect tenses; (2) following *be, am, is, are, was, were, being,* or *been* to form the passive voice; and (3) as participles modifying nouns or pronouns. The perfect tenses are listed on page 272. The passive voice is discussed in 48b, participles in 49c.

▶ Joan has ~~work~~ as a clerk-typist for seven years.
  *worked*

  *Has worked* is the present perfect tense (*has* or *have* followed by a past participle).

▶ Though it is not a new phenomenon, wife-beating is being
  ~~publicize~~ more frequently.
  *publicized*

*Is being publicized* is the passive voice (a form of *be* followed by a past participle).

▶ All aerobics classes end in a cool-down period to loosen
*tightened*
~~tighten~~ muscles.
  ∧

*Tightened* is a participle, a verb form functioning as an adjective modifying the noun *muscles*.

## EXERCISE 29–1

Edit the following sentences to conform to the rules of standard English. Some sentences are correct. Example:

*asked*
After the interview was over, the personnel manager ~~ask~~,
                                                        ∧

"Weren't you the person I talked to on the phone last

week?"

a. Our captain talked so much at meals that we learned to ignore him so we could have some conversation among ourselves.
b. The troop had grown accustom to expecting the worst.
c. That line of poetry can be express more dramatically.
d. England, France, and the United States had already signed a treaty before the war intensified.
e. How would you feel if your mother or a love one had been a victim of a crime like this?

1. The police are use to helping lost tourists.
2. Many people in my hometown have been ask to help with the rally.
3. After getting her car fix, Gloria came to school to talk to a counselor about her financial problems.
4. Staggered working hours have lessen traffic jams and have save many motorists gallons of gas.
5. Our church has a close-circuit television.

# 30

---

## Use standard English forms of irregular verbs.

---

For all regular verbs, the past-tense and past-participle forms are the same (ending in *-ed* or *-d*), so there is no danger of confusion. This is not true, however, for irregular verbs, such as the following.

| INFINITIVE | PAST TENSE | PAST PARTICIPLE |
|------------|------------|-----------------|
| write | wrote | written |
| ring | rang | rung |
| draw | drew | drawn |

You will find a list of frequently used irregular verbs on page 179.

When in doubt about the standard English forms of irregular verbs, consult the list on page 179 or look up the infinitive form of the verb in the dictionary, which also lists any irregular forms. The past-tense form will appear first, the past participle second. If only one additional form is listed, the past-tense and past-participle forms are the same. If no additional forms are listed, the verb is regular, not irregular. (See 29.)

**30a** Do not confuse the past-tense and past-participle forms of irregular verbs.

The past-tense form of a verb, used to express action that occurred entirely in the past, never has a helping verb.

Last week Chris *went* to Harbor Island.

The past-participle form is used with a helping verb: either with *has*, *have*, or *had* to form one of the perfect tenses (see 47c) or with *be*, *am*, *is*, *are*, *was*, *were*, *being*, or *been* to form the passive voice (see 48b).

Betty *has fought* for equal rights for women.

We *were torn* between two of the alternatives proposed by the committee.

In nonstandard speech, the past-tense and past-participle forms are not always used in conformity with the rules of standard English, as in the following sentences.

▶ Yesterday we ~~seen~~ *saw* an unidentified flying object.

We don't yet know who ~~done~~ *did* it.

Because there are no helping verbs, the past-tense forms *saw* and *did* are required.

▶ The driver had apparently ~~fell~~ *fallen* asleep at the wheel.

The teacher asked Dwain if he had ~~did~~ *done* his homework.

Because of the helping verbs, the past-participle forms are required: *had fallen*, *had done*.

**30b** Do not treat irregular verbs as if they were regular.

▶ This change hurt~~ed~~ my co-workers and me.

The past-tense form of *hurt* is *hurt*.

▶ The school is run~~ned~~ for children of military personnel.

The past participle of *run* is *run*.

## 30c Distinguish among the forms of *lie* and *lay*.

Writers and speakers frequently confuse the various forms of *lie* (meaning recline or rest on a surface) and *lay* (meaning put or place).

| INFINITIVE | PAST TENSE | PAST PARTICIPLE |
|---|---|---|
| lie | lay | lain |
| lay | laid | laid |

*Lie* is an intransitive verb; it does not take a direct object: *The tax forms lie on the coffee table. Lay* is transitive; it takes a direct object: *Please lay the tax forms on the coffee table.* (See 48b and 48c.)

In addition to confusing the meanings of *lie* and *lay*, writers and speakers are often unfamiliar with the standard English past-tense and past-participle forms of these verbs.

*lay*
▶ Sue was so exhausted that she ~~laid~~ down for a nap.

The past-tense form of *lie* is *lay*.

*lain*
▶ The patient had ~~laid~~ in an uncomfortable position all night long.

The past-participle form of *lie* is *lain*.

*laid*
▶ Mary ~~lay~~ the baby on my lap.

The past-tense form of *lay* is *laid*.

## Common irregular verbs

| INFINITIVE | PAST TENSE | PAST PARTICIPLE |
|---|---|---|
| arise | arose | arisen |
| awake | awoke | awaked |
| be | was | been |
| beat | beat | beaten, beat |
| begin | began | begun |
| bend | bent | bent |
| bite | bit | bitten, bit |
| blow | blew | blown |
| break | broke | broken |
| bring | brought | brought |
| build | built | built |
| burst | burst | burst |
| catch | caught | caught |
| choose | chose | chosen |
| come | came | come |
| cost | cost | cost |
| deal | dealt | dealt |
| dig | dug | dug |
| dive | dove, dived | dived |
| do | did | done |
| drag | dragged | dragged |
| draw | drew | drawn |
| dream | dreamed, dreamt | dreamed, dreamt |
| drink | drank | drunk |
| drive | drove | driven |
| drown | drowned | drowned |
| eat | ate | eaten |
| fall | fell | fallen |
| fight | fought | fought |
| find | found | found |
| fly | flew | flown |
| forget | forgot | forgotten, forgot |
| freeze | froze | frozen |
| get | got | gotten, got |
| give | gave | given |
| go | went | gone |

| INFINITIVE | PAST TENSE | PAST PARTICIPLE |
|---|---|---|
| grow | grew | grown |
| hang (suspend) | hung | hung |
| hang (execute) | hanged | hanged |
| have | had | had |
| hear | heard | heard |
| hurt | hurt | hurt |
| keep | kept | kept |
| know | knew | known |
| lay (put) | laid | laid |
| lead | led | led |
| lend | lent | lent |
| let (allow) | let | let |
| lie (recline) | lay | lain |
| lose | lost | lost |
| make | made | made |
| read | read | read |
| ride | rode | ridden |
| ring | rang | rung |
| rise (get up) | rose | risen |
| run | ran | run |
| say | said | said |
| see | saw | seen |
| send | sent | sent |
| set (place) | set | set |
| shake | shook | shaken |
| shoot | shot | shot |
| shrink | shrank | shrunk |
| sing | sang | sung |
| sink | sank | sunk |
| sit (be seated) | sat | sat |
| slay | slew | slain |
| sleep | slept | slept |
| speak | spoke | spoken |
| spin | spun | spun |
| spring | sprang | sprung |
| stand | stood | stood |
| steal | stole | stolen |
| sting | stung | stung |

| INFINITIVE | PAST TENSE | PAST PARTICIPLE |
|---|---|---|
| strike | struck | struck, stricken |
| swear | swore | sworn |
| swim | swam | swum |
| swing | swung | swung |
| take | took | taken |
| teach | taught | taught |
| throw | threw | thrown |
| wake | waked, woke | waked |
| wear | wore | worn |
| wring | wrung | wrung |
| write | wrote | written |

## EXERCISE 30-1

Edit the following sentences to conform to the rules of standard English. Some sentences are correct. Example:

> saw
> Was it you I ~~seen~~ last night at the concert?
> ∧

a. Last June my cousin Albert swum the length of the lake in forty minutes.

b. The police officer asked, "How did you know that your partner had went to Trinidad?"

c. The team of engineers watched in horror as the newly built dam bursted and flooded the small valley.

d. The young girl looked soulfully into her mother's eyes as she laid the wheezing puppy on its mat.

e. Have you ever dreamed that you were falling from a cliff or flying through the air?

1. My parents sented Granddad to a nursing home.

2. When Sarah seen Mr. Johnson coming home from the corner store, she ran over to him to see if he had brung her some candy.

3. How many times have you swore to yourself, "I'll diet tomorrow, after one more piece of cheesecake"?

4. Joel brought flowers, but Susan choosed to ignore them.

5. Have you rode on the new subway yet?

# 31

**Be alert to a variety of differences between standard and nonstandard English.**

## 31a Do not omit needed verbs.

Although standard English allows some linking verbs and helping verbs to be contracted, at least in informal contexts, it does not allow them to be omitted.

Linking verbs, used to link subjects to subject complements, are nearly always a form of *be: be, am, is, are, was, were, being, been.* (See 48b.) Some of these forms may be contracted (*I'm, she's, we're*), but they should not be omitted altogether.

▶ Alvin *is* a man who can defend himself.

▶ When you *are* out there in the evening, you often hear the helicopters circling above.

Helping verbs, used with main verbs, are forms of *be, do,* and *have* or the words *can, will, shall, could, would, should, may, might,* and *must.* (See 47c.) Some helping verbs may be contracted (*he's leaving, we'll celebrate, they've been told*), but they should not be omitted altogether.

▶ My sister *is* coming home tomorrow.

▶ We *have* been in Chicago since last Thursday.

▶ Do you know someone who *would* be good for the job?

**31b**  Use -s endings on most nouns to show plurality.

In some dialects the plural marker -s is commonly dropped when a noun is preceded by a number or some other indication of quantity. Speakers of these dialects may feel that the -s ending is redundant and therefore unnecessary in such constructions. In standard English, however, the absent -s ending is quite conspicuous, especially in writing.

▶ For most ~~tourist~~, the first few days in Hawaii are spent in
*tourists*
∧
Honolulu.

▶ We could afford only three ~~gallon~~ of gas.
*gallons*
∧

   Some nouns form plurals irregularly (*man, men; child, children; deer, deer; goose, geese*). Do not add -s endings to these nouns. When in doubt, consult the dictionary.

▶ The childrens in my neighborhood all walked to school.

**31c**  Use an apostrophe and an -s to show possession.

Standard English requires an apostrophe and an s to show possession: *Bill's horse, my friend's house.* At least one dialect allows both the apostrophe and the s to be omitted (*my friend house*) because the juxtaposed nouns and the context normally make the meaning clear. To speakers of standard English, even those who are tolerant of an occasional dropped apostrophe, the omission of both the apostrophe and the s is quite distracting. For more about the apostrophe, see 36.

▶ My union representative accompanied me to the assistant
*director's*
~~director~~ office.
∧

*cousin's*
▶ Sandra gave Joe directions to her ~~cousin~~ house.
∧

## 31d Use the article *an* when standard English requires it.

In some dialects, the article *an* does not appear. Standard English requires *an*, not *a*, in front of vowels and vowel sounds. See the Glossary of Usage.

*an*
▶ I would be happier digging a ditch or working on ~~a~~ assembly
∧
line.

*an*
▶ Herb's younger sister is ~~a~~ X-ray technologist.
∧

## 31e Avoid double negatives.

Standard English allows two negatives only if a positive meaning is intended: *The runners were not unhappy with their performance.* Double negatives used to emphasize negation are nonstandard.

*anything*
▶ Management is not doing ~~nothing~~ to see that the trash is
∧
picked up.

*ever*
George won't ~~never~~ forget that day.
∧

I enjoy living alone because I don't have to answer to
*anybody*
~~nobody~~.
∧

The double negatives *not . . . nothing*, *won't never*, and
*don't . . . nobody* are nonstandard.

The word *hardly* is considered as a negative, so it should
not be used with negatives such as *not* or *never*.

▶ Maxine is so weak she ~~can't~~ hardly climb stairs.
  *can*
  ∧

## EXERCISE 31 – 1

Edit the following sentences to conform to the rules of standard
English. Some sentences are correct. Example:

Marianne doesn't know ~~nothing~~ about computers.
  *anything*
  ∧

a. The pediatrician gave my daughter a injection for her allergy.
b. They skate swiftly, waving and dodging as they drive the pucks
   down the ice in the direction of the opposing team goal.
c. Chris didn't know about Marlo's death because he never listens.
   He always talking.
d. Though the meals are free, donations are accepted to help pay
   operational cost.
e. James is religious, but he is tolerant of people who aren't.

1. Janet's husband died about three month ago.
2. The rate of unemployment for teenagers is several time that for
   adults.
3. The plan allows employees without a annual leave balance to
   substitute their day off for the approved leave.
4. School officials must use many methods to ensure the teacher
   right to teach and the student right to learn.
5. With the budget deadline approaching, our office hasn't hardly
   had time to handle routine correspondence.

# PART VII

# Editing for Punctuation

# 32

## The comma

The comma was invented to help readers. Without it, sentence parts can collide into one another unexpectedly, causing misreadings.

> **CONFUSING**   If you cook Elmer will do the dishes.

> **CONFUSING**   While we were eating a rattlesnake approached our campsite.

Add commas in the logical places (after *cook* and *eating*), and suddenly all is clear. No longer is Elmer being cooked, the rattlesnake being eaten.

Various rules have evolved to prevent such misreadings and to speed readers along through complex grammatical structures. Those rules are detailed below.

### 32a   Use a comma before a coordinating conjunction joining independent clauses.

Coordinating conjunctions (*and, but, or, nor, for, so, yet*) join coordinate elements, word groups of equal grammatical rank. When coordinating conjunctions connect two or more independent clauses — word groups that might have been punctuated as separate sentences — a comma is required.

▶ Nearly everyone has heard of love at first sight, but I fell in

love at first dance.

> Together the comma and the coordinating conjunction *but* signal that one statement has come to a close and that another, equally important, is about to begin.

▶ Along the walls were arranged glass cubicles, and partitions

ran down the middle of the room.

> Without the comma one is likely to think, on first reading, that
> glass cubicles *and partitions* were arranged along the walls. A
> comma prevents readers from grouping the words in this mis-
> leading way.

**EXCEPTION:** If the two independent clauses are short and there
is no danger of misreading, the comma may be omitted.

> Her eyelashes were singed but she was safe.

**CAUTION:** Do *not* use a comma to separate coordinate word
groups that are not independent clauses. See 33a.

> A good money manager controls expenses and invests surplus
> dollars to meet future needs.

## 32b Use a comma after an introductory clause or phrase.

The most common introductory word groups are clauses and
phrases functioning as adverbs. Such word groups usually
tell when, where, how, why, or under what conditions the
main action of the sentence occurred. See 49a, 49b, and 49c.

▶ Under Title IV of the Interpersonnel Act of 1970, our office

has entered into an agreement with the University of

Arkansas.

> The comma is a useful signal that the introductory phrase is
> over and that the main part of the sentence is about to begin.

▶ When Irwin was ready to eat ⌄ his cat jumped onto the table.

Without the comma, readers may have Irwin eating his cat. The comma signals that *his cat* is the subject of a new clause, not part of the introductory one.

**EXCEPTION:** The comma may be omitted after a short adverb clause or phrase if there is no danger of misreading.

In no time we were at 2,800 feet.

Sentences also frequently open with phrases describing the noun or pronoun immediately following them. The comma tells readers that they are about to hear that noun or pronoun; therefore, the comma is usually required even when the phrase is short. See 49c.

▶ Knowing that he couldn't outrun a car ⌄ Kevin took to the fields.

Excited about the move ⌄ Alice and Don began packing their books.

The commas tell readers that they are about to hear the nouns described: *Kevin* in the first sentence, *Alice and Don* in the second.

## EXERCISE 32–1

Add or delete commas where necessary in the following sentences. Some sentences are correct. Example:

Because it rained all Memorial Day ⌄ our picnic was rather soggy.

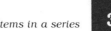

a. He pushed the car beyond the toll gate, and dashed a bucket of water on the smoking hood.
b. The man at the next table complained loudly and the waiter stomped off in disgust.
c. Between the heavy rain and the thick fog, the driving was bad.
d. After I won the hundred-yard dash I found a bench in the park and collapsed.
e. Knowing what she knows about the way nurses are treated in that hospital she was brave to complain about Dr. Michaels.

1. Nursing is physically, and mentally demanding, yet the pay is low.
2. After everyone had eaten Lu and George cut the cake.
3. Lighting the area like a second sun, the helicopter circled the scene.
4. Employees must report to work no later than 9:30 A.M., and leave no later than 6:00 P.M.
5. As cucumbers grow their vines need room to expand.
6. Instead of eating half a cake or two dozen cookies, I now grab a banana or an orange.
7. The temperature was 104 degrees and Eric's car was not equipped with air conditioning.
8. While one of the robbers tied Laureen to a chair, and gagged her with an apron, the other emptied the contents of the safe into a knapsack.
9. Changes in the itinerary are made in a different color ink and the date of change is entered in the margin.
10. Being a confirmed bachelor and having just been divorced from Uncle Sam I did not want to rush into any kind of relationship.

## **32c** Use a comma between all items in a series.

When three or more items are presented in a series, those items should be separated from one another with commas. Items in a series may be single words, phrases, or clauses.

> At Dominique's one can order fillet of rattlesnake, bison burger, or pickled eel.

Although some writers view the comma between the last two items as optional, most experts agree that it is better to put it in because its omission can result in ambiguity or misreading.

▶ My uncle willed me all of his property, houses **,** and

 warehouses.

> Without the comma after *houses*, this sentence is ambiguous. Readers cannot tell whether the uncle has willed property *and* houses *and* warehouses or simply property consisting of houses and warehouses.

▶ The activities include a search for lost treasure, dubious

 financial dealings, much discussion of ancient heresies **,** and

 midnight orgies.

> Without the comma this sentence is easily misread. The people seem to be discussing orgies, not having them. The comma makes it clear that *midnight orgies* is a separate item in the series.

**32d** Use a comma between coordinate adjectives not joined by *and*. Do not use a comma between cumulative adjectives.

When two or more adjectives each modify a noun separately, they are coordinate.

> Mother has become a *strong, confident, independent* woman.

Adjectives are coordinate if they can be joined with *and* (strong *and* confident *and* independent) or if they can be scrambled (an independent, strong, confident woman).

Adjectives that do not modify the noun separately are cumulative.

> *Three large gray* shapes moved slowly toward us.

Beginning with the adjective closest to the noun *shapes*, these modifiers lean on one another, piggyback style, with each modifying a larger word group. *Gray* modifies *shapes*, *large* modifies *gray shapes*, and *three* modifies *large gray shapes*. Notice that we cannot insert the word *and* between cumulative adjectives: Three *and* large *and* gray shapes. Nor can we scramble them: Gray three large shapes.

**COORDINATE ADJECTIVES**

▶ Robert is a warm, gentle, affectionate father.

The adjectives *warm*, *gentle*, and *affectionate* each modify *father* separately. They can be connected with *and* (warm *and* gentle *and* affectionate), and they can be scrambled (an affectionate, warm, gentle father).

**CUMULATIVE ADJECTIVES**

▶ Ira ordered a rich/chocolate/layer cake.

Ira didn't order a cake that was rich and chocolate and layer: He ordered a *layer cake* that was *chocolate*, a *chocolate layer cake* that was *rich*. These cumulative adjectives cannot be scrambled: a layer chocolate rich cake.

## EXERCISE 32–2

Add or delete commas where necessary in the following sentences. Some sentences are correct. Example:

It was a small, unimportant point.

a. She wore a black silk cape, a rhinestone collar, satin gloves and army boots.
b. I called the fire department, ran downstairs to warn my neighbors, and discovered that they had set the fire on purpose.
c. He was an impossible demanding guest.
d. Juan walked through the room with casual elegant grace.
e. My cat's pupils had constricted to small black shining dots.

1. I don't know when I began to fear snakes. I'm sure it wasn't the day my brother and I found a dead garter snake, picked it up and placed it on Miss Eunice's doorstep.
2. Movies have often portrayed bootleggers as mean cutthroat racketeers.
3. Rick James appeared in a glittering, silver jumpsuit and platinum, platform boots.
4. For breakfast the children ordered cornflakes, English muffins with peanut butter and cherry Cokes.
5. Mark was clad in a luminous orange rain suit and a brilliant white helmet.
6. An ambulance threaded its way through police cars fire trucks and irate citizens.
7. Handguns, knives, and other weapons are turning up in locker checks at our local junior high school.
8. A toned, firm body is now considered more attractive than a thin, flabby one.
9. Janice's costume was completed with high-heeled red snakeskin sandals.
10. My once-timid mother fired the building superintendent, hired a replacement and began serving legal notices against delinquent tenants.

**32e** Use commas to set off nonrestrictive elements. Do not use commas to set off restrictive elements.

Word groups providing information about nouns or pronouns (adjective clauses, adjective phrases, and appositives) are classified as restrictive or nonrestrictive. A restrictive element limits the meaning of the noun or pronoun and is therefore essential to the meaning of the sentence.

**RESTRICTIVE**

For camp the children needed clothes *that were washable*.

Dick played with a ball *made out of old socks rolled together*.

Landscaper *Steve Zimmerman* put in that weeping cherry tree.

When a restrictive element is removed from the sentence, the meaning changes significantly, becoming more general than the writer intended. The writers of the above sentences, for example, do not mean that the children needed clothes in general, that Dick played with an ordinary ball, or that an unspecified landscaper put in the tree. In each instance, the intended meaning is more precise.

A nonrestrictive element comments on a noun or pronoun that has already been clearly limited.

**NONRESTRICTIVE**

For camp the children needed sturdier shoes, *which were expensive*.

The guard, *making sure not to touch me*, slid my identification through the slot.

Bud, *the man next door*, observed my aunt in one of her zanier moments.

When a nonrestrictive element is removed from the sentence, the meaning remains essentially the same. It does not become more general than the writer intended.

Nonrestrictive elements should be set off by commas; restrictive elements should not.

*Adjective clauses*

Adjective clauses are patterned like sentences, containing subjects and verbs, but they function within sentences as modifiers of nouns or pronouns. They always follow the word modified, usually immediately. Adjective clauses begin with a relative pronoun (*who, whom, whose, which, that*) or with a relative adverb (*where, when*).

**NONRESTRICTIVE CLAUSE**

▶ Ed's country house, which is located on thirteen acres, was completely furnished with bats in the rafters and mice in the kitchen.

The clause *which is located on thirteen acres* does not restrict the meaning of *house*, so the information is nonessential. If Ed had two country houses and the purpose of the clause were to identify which house was being discussed, then the information would be essential.

**RESTRICTIVE CLAUSE**

▶ An office manager for a corporation/ that had government contracts/ asked her supervisor if she could reprimand her co-workers for smoking.

Because the adjective clause *that had government contracts* identifies the corporation, the information is essential.

**NOTE:** The relative pronoun *which* is usually reserved for nonrestrictive clauses, the ones requiring commas. *That* is used only for restrictive clauses, the ones requiring no commas.

## Phrases functioning as adjectives

Prepositional or verbal phrases functioning as adjectives may be restrictive or nonrestrictive.

**NONRESTRICTIVE PHRASE**

▶ The helicopter‸ with its 100,000-candlepower spotlight illuminating the area‸ circled above.

The *with* phrase is nonessential because its purpose is not to identify which of two or more helicopters is being discussed.

**RESTRICTIVE PHRASE**

▶ One corner of the attic was filled with newspapers/dating from the turn of the century.

*Dating from the turn of the century* restricts the meaning of *newspapers*, so the comma should be omitted.

## Appositives

An appositive is a noun or noun phrase that renames a noun immediately preceding it. Most appositives are nonrestrictive and should be set off with commas; the few that are restrictive require no commas.

**NONRESTRICTIVE APPOSITIVE**

▶ The author thanked her husband‸ Gerald‸ for his help.

The appositive *Gerald* does not restrict the meaning of husband by identifying which of two or more husbands is meant. Presumably the author has only one husband, in which case the appositive is nonrestrictive.

**RESTRICTIVE APPOSITIVE**

▶ The song͵ "Fire It Up͵" was blasted out of amplifiers ten feet
tall.

Once they've read *song,* readers still don't know precisely which
song is meant. The appositive following this noun identifies it,
so it is restrictive.

## EXERCISE 32 – 3

Add or delete commas where necessary in the following sentences.
Some sentences are correct. Example:

Many musicians͵ who lived in Bach's time͵ played several

instruments.

a. He was a star in the circus where six hundred people watched
   his triple somersault.
b. Ignoring several openings, Mary waited for a job, with no overtime, to become available.
c. Shakespeare's tragedy, *King Lear,* was given a splendid performance by the actor, Laurence Olivier.
d. The woman running for the council seat in the fifth district had
   a long history of community service.
e. My youngest sister who plays left wing on the team now lives at
   The Sands, a beach house near Los Angeles.

1. I had the pleasure of talking to a woman, who had just returned
   from India, where she had lived for ten years.
2. We bought a home in Upper Marlboro where my husband worked
   as a mail carrier.
3. The man, whom you recommended to us, is an excellent addition
   to our staff.
4. Ms. Smith's favorite is the youngest brother, Tommie.
5. Greg's cousin, Albert, lives in Huntington Beach. [*Greg has more
   than one cousin.*]
6. The whiskey stills run mostly by farmers and fishermen were
   about twenty miles from home.

7. I passed up the dessert, made with fresh raspberries, in favor of the chocolate torte.
8. We encountered no problems until reaching Cripple Creek, where the trail forked.
9. The second phone number 383-1351, is used for business.
10. The cranky professor singled out the student, scribbling madly in his notebook, and made him recite the stanza aloud.

**32f** Use commas to set off transitions, conjunctive adverbs, and supplemental information.

Transitions are bridges between sentences or parts of sentences. *For example, in other words, in fact, in the first place,* and *as a matter of fact* are common examples.

▶ As a matter of fact, American football was established by

    ∧

fans who wanted to play a more organized game of rugby.

▶ Celery, for example, contains more sodium than most

  ∧     ∧

people would imagine.

Conjunctive adverbs include words such as *however, therefore, furthermore, moreover, nevertheless, thus,* and *consequently.* When such words are used to join independent clauses, they are preceded by a semicolon and followed by a comma. (See 34.) Otherwise they are separated from the rest of the sentence with commas.

▶ This prospective babysitter was very kind; however, she was

         ∧

busy every Saturday for a month.

▶ The major benefit of flexitime to working parents, however,

        ∧      ∧

is the opportunity to spend more time with their children.

**EXCEPTION:** If a transition or conjunctive adverb blends smoothly with the rest of the sentence, it does not need to be set off with a comma.

*Of course* we are planning to attend the wedding.

Bill's typewriter is broken; *therefore* you will need to use Sue's.

Supplemental information that interrupts the natural flow of a sentence should be set off with commas.

▶ Evolution, so far as we know, doesn't work this way.

▶ The bass weighed about twelve pounds, give or take a few ounces.

## 32g Use commas to set off absolute phrases.

An absolute phrase, which modifies the whole sentence, consists of a noun followed by a participle or participial phrase. (See 49e.)

▶ Brenda was forced to rely on public transportation, her car having been wrecked the week before.

▶ Her tennis game at last perfected, Chris won the cup.

## 32h Use commas to set off contrasted elements.

▶ Jane talks to me as an adult and friend, not as her little sister.

▶ Celia , unlike Robert , had no loathing for dance contests.
    ∧                    ∧

**32i**  Use commas to set off nouns of direct address, the words *yes* and *no*, and mild interjections.

▶ Forgive us , Dr. Spock , for spanking Bryan.
      ∧           ∧

▶ Yes , the loan will very likely be approved.
    ∧

▶ Well , what can one expect in circumstances like these?
     ∧

**32j**  Use commas with expressions such as *he said* to set off direct quotations. (See also 37e.)

▶ Naturalist Arthur Cleveland Bent remarked , "In part the
                                           ∧
peregrine declined unnoticed because it is not adorable."

▶ "Convictions are more dangerous foes of truth than lies ,"
                                                        ∧
wrote philosopher Friedrich Nietzsche.

**32k**  Use commas with dates, addresses, and titles.

In dates, the year is set off from the rest of the sentence with a pair of commas.

▶ On December 12 , 1890 , orders were sent out for the arrest
               ∧       ∧
of Sitting Bull.

**EXCEPTIONS:** If the date is inverted, commas are not needed.

On 15 April 1983 Congress voted on important legislation.

If only the month and year are given, commas are not needed.

January 1982 was an extremely cold month.

The elements of an address or place name are followed by commas. A zip code, however, is not preceded by a comma.

▶ John Lennon was born in Liverpool, England, in 1940.

▶ Please send the package to Greg Tarvin at 708 Spring Street,

Washington, Illinois 61571.

If a title follows a name, separate it from the rest of the sentence with a pair of commas.

▶ Sandra Barnes, M.D., performed the surgery.

EXERCISE 32 – 4: Review

Add or delete commas where necessary in the following sentences. Some sentences are correct. Example:

Although we invited him to the party, Gerald decided to

spend another late night in the computer room.

a. Each morning this seventy-year-old woman cleans the barn, shovels manure and spreads clean hay around the milking stalls.
b. Good technique does not guarantee however, that the power you develop will be sufficient for Kyok Pa competition.
c. "The last flight" she said with a sigh "went out five minutes before I arrived at the airport."

d. My only brother, George, worked as a congressional aide last summer.

e. We wondered how our heavy, white-haired grandmother could have been the pretty bride she described.


1. Mr. Mundy was born on July 22, 1939 in Arkansas.

2. You will be unable to answer all their questions, or solve all their problems.

3. The students of Highpoint are required to wear dull green, polyester pleated skirts.

4. As we approached a crumpled figure lying on the mud trail fired on us and forced us to the ground.

5. Draped in scarlet, green, and navy blankets the horses threaded their way through town.

6. Siddhartha decided to leave his worldly possessions behind and live in the forest by a beautiful river.

7. When, we noticed her difficulty Cynthia became even more frustrated.

8. Evolution, so far as we know, doesn't work this way.

9. Just as she barged in the telephone rang.

10. He said, he wanted to be left alone.

11. Julia lives in Sawbridgeworth, Hertfordshire, England for most of the year.

12. The next verbal duel, in which I was an unwilling participant took place in rapid-fire order.

13. When she was fifteen, she moved to Virginia where her aunt and two cousins lived.

14. Please make the check payable to David Kerr D.D.S.

15. Ms. Gilroy did not answer the second letter we wrote until January 30 1984.

16. At the sound of a starting pistol the horses surged forward toward the first obstacle a sharp incline three feet high.

17. Duchamp's *Bicycle Wheel,* simply a bicycle wheel mounted on a stool demonstrates that an everyday object can have a beauty of its own.

18. "It's simply too much" he groaned.

19. The Darby River, a branch of the Delaware, flows by our house in the mountains.

20. I found Bill my pet piranha belly up in the tank one day.

# 33

## Unnecessary commas

**33a**  Do not use a comma between compound elements that are not independent clauses.

Though a comma should be used before a coordinating conjunction joining independent clauses (see 32a), this rule should not be extended to other compound word groups.

▶ The director led the cast members to their positions / and

gave an inspiring last-minute pep talk.

The word group following *and* is not an independent clause because it lacks a subject; *and* connects the verbs *led* and *gave*.

▶ Jake still doesn't realize that his illness is serious / and that

he will have to alter his diet to improve.

The word group following *and* is not an independent clause. The *and* connects two subordinate clauses, each beginning with *that*.

**33b**  Do not use a comma to separate the subject from the verb or the verb from its object or complement.

A sentence should flow from subject to verb to object without unnecessary pauses. Commas may appear between these major sentence elements only when a specific rule calls for them.

▶ Abiding by the 55-mile-per-hour speed limit / can save

considerable gasoline.

The gerund phrase *abiding by the 55-mile-per-hour speed limit* is the subject of the verb *can save*, and it should not be separated from that verb. In fact, a comma here would lead to misreading, for readers would expect a sentence like this one, opening with a participial phrase: *Abiding by the 55-mile-per-hour speed limit, we can save considerable gasoline.*

▶ Fran explained to Mr. Dospril/ that she was busy and would have to see him later.

The *that* clause is the direct object of the verb *explained*. The writer has mistakenly used a comma to separate the verb from its object.

## 33c Do not use a comma before the first or after the last item in a series.

Though commas are required between items in a series (32c), do not place them either before or after the series.

▶ Other causes of asthmatic attacks are/ stress, change in temperature, humidity, and cold air.

▶ Ironically, this job that appears so glamorous, carefree, and easy/ carries a high degree of responsibility.

## 33d Do not use a comma between cumulative adjectives or between an adjective and the noun that follows it.

Though commas are required between coordinate adjectives (those that can be separated with *and*), they do not belong between cumulative adjectives (those that cannot be sepa-rated with *and*). For a full discussion, see 32d.

▶ In the corner of the closet we found an old⁄ maroon hatbox

from Sears.

A comma should never be used to separate an adjective from the noun that follows it.

▶ It was a senseless, dangerous⁄mission.

## 33e Do not use commas to set off restrictive elements.

Restrictive elements are adjectival modifiers or appositives necessary for identifying the nouns they follow. For a full dis-cussion, see 32e.

▶ Drivers⁄ who think they own the road⁄ make cycling a

dangerous sport.

The modifier *who think they own the road* restricts the drivers being discussed, identifying the exact group the sentence is about. The writer who puts commas around this modifier falsely sug-gests that all drivers think they own the road.

▶ Margaret Mead's book⁄ *Coming of Age in Samoa*⁄ has stirred

up considerable controversy in recent years.

Since Margaret Mead wrote more than one book, the appositive contains information essential to the meaning of the sentence.

**33f**  Do not use a comma to set off a concluding adverbial element that is essential to the meaning of the sentence.

Adverbial elements provide information about verbs, usually specifying when, where, how, why, or under what conditions the action occurred. When such elements introduce a sentence, they are nearly always followed by a comma. (See 32b.) When they conclude a sentence, however, they are ordinarily not set off with a comma because their content is usually essential to the meaning of the earlier part of the sentence.

▶ Don't visit Paris at the height of the tourist season/unless

you have booked hotel reservations.

The *unless* clause is essential. Without it, the sentence would be advising us not to visit Paris at the height of the tourist season, even if we had booked reservations.

**EXCEPTION:** If a concluding adverbial element is clearly nonessential, it should be preceded by a comma.

The lecture seemed to last only a short time, though the clock said it had gone on for more than an hour.

**33g**  Do not use a comma before a parenthesis.

▶ At MCI Sylvia began at the bottom/(with only three and a

half walls and a swivel chair), but within five years she had

been promoted to supervisor.

**33h** Do not use a comma after *such as* or *like.*

▶ Many shade-loving plants, such as / begonias, impatiens, and coleus, can add color to a shady garden.

**33i** Do not use a comma before *than.*

▶ Touring Crete was more thrilling for us / than visiting the Greek islands frequented by the jet set.

EXERCISE 33 – 1

Add or delete commas where necessary in the following sentences. Some sentences are correct. Example:

Before he noticed / the strangers in the room, they left.

a. Don't sign up for Logic 101, unless you are prepared to change the way you think.
b. At last he was able to move, his speakers, stereo, video cassette recorder, cameras, screens, and all the rest of his equipment, into his own studio.
c. The man, who escaped, was the one we wanted.
d. Being prepared for the worst is one way to avoid disappointment.
e. He went out into the cold, and hailed a cab.

1. She was born on 4, July, 1960, and each year she celebrated her birthday with fireworks.
2. Mesquite, the hardest of the soft woods, grows primarily in the Southwest.
3. My father said, that if he could live his life over again, he would move to California.
4. He wore a thick, black, wool coat over army fatigues and a spotted, T-shirt.

5. When he heard the groans, he opened the door, and ran out.
6. She loved early spring flowers such as, crocuses, daffodils, forsythia, and irises.
7. What was the difference in weather between January, 1983 and January, 1984?
8. My favorite film, (Woody Allen's *Love and Death*) is a movie my sister refuses to see.
9. Her address is 27, Darkhorse Avenue, Boston Massachusetts, 02116.
10. We'd rather spend our money on blue-chip stocks, than speculate on porkbellies.

# 34

## The semicolon

The semicolon is used to join major sentence elements of equal grammatical rank.

**34a**  Use a semicolon to connect closely related independent clauses not joined by a coordinating conjunction.

When related independent clauses appear in one sentence, they are ordinarily connected with a comma and a coordinating conjunction (*and, but, or, nor, for, so, yet*). The coordinating conjunction signals the relation between the clauses. If the relation is clear without the conjunction, a writer may choose to connect the clauses with a semicolon instead.

A minority may be right; a majority is always wrong.

Injustice is relatively easy to bear; what stings is justice.

The semicolon must be used whenever the coordinating conjunction has been omitted between independent clauses. To use merely a comma creates a serious error known as a comma splice. (See 20.)

▶ Evita didn't rise through hard work and dedication/; she

found other means.

▶ Some of the inmates were young and strung out on drugs/;

others looked as if they might kill at any moment.

## 34b Use a semicolon before a conjunctive adverb linking independent clauses.

Conjunctive adverbs such as *however, nevertheless, moreover,* and *therefore* can never be pressed into service as coordinating conjunctions. The only coordinating conjunctions are *and, but, or, nor, for, so,* and *yet.* Whenever a conjunctive adverb is used to link independent clauses, it must be preceded by a semicolon. (See 20.)

▶ I learned all the rules and regulations/; however, I never

really learned to control the ball.

## 34c Use a semicolon between independent clauses containing internal punctuation even when a coordinating conjunction links the clauses.

Ordinarily a semicolon is not used before a coordinating conjunction linking independent clauses. However, if the clauses contain internal punctuation, a semicolon may be used.

> As a vehicle [the Model T] was hard-working, commonplace,
> and heroic; and it often seemed to transmit those qualities to
> the persons who rode in it.　　　　　　　*— E. B. White*

Though a comma would also be correct in this sentence, the
semicolon is more effective, for it indicates the relative weights
of the pauses.

**34d** Use a semicolon between items in a series
containing internal punctuation.

▶ Classic science fiction sagas are *Star Trek*, with Mr. Spock
and his large pointed ears/; *Battlestar Galactica*, with its
　　　　　　　　　　　　　　　∧
Cylon Raiders/; and *Star Wars*, with Han Solo, Luke
　　　　　　　∧
Skywalker, and Darth Vader.

Without the semicolons the reader would have to sort out the
major groupings, distinguishing between important and less important pauses according to the logic of the sentence. By insert-
ing semicolons at the major breaks, the writer does this work
for the reader.

**34e** Do not use a semicolon to separate a subordinate
clause from the rest of the sentence.

The semicolon should be used only between items of equal
grammatical rank. Subordinate clauses are less important
grammatically than the independent clauses in which they
appear. (See 49b.)

▶ Unless you brush your teeth within ten or fifteen minutes
after eating/, brushing does almost no good.
　　　　　∧

The *unless* clause is subordinate. Introductory subordinate clauses are usually followed by a comma (32b), never by a semicolon.

EXERCISE 34 – 1

Combine each set of sentences below into one sentence using semicolons to link independent clauses or to separate items in a series. You may have to add, delete, or rearrange words. Example:

**Museum exhibits about the Beatles, like the current exhibit**

**at the Museum of Broadcasting, show the lasting popularity**

**of the group; Furthermore, continuing sales of their records**

**attest to a new generation's fascination with them.**

a. The noise — the bass guitarist upstairs, the disco music downstairs, the wailing car alarm on the street, the garbage truck in the alley — was deafening. It's said that such noise raises the heart rate and the blood pressure.

b. Fashion advertising is big business. Millions are spent every year in this country just on magazine ads.

c. Among the TV movies to choose from tonight are a spy thriller with Charles Bronson, who has a photographic memory. There is also a screwball comedy with Clark Gable and Claudette Colbert, featuring the classic hitchhiking scene. There is a sci-fi picture, dubbed from Japanese into English, with an oversized lizard and a giant gorilla.

d. We were very angry with the cousins for not telling us they were coming. Moreover, they stayed two weeks and never even helped with the dishes.

e. We brought her the lumber scraps left over from the bookcase. We couldn't understand why she wanted them.

1. When you play college football, you may have a difficult academic career, which will hamper you in the future. You may have injuries, which will bother you for the rest of your life.

2. She bought a dark skirt, which had a slit up one side. She bought a handsome blazer, which matched the skirt perfectly. She bought a pale silk blouse. And she bought a dashing silk scarf with a delicately scalloped edge.

3. Margaret Mead maintained that adolescence in Samoa was a calm and neurosis-free progression into adulthood. However, her views have been challenged recently.

4. Her interviewer had a gruff voice, an impatient manner, and an unpleasantly sardonic sense of humor. Most important, he didn't seem to know much about the job.

5. In David Rabe's plays about the war in Vietnam, the good soldier is open to question. His eagerness to fight in an unjust war indicates a serious moral flaw.

6. Turn left at the second stoplight. Drive twenty-three blocks until you see the Murphy's Superette billboard. Turn right and drive past the gas station, a row of burned-out buildings, and a church. Then pull into the last driveway on the left.

7. Virginia Woolf complained about the emphasis on competition in the education of males. She felt it prepared them to anticipate war as a desirable occupation.

8. She didn't want to be the receptionist in a law firm. She didn't want to work as a clerk in a store during Christmas rush. She didn't want to drive a taxi. But she would take any other job.

9. Health clubs are the latest fad in fitness. Many joggers, plagued by knee injuries, have turned to exercise machines.

10. Tragedy explores the situation of the individual confronted with the fact of death. In contrast, comedy explores the adaptability and ongoing survival of human society.

# 35

## The colon

The colon is used primarily in formal writing to call attention to the words that follow it.

**35a**   Use a colon before items that have been introduced with an independent clause.

> To bring law and order to the fish tank, I had several alternatives: I could separate the villain from the victim, I could destroy the evil one, or I could hire a policeman.

> The daily routine should include at least the following: 20 knee bends, 50 sit-ups, 15 leg lifts, and five minutes of running in place.

**35b**   Use a colon before a quotation that has been formally introduced.

When a quotation is formally introduced, it is preceded by a full independent clause, not just an expression such as *he said* or *she remarked.* For other ways of introducing quotations, see 37e.

> Consider, for example, the words of John F. Kennedy: "Ask not what your country can do for you; ask what you can do for your country."

**35c**   Use a colon before an appositive that has been formally introduced.

An appositive is a noun or noun phrase that renames a noun that precedes it. Most appositives are set off with commas (32e), but when an appositive appears at the end of an independent clause, it may be introduced with a colon.

> Karate teaches respect: respect for your elders, for your country and flag, for your fellow students, for yourself.

## 35d   Use a colon between independent clauses if the second summarizes or explains the first.

Faith is like love: It cannot be forced.

**NOTE:** When an independent clause follows a colon, it may begin with a lowercase or a capital letter.

## 35e   Use a colon after the salutation in a formal letter, to indicate hours and minutes, to show proportions, and between city and publisher in bibliographic entries.

Dear Sir:

5:30 P.M.

Martinis should be mixed about 5:1.

New York: St. Martin's Press, 1984

## 35f   Do not use a colon before a list unless the list is preceded by an independent clause.

▶ Some important vitamins found in vegetables are:/vitamin A, thiamine, niacin, and vitamin C.

The area to be painted consisted of:/three gable ends, trim work, sixteen windows, and a front and back porch.

The lists in these sentences are not introduced with independent clauses. The list in the first sentence is simply a subject complement following the verb *are;* the list in the second sentence is the object of the preposition *of.*

## EXERCISE 35–1

Edit the following sentences to correct errors in the use of the comma, the semicolon, or the colon. Some sentences are correct. Example:

> **Do not volunteer for any leadership position / unless you are**
>
> **certain that you can fulfill all the responsibilities.**

a. Among the canceled classes were: calculus, physics, advanced biology, and English 101.

b. I entered this class feeling jittery and incapable, I leave feeling poised and confident.

c. Veterans exposed to Agent Orange went to court to demand justice: justice for their wives, who suffered with the veterans in their illnesses, and justice for their children, who suffered damaging illnesses of their own.

d. The second and most memorable week of survival school consisted of five stages: orientation; long treks; POW camp; escape and evasion; and return to civilization.

e. In the introduction to his wife's book on gardening, E. B. White describes her writing process; "The editor in her fought the writer every inch of the way; the struggle was felt all through the house. She would write eight or ten words, then draw her gun and shoot them down."

1. Severe, unremitting pain is a ravaging force; especially when the patient tries to hide it from others.

2. There are two types of leave: annual leave, which is used for vacations and personal reasons; and sick leave, which is used for medical appointments and illness.

3. For example: When a student in private school is caught with drugs, he or she is immediately expelled.

4. I'm from Missouri, you must show me.

5. Most universities have settled on one of two alternatives; "core" multidisciplinary courses required of all students; or "distribution requirements," prescribed choices of courses housed within traditional academic departments.

6. Not everyone would fall in love with the Bethesda Co-op; I can't imagine a corseted, properly hatted matron staying long enough to discover what it's all about.

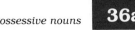
7. The office work includes: typing reports and briefing materials; editing drafts for grammar and punctuation; and answering the phone.
8. Mary was an extremely ambitious student; however, she did not let her ambition ruin her relationships with others.
9. The first requirement is honesty, everything else follows.
10. By 2.30 that afternoon the odds were 4;1 against him.

# 36

## The apostrophe

**36a** Use an apostrophe to indicate that a noun is possessive.

Possessive nouns usually indicate ownership, as in *Tim's hat* or *the lawyer's desk.* Frequently, however, ownership is only loosely implied: *the tree's roots, a day's work.* If you are not sure whether a noun is possessive, try turning it into an *of* phrase: *the roots of the tree, the work of a day.*

1. If the noun does not end in *-s*, add *-'s.*

   Roy managed to climb out on the driver's side.

   Thank you for refunding the children's money.

2. If the noun is singular and ends in *-s*, add *-'s.*

   Lois's sister spent last year in India.

**EXCEPTION:** If pronunciation would be awkward with the added *-'s*, omit it.

   Euripides' plays are among my favorites.

3. If the noun is plural and ends in -*s*, add only an apostrophe.

> Both actresses' jewels were stolen.

4. To show joint possession, use an apostrophe with the last noun only; to show individual possession, make all nouns possessive.

> Have you seen Joyce and Greg's new camper?

> John's and Marie's expectations of marriage couldn't be more different.

In the first sentence, Joyce and Greg jointly possess one camper. In the second sentence, John and Marie individually have different expectations.

5. If a noun is hyphenated or compound, use an apostrophe with the last element.

> Her father-in-law's sculpture won first place.

**36b** Use an apostrophe to indicate that an indefinite pronoun is possessive.

Indefinite pronouns are those that refer to no specific person or thing: *everyone, someone, no one, something.* (See 47b.)

> Someone's raincoat has been left behind.

> This diet will improve almost anyone's health.

**36c** Use an apostrophe to mark contractions.

In contractions the apostrophe takes the place of a missing letter.

If that's not love, what would you call it?

Doesn't Frank plan to go on the tour?

*That's* stands for *that is*, *doesn't* for *does not*.

## 36d Use an apostrophe to pluralize numbers mentioned as numbers, letters mentioned as letters, words mentioned as words, and abbreviations.

Peggy skated nearly perfect figure *8*'s.

The bleachers in our section were marked with large red *J*'s.

We've heard enough *maybe*'s.

You must ask to see their I.D.'s.

## 36e Avoid common misuses of the apostrophe.

1. Do not use an apostrophe with nouns that are not possessive.

▶ Some ~~outpatient's~~ *outpatients* are given special parking permits.

2. Do not use an apostrophe in the possessive pronouns *its*, *whose*, *his*, *hers*, *ours*, *yours*, and *theirs*.

▶ Each area has ~~it's~~ *its* own conference room.

*It's* means *it is*. The possessive pronoun *its* contains no apostrophe, despite the fact that it is possessive.

▶ This course was taught by a professional florist ~~who's~~ *whose*

technique was oriental.

*Who's* means *who is*. The possessive pronoun is *whose*.

**EXERCISE 36 – 1**

Edit the following sentences to correct errors in the use of the apostrophe. Some sentences are correct. Example:

> Marietta lived above the only bar in town, Smiling ~~Jacks~~ Jack's.

a. In a democracy anyones vote counts as much as mine.
b. He received two *A*'s, three *B*'s and a *C*.
c. The puppy's favorite activity was chasing it's tail.
d. *Bubbling Brown Sugar* is one of the best musicals I've ever seen.
e. A crocodiles' life span is about thirteen years.

1. The snow does'nt rise any higher than the horses' fetlocks. [*more than one horse*]
2. For a bus driver, complaints, fare disputes, and robberies are all part of a days work.
3. Each day the menu features a different European countries' dish.
4. After a good nights rest, we headed for the chairlift's.
5. Ms. Jacobs is unwilling to listen to students complaints.
6. The employees names will be listed next to each work station.
7. Ethiopians's meals were served on fermented bread.
8. Kevins girl friend often calls late at night.
9. Luck is an important element in a rock musician's career.
10. Sue went to a party for a friend of theirs'.

# 37

## Quotation marks

**37a** Use quotation marks to enclose exact, word-for-word quotations from printed material.

> Robert Lewis Stevenson wrote that "no human being ever spoke of scenery for above two minutes at a time, which makes me suspect that we hear too much of it in literature."

In *Walden* Thoreau offers this advice: "As long as possible live free and uncommitted. It makes but little difference whether you are committed to a farm or the county jail."

See 51i and 51k for further discussion.

## 37b Use quotation marks to enclose a person's spoken words or unspoken thoughts.

In a husky voice Ali bragged, "My opponent will be on the floor in round four. He'll take a dive in round five. In round nine he'll be all mine."

I thought to myself, "This is a jail, so what does he expect?"

## 37c Use single quotation marks to enclose a quotation within a quotation.

According to Paul Eliott, Eskimo hunters "chant an ancient magic song to the seal they are after: 'Beast of the sea! Come and place yourself before me in the early morning!' "

## 37d Use quotation marks around the titles of newspaper or magazine articles, poems, short stories, songs, television or radio programs, and chapters or subdivisions of books.

Katherine Mansfield's "The Garden Party" provoked a lively discussion in our short-story class last night.

**NOTE:** Titles of books, plays, and films and names of magazines and newspapers are put in italics or underlined. See 42a.

**37e** Use punctuation with quotation marks according to convention.

1. Place periods and commas inside quotation marks.

"This is a stick-up," said the well-dressed young couple. "We want all your money."

2. Put colons and semicolons outside quotation marks.

Harold wrote that he was "unable to attend the fundraiser for Ground Zero"; his letter, however, contained a substantial contribution.

3. Put question marks and exclamation points inside quotation marks unless they apply to the sentence as a whole.

Contrary to tradition, bedtime at my house is marked by "Mommy, can I tell you a story now?"

Have you heard the old proverb "Do not climb the hill until you reach it"?

In the first sentence, the question mark applies only to the quoted question. In the second sentence, the question mark applies to the whole sentence.

4. After a word group introducing a quotation, choose a colon, a comma, or no punctuation at all—whichever is appropriate in the context.

If a quotation has been formally introduced, a colon is appropriate. A formal introduction is a full independent clause, not just an expression such as *he said* or *she remarked*.

Freuchen points out that the diet is not as monotonous as it may seem: "When you have meat and meat, and meat again, you learn to distinguish between the different parts of an animal."

If a quotation is introduced with an expression such as *he said* or *she remarked* — or if it is followed by such an expression — a comma is needed.

> Robert Frost said, "You can be a little ungrammatical if you come from the right part of the country."

> "You can be a little ungrammatical if you come from the right part of the country," said Robert Frost.

When a quotation is blended into the writer's own sentence, either a comma or no punctuation is appropriate, depending on the way in which the quotation fits into the sentence structure.

> The future champion could, as he put it, "float like a butterfly and sting like a bee."

> Charles Hudson noted that "Cooacoochee and a companion escaped from prison by squeezing through a tiny window eighteen feet above the floor of their cell."

If a quotation appears at the beginning of a sentence, set it off with a comma unless the quotation ends with a question mark or an exclamation point.

> "We shot them like dogs," boasted Davy Crockett, who was among Jackson's troops.

> "What is it?" I asked, bracing myself.

If a quoted sentence is interrupted by explanatory words, use commas to set off the explanatory words.

> "A great many people think they are thinking," wrote William James, "when they are merely rearranging their prejudices."

If two successive quoted sentences from the same source are interrupted by explanatory words, use a comma before the explanatory words and a period after them.

> "I was a flop as a daily reporter," admitted E. B. White. "Every piece had to be a masterpiece — and before you knew it, Tuesday was Wednesday."

**37f** Do not use quotation marks to draw attention to familiar slang or to justify an attempt at humor.

▶ Greasers shout at their mothers, cruise the streets at night, and punch each other out ~~"just for fun."~~

## EXERCISE 37 – 1

Add or delete quotation marks as needed and make any other necessary changes in punctuation in the following sentences. Some sentences are correct. Example:

> After the movie Vicki said, "The reviewer called this flick
> "trash of the first order." I guess you can't believe
> everything you read."

a. Fire and Ice is one of Robert Frost's most famous poems.

b. As Emerson said back in 1849, I hate quotations. Tell me what you know.

c. Joggers have to run up the hills and then back down, but bicyclers, once they reach the top of a hill, get a "free ride" back down.

d. Joan was a self-proclaimed "rabid Celtics fan;" she went to every home game and even flew to L.A. for the play-offs.

e. Despite our earlier argument, Debbie approached me after work and said "How about a game of Ms. Pac-Man, John"?

1. Fido jumped on my bed and said "good morning" with her three-inch tongue.
2. The dispatcher's voice cut through the still night air: "Scout 41, robbery in progress, alley rear of 58th and Blaine.
3. After leaving the scene of the domestic quarrel, the officer said that "he had to make his hourly round to the nearest 7-Eleven for a coffee break."
4. In order for the body to turn sugar into glucose, other nutrients in the body must be used. Sugar "steals" these other nutrients from the body.
5. Historians Segal and Stineback tell us that the English settlers considered these epidemics "the hand of God making room for His followers in the "New World"."

# 38

## End punctuation

## 38a The period

1. Use a period to end all sentences except direct questions or genuine exclamations.

Everyone knows that a period should be used to end most sentences. The only problems that arise concern the choice between a period and a question mark or between a period and an exclamation point.

If a sentence reports a question instead of asking it directly, it should end with a period, not a question mark.

Celia wondered whether the picnic would be canceled.

If a declarative or an imperative sentence is not a genuine exclamation, it should end with a period, not an exclamation point.

> After years of working her way through school, Pat finally graduated with high honors.

> Fill out the travel form in triplicate, and then send it to the main office.

2. Use periods in abbreviations according to convention. A period is conventionally used in abbreviations such as the following:

| | | | |
|---|---|---|---|
| Dr. | M.A. | A.M. | i.e. |
| Mr. | Ph.D. | B.C. | e.g. |
| Ms. | R.N. | A.D. | etc. |

Ordinarily a period is not used in abbreviations of organization names:

| | | | |
|---|---|---|---|
| NATO | UNESCO | AFL-CIO | FCC |
| TVA | IRS | SEC | IBM |
| USA (or U.S.A.) | NAACP | PUSH | FTC |

Usage varies, however. When in doubt, consult a dictionary or style manual.

# 38b The question mark

1. Use a question mark after a direct question.

Obviously a direct question should be followed by a question mark:

> What is the horsepower of a 747 engine?

If a polite request is written in the form of a question, it too should be followed by a question mark:

> Would you please send me your catalog of lilies?

2. Do not use a question mark after a reported question. Use a period instead.

> He asked me who was teaching the mythology course.

## 38c The exclamation point

1. Use an exclamation point after a word group or sentence that expresses exceptional feeling or deserves special emphasis.

> The medic shook me and kept yelling, "He's dead! He's dead! Can't you see that?"

2. Do not overuse the exclamation point.

▶ In the fisherman's memory the fish lives on, increasing in

length and weight with each passing year, until at last it is

big enough to shade a fishing boat/.

This sentence doesn't need to be pumped up with an exclamation point. It is emphatic enough without it.

▶ Whenever I see Billie Jean lunging forward to put away an

overhead smash, it might as well be me/ She does it just the

way that I would!

The first exclamation point should be deleted so that the second one will have more force.

### EXERCISE 38–1

Add appropriate end punctuation in the following paragraph.

Although I am generally rational, I am superstitious I never walk under ladders or put shoes on the table If I spill the salt, I go into frenzied calisthenics picking up the grains and tossing them over my left shoulder As a result of these curious activities, I've always wondered whether knowing the roots of superstitions would quell my irrational responses Superstition has it, for example, that one should never place a hat on the bed This superstition arises from a time when head lice were quite common and placing a guest's hat on the bed stood a good chance of spreading lice through the host's bed Doesn't this make good sense And doesn't it stand to reason that if I know that none of my guests has lice I shouldn't care where their hats go Of course it does It is fair to ask, then, if I have changed ways and place hats on beds Are you kidding I wouldn't put a hat on a bed if my life depended on it

# 39

## Other punctuation marks: the dash, parentheses, brackets, the ellipsis mark

## 39a The dash

When typing, use two hyphens to form a dash (--). Do not put spaces before or after the dash.

1. Use dashes to set off parenthetical material that deserves emphasis.

> Everything that went wrong — from the peeping Tom at her window to my head-on collision — was blamed on our move.

> After the initial contact, no more touching was permitted — not even holding hands.

2. Use dashes to set off appositives that contain commas.

An appositive is a noun or noun phrase that restates a noun preceding it. Ordinarily most appositives are set off with commas (32e), but when the appositive contains commas, readers need a pair of dashes to help them see the relative importance of all the pauses.

> In my hometown the basic needs of people — food, clothing, and shelter — are less costly than in Los Angeles.

3. Use a dash to prepare for a list, a restatement, an amplification, or a dramatic shift in tone or thought.

> Along the left wall are the bulk liquids — sesame seed oil, honey, safflower oil, and that half-liquid "peanuts only" peanut butter.

> Consider the amount of sugar in the average person's diet — 104 pounds per year, 90 percent more than that consumed by our ancestors.

> Everywhere we looked there were little kids — a box of Cracker Jacks in one hand and mommy or daddy's sleeve in the other.

> Kiere took a few steps back, came running full speed, kicked a mighty kick — and missed the ball.

4. Do not overuse the dash.

Unless there is a specific reason for using the dash, avoid it. Unnecessary dashes create a choppy effect.

▶ Seeing that our young people learn to use computers as instructional tools ╱ for information retrieval ╱ makes good sense. Herding them ╱ sheeplike ╱ into computer technology does not.

# 39b   Parentheses

1. Use parentheses to enclose supplemental material, minor digressions, and afterthoughts.

> After taking her temperature, pulse, and blood pressure (routine vital signs), the nurse made her as comfortable as possible.

> The weights James was first able to move (not lift, mind you) were measured in ounces.

2. Use parentheses to enclose letters or numbers labeling items in a series.

> Regulations stipulated that only the following equipment could be used on the survival mission: (1) a knife, (2) thirty feet of parachute line, (3) a book of matches, (4) two ponchos, (5) an *E* tool, and (6) a signal flare.

3. Do not overuse parentheses.

Rough drafts are likely to contain more afterthoughts than necessary. As writers head into a sentence, they often think of additional details, occasionally working them in as best they can with parentheses. Usually such sentences should be revised so that the additional details no longer seem to be afterthoughts.

▶ Tucker's Restaurant serves homestyle breakfasts with fresh
eggs, buttered toast ~~(which is still warm)~~, sausage, bacon,
  ⌃ *warm*
waffles, pancakes, and even kippers.

▶ Researchers have said that ~~ten million (estimates run as~~
  ⌃ *from ten to fifty million*
~~high as fifty million)~~ Americans have hypoglycemia.

## **39c** Brackets

Use brackets to enclose any words or phrases that you have inserted into an otherwise word-for-word quotation.

> *Audubon* reports that "if there are not enough young to balance deaths, the end of the species [California condor] is inevitable."

The *Audubon* article did not contain the words *California condor,* since the context made clear what species was meant, so the writer in this example needed to add the name in brackets.

## **39d** The ellipsis mark

Use an ellipsis mark to indicate that you have deleted material from an otherwise word-for-word quotation. For a full discussion, see 51k.

> Reuben reports that "when the amount of cholesterol circulating in the blood rises over . . . 300 milligrams per 100, the chances of a heart attack increase dramatically."

### EXERCISE 39 – 1

Edit the following sentences to correct errors in use of the dash, parentheses, brackets, and ellipsis marks. Some sentences are correct. Example:

Social insects⁄ bees, for example⁄ are able to communicate quite complicated messages to their fellows.

a. Of the three basic schools of detective fiction, the tea-and-crumpet, the hard-boiled detective, and the police procedural, I find the quaint, civilized quality of the tea-and-crumpet school the most appealing.

b. The professional pool player needs to contend not only with abstract theories of math and physics but also with concrete details like the nap of the felt, usually running lengthwise, and the resiliency of the rails.

c. Vin, an accomplished Eagle Scout, packed carefully for his camping trip, remembering his sleeping bag, tent, mess kit, insect repellent, and custom-made marshmallow toaster.

d. *InfoWorld* reports that "customers without any particular aptitude for computers can easily learn to use it (the Bay Area Teleguide) through simple, three-step instructions located at the booth."

e. Pat helped Geoff put the tail on his kite — which was made of scraps from old dresses — and off they went to the park.

1. For the basic cheese sauce, use ½ cup sharp cheese, 2 tablespoons flour, 1 tablespoon butter, ½ cup milk, and a pinch of paprika (if desired).

2. Every night after her jazzercise class, Elizabeth bragged about how great she felt — but she always looked exhausted.

3. There are three points of etiquette in poker: 1. always allow someone to cut the cards, 2. don't forget to ante up, and 3. never stack your chips.

4. In *Lifeboat* (a film that takes place entirely on the open sea in a lifeboat) Alfred Hitchcock appears in a newspaper advertisement for weight loss.

5. The picnic offered many regional specialties, Chuck's buffalo chicken wings, Marge's traditional baked beans, and Janet's ratatouille, and every one was delicious.

**EXERCISE 39 – 2: Review**

Punctuate the following letter.

27 Latches Lane
Missoula Missouri 55432
April 16 1984

Dear Rosalie

I have to tell you about the accident We were driving home at around 5 30 PM of course wed be on the Schuylkill Expressway at rush hour when a tan Cutlass smashed us in the rear Luckily we all had our seatbelts fastened Dr Schabbles who was in the back seat and my husband Bob complained of whiplash but really we got off with hardly a scratch

The mother and daughter in the Cutlass however werent as fortunate They ended up with surgical collars and Ace bandages but their car certainly fared better than ours

The driver of the third car involved in the accident confused everyone Although her car was in the front of the line she kept saying I hit the tan car I hit the tan car We didnt understand until she told us that a fourth car had hit her in the rear and had pushed her ahead of all the rest Can you imagine how frustrated we were when we found out that this man the one who had started it all had left the scene of the accident You were the last car in line someone said No you were we answered The policeman had to reconstruct the disaster from the hopeless babble of eight witnesses

Its uncanny Out of 34800 cars on the expressway on April 14 the police keep count you know our car had to be the one in front of that monstrous tan Cutlass

Well I just wanted to send you a report I hope your days are less thrilling than mine

Yours

Marie

# PART VIII

# *Editing for Mechanics*

# 40

## Abbreviations

**40a** Abbreviate titles immediately before and after proper names.

| TITLES BEFORE PROPER NAMES | TITLES AFTER PROPER NAMES |
|---|---|
| Mr. Ralph Meyer | William Albert, Sr. |
| Mrs. Edward Horn | Thomas Hines, Jr. |
| Ms. Nancy Linehan | Anita Lor, Ph.D. |
| Dr. Margaret Simmons | Robert Simkowski, M.D. |
| Rev. John Stone | William Lyons, M.A. |
| St. Joan of Arc | Margaret Chin, LL.D. |

Do not abbreviate a title if it is not used with a proper name.

> ▶ My history ~~prof.~~ professor was a specialist on America's use of the
>
> atomic bomb in World War II.

**40b** Use commonly accepted abbreviations for the names of organizations, corporations, and countries.

Familiar abbreviations, often written without periods, are acceptable:

    CIA, FBI, AFL-CIO, NAACP
    IBM, UPI, CBS
    USA, USSR (or U.S.A., U.S.S.R.)

> ▶ While in Washington the schoolchildren toured the ~~Federal~~ FBI
>
> ~~Bureau of Investigation~~ building.

YMCA
▶ The ~~Young Men's Christian Association~~ has opened a new
  ∧
gym.

**NOTE:** When using an unfamiliar abbreviation (such as UAW for United Auto Workers) throughout a paper, write the full name followed by the abbreviation in parentheses at the first mention of the name. Then use the abbreviation throughout the rest of the paper.

**40c**  Use the following commonly accepted abbreviations: B.C., A.D., A.M. (or a.m.), P.M. (or p.m.), $, No. (or no.).

| | |
|---|---|
| 40 B.C. (follows the date) | $100 |
| A.D. 44 (precedes the date) | No. 12 |
| 4:00 A.M. | |

**NOTE:** Use the abbreviations No. and $ only with specific numbers and amounts. Otherwise, write out the words.

number
▶ There were an odd ~~no.~~ of seats in the room.
  ∧

**40d**  Use commonly accepted English and Latin abbreviations in footnotes and bibliographies and in informal writing for comments in parentheses.

cf. (Latin *confer*, "compare")
e.g. (Latin *exempli gratia*, "for example")
et al. (Latin *et alii*, "and others")
etc. (Latin *et cetera*, "and so forth")
i.e. (Latin *id est*, "that is")
N.B. (Latin *nota bene*, "note well")

She hated the slice-and-dice genre of horror movies (e.g., *Happy Birthday to Me, Psycho, Friday the Thirteenth*).

Harold Simms et al., *The Race for Space*

In formal writing use the appropriate English phrases.

▶ Many obsolete laws remain on the books, ~~e.g.~~, a law in *for example*

Vermont forbidding an unmarried man and woman to sit less

than six inches apart on a park bench.


**40e**  Do not abbreviate personal names, units of measurement, days of the week, holidays, months, courses of study, divisions of written works, states and countries (except in addresses and except Washington, D.C.). Do not abbreviate Company, Incorporated, and Brothers unless their abbreviated forms are part of an official name.

**PERSONAL NAME**  Charles (not Chas.)

**UNITS OF MEASUREMENT**  pounds (not lb.)

**DAYS OF THE WEEK**  Monday through Friday (not Mon. through Fri.)

**HOLIDAYS**  Christmas (not Xmas)

**MONTHS**  January, February, March (not Jan., Feb., Mar.)

**COURSES OF STUDY**  political science, psychology (not poli. sci., psych.)

**DIVISIONS OF WRITTEN WORKS**  chapter, page (not ch., p.)

**STATES AND COUNTRIES**  Massachusetts, New York (not MA or Mass., NY)

**PARTS OF A BUSINESS NAME**   Adams Lighting Company (not Adams Lighting Co.); Fletcher and Brothers, Incorporated (not Fletcher and Bros., Inc.)

▶ Eliza promised to buy me one ~~lb.~~ *pound* of Godiva chocolate for my birthday, which was last ~~Fri.~~ *Friday.*

## EXERCISE 40 – 1

Edit the following sentences to correct errors in abbreviations. Some sentences contain more than one error. Some sentences are correct. Example:

This year ~~Xmas~~ *Christmas* will fall on a ~~Fri.~~ *Friday.*

a. Marlon Mansard, a reporter for Columbia Broadcasting System, received a congressional citation for his work in Lebanon.

b. My grandmother told me that of all the subjects she studied, she found poli. sci. the most challenging.

c. Reverend Martin Luther King, Senior, spoke eloquently about his son's work against segregation in the South.

d. Julius Caesar was born in B.C. 100 and died in 44 B.C.

e. When she arrived in Poughkeepsie to work at International Business Machines, Pauline was overwhelmed by the sophistication and variety of product prototypes.

1. Pardulio's Meat Market has every conceivable kind of meat: moose, bear, buffalo, deer, whale, chicken, beef, etc.

2. Three interns were selected to assist the chief surgeon, Doctor Paul Hunter, in the hospital's first heart-lung transplant.

3. Some historians think that the New Testament was completed by A.D. 100.

4. A no. of govt. officials have been reviewing the records of some small brokerage firms in the area.

5. The patient handed the dental assistant a check for $40 and rushed out the door.

# 41

## Numbers

**41a**  Spell out numbers of one or two words. Use figures for numbers that require more than two words to spell out.

▶ Now, some ~~8~~ *eight* years later, Muffin is still with us.

▶ I counted ~~one hundred and seventy-six~~ *176* records on the shelf.

If a sentence begins with a number, spell out the number or rewrite the sentence.

▶ *One hundred and fifty* ~~150~~ children in our program need expensive dental treatment.

Rewriting the sentence will also correct the error and may be less awkward if the number is long: *There are 150 children in our program who need expensive dental treatment.*

**41b**  Use figures for dates, addresses, percentages, fractions, decimals, scores, statistics and other numerical results, exact amounts of money, divisions of books and plays, pages, identification numbers, and the time.

**DATES**  July 4, 1776, 56 B.C., A.D. 30

**ADDRESSES**  77 Latches Lane, 519 West 42nd Street

**PERCENTAGES, FRACTIONS, DECIMALS**  55 percent, ½, 0.047

**SCORES**  7 to 3

**STATISTICS**     average age 37, average weight 180

**SURVEYS**     4 out of 5

**EXACT AMOUNTS OF MONEY**     $105.37, $106,000, $0.05

**DIVISIONS OF BOOKS**     volume 3, chapter 4, page 189

**DIVISIONS OF PLAYS**     Act I, scene iii

**IDENTIFICATION NUMBERS**     serial number 10988675

**TIME OF DAY**     4:00 P.M., 1:30 A.M.

▶ Several doctors put up ~~two hundred and fifty-five thousand dollars~~ for the construction of a golf course.

*$255,000*

▶ Though I was working on a ~~nineteen thirty-nine~~ sewing machine, my costume turned out well.

*1939*

**NOTE:** You may spell out *first, second, fifth,* or use *1st, 2nd, 5th* in dates when the year is omitted (*fifth of June, April 1st*).

When not using A.M. or P.M., write out the time in words (*four o'clock in the afternoon, twelve noon, one in the morning*).

EXERCISE 41 – 1

Edit the following sentences to correct errors in the use of numbers. Some sentences are correct. Example:

By the end of the evening Brandon had only ~~three dollars and six cents~~ left.

*$3.06*

a. The president of Forti Motor Company announced that all shifts would report back to work at the Augusta plant on Monday, June six.

b. I didn't really notice any change in my life when I turned 21.

c. The score was tied at five to five when the momentum shifted and carried the Standards to a decisive twelve to five win.

d. Between 1970 and 1980 there was a fifty-eight percent increase in the number of U.S. households headed by single mothers.

e. In nineteen eighty-four, only one percent of all male high school students planned to make a career of teaching.

1. One of my favorite scenes in Shakespeare is the property division scene in Act One of *King Lear*.

2. The president's plane will arrive in Houston at 6:30 P.M. on March 14.

3. 12 percent of all American marriages occur in June.

4. After her 5th marriage ended in divorce, Melinda decided to give up her quest for the perfect husband.

5. The study showed that three out of four local high school seniors apply to college.

# 42

## Italics (underlining)

In handwritten or typed papers <u>underlining</u> represents *italics*, a slanting typeface used in printed material.

**42a**  Underline the titles of books, plays, films, long poems, musical compositions, works of visual art, magazines, newspapers, pamphlets, and radio and television shows.

> **TITLES OF BOOKS**   *The Great Gatsby, David Copperfield*
>
> **PLAYS**   *Julius Caesar, Death of a Salesman*
>
> **FILMS**   *The French Connection, Star Wars*

**LONG POEMS** T. S. Eliot's *The Waste Land*, Milton's *Paradise Lost*

**MUSICAL COMPOSITIONS** Handel's *Messiah*, Gershwin's *Porgy and Bess*

**WORKS OF VISUAL ART** Rodin's *The Thinker*, da Vinci's *The Last Supper*

**MAGAZINES** *Time, Scientific American*

**NEWSPAPERS** *The New York Times, The Boston Globe*

**PAMPHLETS** Thomas Paine's *Common Sense*

**RADIO AND TELEVISION SHOWS** *All Things Considered, Saturday Night Live*

The titles of other works, such as short stories, essays, songs, and short poems, are enclosed in quotation marks.

**NOTE:** Be precise. Underline articles (*a, an, the*) only if they are part of the title. Articles and the names of cities may or may not be part of the titles of particular newspapers and magazines (*The New Republic*, but the *New Haven Register*).

Do not underline the Bible or the titles of books in the Bible (Genesis, not *Genesis*); the titles of legal documents (the Constitution, not the *Constitution*); or the titles of your own papers.

**42b** Underline the names of spacecraft, aircraft, ships, and trains.

*Apollo VIII, Hindenburg, Titanic, Silver Streak*

▶ The success of the Soviet's <u>Sputnik</u> galvanized the U.S.

space program.

**42c**  Underline foreign words used in an English sentence.

▶ Although Joe's method seemed to be successful, I decided to

establish my own <u>modus operandi</u>.

**EXCEPTION:** Do not underline foreign words that have become part of the English language — "dilemma," "bourgeois," and "karate," for example. When in doubt, consult a dictionary.

**42d**  Underline words mentioned as words, letters mentioned as letters, and numbers mentioned as numbers.

▶ Tim assured us that the howling probably came from his

bloodhound, Hill Billy, but his <u>probably</u> stuck in our minds.

▶ Sarah called her father by his given name, Johnny, but she

was unable to pronounce <u>J</u>.

▶ A big <u>3</u> was painted on the door.

**42e**  Avoid excessive underlining for emphasis.

The best strategies for achieving emphasis are rhetorical. Underlining to highlight words or ideas is a shortcut and should be used sparingly.

▶ Tennis is a sport that has become an <u>addiction</u>.

## EXERCISE 42–1

Edit the following sentences to correct errors in the use of italics. Some sentences are correct. Example:

**Do you think that all children should have a thorough**

**understanding of the** ~~Bill of Rights~~?

a. I find it impossible to remember the second l in llama.
b. Howard Hughes commissioned the Spruce Goose, a beautifully built but thoroughly impractical wooden aircraft.
c. Coach Jones shouted, "Give us your *best* try and we'll *go* the *distance!*"
d. Bernard watched as Eileen stood transfixed in front of Vermeer's Head of a Young Girl.
e. I will never forget the way he whispered the word finished.

1. Even though it is almost always hot in Mexico in the summer, you can usually find a cool spot on one of the park benches in the town's zócalo.
2. The preacher was partial to quotations from Exodus.
3. William Faulkner's *A Rose for Emily* is a brilliant but terrifying short story.
4. *Leaves of Grass* by Walt Whitman was quite controversial when it was published a century ago.
5. In her first calligraphy lesson, Susanne learned how to make a Romanesque B.

# 43

## Spelling

You learned to spell from repeated experience with words in both reading and writing, but especially in writing. Words have a look, a sound, and even a feel to them as the hand moves across the page. From your experience with words, you have no doubt developed a "suspicion quotient," an ability to spot particularly tricky words that are worth looking up. Is it *license* or *liscence* or *lisence*? If you don't know, you probably have enough sense to know that you don't know. The solution in such cases is obvious: Look up the word in a dictionary.

To develop your suspicion quotient, you can practice with a list of troublesome words, such as the one at the end of this section. Of course the most effective list for you is a compilation of the words you've actually misspelled.

You can improve your spelling by working at it. Visualize a difficult word. Or, after looking it up in the dictionary, practice writing the word a number of times to give yourself the experience of writing it correctly and remembering it. Some people use mnemonics (memory aids) to help them with habitually misspelled words. For example, *commitment* and *committee* are two words that often give people trouble because of the *t* or *t*'s in the middle. You might remember that commitment is a single thing and then associate that singleness with one *t*; a committee, on the other hand, involves more than one person, so you might remember that the word has more than one *t*. Obviously, your own memory devices for words will be the most effective techniques for you.

Pronouncing a word carefully before writing it can also help your spelling. Don't add extra syllables. Many people say *ath-e-lete* and so misspell the word by adding an extra *e* in the middle. Likewise, don't omit necessary syllables. People often slur syllables in a word and therefore omit them in writing the word. A good example is the word *incidentally*, which people often pronounce *incidently* and so misspell.

## 43a Discriminate between words that sound alike but have different meanings.

Pronunciation can be a useful guide, but don't rely too heavily on it. As you know by now, words are not always spelled as they sound, especially in English. Think of the different sounds for *-ough* in the following words: *rough, thorough, through, slough.* Other sets of words that cause spelling troubles are homophones, words sounding alike but having different meanings and spellings.

### HOMOPHONES (WORDS WITH SIMILAR PRONUNCIATION AND DIFFERENT MEANINGS)

accept (to receive)
except (to take or leave out)

affect (v., to exert an influence)
effect (v., to accomplish; n., result)

ascent (a climb)
assent (agreement)

brake (something used to stop movement)
break (to split or smash into pieces)

capital (seat of government)
capitol (building in which a legislative body meets)

cite (to quote)
sight (vision)
site (position, place)

complement (something that completes)
compliment (praise)

coarse (of ordinary or inferior quality)
course (path, policy chosen)

desert (v., to withdraw from; n., uninhabited and arid land)
dessert (sweet course at the end of a meal)

discreet (prudent, tactful)
discrete (constituting a separate entity)

elicit (to draw or bring out)
illicit (illegal)

eminent (famous, respected)
immanent (indwelling, inherent)
imminent (ready to take place)

formally (in a customary manner)
formerly (in time past)

hole (hollow place)
whole (entire, unhurt)

its (of or belonging to it)
it's (contraction for *it is*)

lead (n., metal; v., to guide)
led (past tense of the verb *lead*)

loose (free, not securely attached)
lose (to fail to keep, to be deprived of)

manner (way)
manor (house)

pair (set of two)
pare (to prepare, trim)
pear (a fruit)

passed (past tense of the verb *pass*)
past (belonging to a former time)

principal (most important; a person who has authority)
principle (a general or fundamental truth)

rain (water falling in drops)
reign (to rule)
rein (restraining influence)

raise (to lift)
raze (to destroy, lay level with the ground)

stationary (standing still)
stationery (writing paper)

straight (free from curves, bends, or angles)
strait (narrow space or passage)

their (belonging to them)
they're (contraction of *they are*)
there (that place or position)

to (prep., toward)
too (also, excessively)
two (one more than one in number)

weather (state of the atmosphere)
whether (indicating a choice between alternatives)

who's (contraction of *who is*)
whose (possessive of *who*)

your (possessive of *you*)
you're (contraction of *you are*)

**43b** Be aware of the following spelling rules.

1. *i* before *e* except after *c* or when sounded like *ay*, as in *neighbor* and *weigh*.

| | |
|---|---|
| **I BEFORE E** | relieve, believe, sieve, frieze |
| **E BEFORE I** | receive, deceive, sleigh, freight, eight |
| **EXCEPTIONS** | seize, either |

2. Drop the final *e* in a word when adding a suffix that begins with a vowel. Keep the final *e* if the suffix begins with a consonant.

desire, desiring; remove, removable

achieve, achievement; care, careful

3. When adding a suffix to words ending in *y*, change *y* to *i* when the *y* is preceded by a consonant but not when it is preceded by a vowel.

comedy, comedies; dry, dried

monkey, monkeys; play, played

4. Double the final consonant of a word when adding a suffix beginning with a vowel if the final consonant of the word is preceded by a single vowel.

bet, betting; sled, sledding

Do not double the final consonant when it is preceded by two vowels or by a vowel and another consonant.

sleep, sleeping; paint, painted; afford, affordable; suggest, suggestible

Do not double the final consonant when the suffix to be added begins with a consonant.

adjust, adjustment; faithful, faithfulness; stupid, stupidly

Double the final consonant in a word of two or more syllables when a single vowel precedes the final consonant and when the accent falls on the last syllable of the stem once the suffix is added.

prefer, preferring; commit, committed

Do not double the final consonant in a word of two or more syllables when the consonant is preceded by two vowels or by a vowel and another consonant or when the accent falls on a syllable in the stem other than the last when the suffix is added.

adjust, adjusting; reward, rewarded; appear, appearance

5. Add -*s* to form the plural of most nouns; add -*es* to words that seem to need an extra syllable for smooth pronunciation of the plural.

table, tables; paper, papers

church, churches; bench, benches

Add -*s* to nouns ending in *o* when the *o* is preceded by a vowel. Add -*es* to nouns ending in *o* preceded by a consonant.

radio, radios; video, videos

hero, heroes; tomato, tomatoes

**NOTE:** English words that derive from other languages (Greek, Latin, Italian, or French) sometimes form the plural as they would in their original language.

medium, media; datum, data; criterion, criteria

## **43c** Learn the following commonly misspelled words.

| | | |
|---|---|---|
| absence | almost | argument |
| academic | although | arising |
| accidentally | altogether | arithmetic |
| accommodate | always | arrangement |
| accomplish | amateur | ascend |
| accumulate | among | association |
| achievement | analyze | athlete |
| acknowledge | annual | athletics |
| acquaintance | answer | attendance |
| acquire | apology | audience |
| across | apparently | bachelor |
| address | appearance | basically |
| aggravate | appropriate | beginning |
| all right | arctic | believe |

benefited
brilliant
Britain
bureau
business
cafeteria
calendar
candidate
category
cemetery
changeable
changing
characteristic
chosen
column
coming
committed
committee
comparative
competitive
conceivable
conference
conferred
conqueror
conscience
conscientious
conscious
convenient
courteous
criticism
criticize
curiosity
dealt
decision
definitely
descendant
describe
description
despair

desperate
develop
dictionary
dining
disagree
disappear
disappoint
disastrous
dissatisfied
eighth
eligible
eliminate
embarrass
eminent
emphasize
entirely
entrance
environment
equivalent
especially
exaggerated
exhaust
existence
experience
explanation
extraordinary
extremely
familiar
fascinate
February
foreign
forty
fourth
friend
government
grammar
guard
guidance
height

humorous
illiterate
imaginary
imagination
immediately
incidentally
incredible
indefinitely
indispensable
inevitable
infinite
intelligence
interesting
irrelevant
irresistible
knowledge
laboratory
legitimate
license
lightning
literature
loneliness
maintenance
maneuver
marriage
mathematics
mischievous
necessary
nevertheless
noticeable
obstacle
occasion
occasionally
occur
occurred
occurrence
optimistic
original
outrageous

pamphlet
parallel
particularly
pastime
perform
permissible
perseverance
perspiration
physically
picnicking
playwright
politics
practically
precede
precedence
preference
preferred
prejudice
preparation
prevalent
primitive
privilege
probably
proceed
professor

prominent
pronunciation
quantity
quiet
quite
quizzes
receive
recognize
recommend
reference
referred
regard
repetition
restaurant
rhythm
rhythmical
roommate
sandwich
schedule
secretary
seize
separate
sergeant
several

similar
sincerely
soliloquy
sophomore
specimen
strictly
subtly
succeed
surprise
temperature
thorough
tragedy
tries
truly
Tuesday
unanimous
unnecessarily
until
usually
vacuum
villain
weird
whether
writing

## EXERCISE 43 – 1

Correct any spelling mistakes in the following list of words. Some are already correct. (Use a dictionary when in doubt.)

ellusive
percieve
maladies
beautiful
anullment
retirment
lonley

beaurocrat
erasible
inconsistent
pulleys
nuclear
promoteable
rodios

twelth
annoint
ryme
traceable
retrieveable
skis

# 44

## The hyphen

**44a**   Consult the dictionary to determine whether a compound word should be treated as a hyphenated compound (*water-repellent*), one word (*waterproof*), or two words (*water table*); if the compound word is not in the dictionary, treat it as two words.

▶ Grandma kept a small note book in her apron pocket.

▶ We could see the forest fire clearly from the look out on top of the mountain.

▶ Alice walked through the looking glass into a backward world.

Use a hyphen to connect two or more words functioning together as an adjective before a noun.

▶ Mrs. Douglas gave Mary a seashell and some newspaper– wrapped fish to take home to her mother.

Slowly we approached the bullet–ridden retreat.

*Newspaper-wrapped* and *bullet-ridden* are adjectives modifying *fish* and *retreat*.

Do not use a hyphen when such compounds follow the noun.

▶ The outside of the mountain retreat was bullet/ridden.

Do not use a hyphen to connect *-ly* modifiers to the words they modify.

▶ A slowly/moving truck tied up traffic.

**44b** Hyphenate the written form of fractions and of compound numbers from twenty-one to ninety-nine.

▶ One—fourth of my income goes to pay off the national debt.
    ∧

**44c** Avoid dividing words. If a word must be divided at the end of a line, divide it correctly.

1. Never divide one-syllable words.

▶ He didn't have the courage or the ~~stren~~
    *strength*
    ~~gth~~ to open the door.
    ∧

2. Never divide a word so that a single letter stands alone at the end of a line or fewer than three letters begin a line.

▶ She'll bring her brother with her when she comes ~~a~~
    *again*
    ~~gain~~.
    ∧

▶ As audience to *The Mousetrap*, Hamlet is a ~~watch~~
    *watcher*
    ~~er~~ watching watchers.
    ∧

3. When dividing a compound word at the end of a line, make the break between the words that form the compound.

▶  My niece is determined to become a long-~~dis~~-
    *distance*
    ~~tance~~ runner when she grows up.
    ∧

4. Use hyphens to avoid ambiguity.

For example, a hyphen distinguishes *re-creation* from *recre-ation*.

> Riding my bicycle in the country is my favorite recreation.

> The film was praised for its astonishing re-creation of nineteenth-century London.

Hyphens may also be used to avoid doubling or tripling vowels or consonants in compound words (*anti-intellectual, meta-analysis*). Always check a dictionary, however, for the standard form of the word.

### EXERCISE 44 – 1

Edit the following sentences to correct errors in hyphenation. Some sentences are correct. Example:

The swiftly⁄moving tugboat pulled alongside the barge and

directed it away from the oil spill in the harbor.

a. Gold is the seventy-ninth element in the periodic table.
b. Many states are adopting laws that limit property taxes for homeowners.
c. Zola's first readers were scandalized by his slice of life novels.
d. Two thirds of the House voted for the amendment.
e. He did fifty push-ups in two minutes and then collapsed.

1. We knew we were driving too fast when our tires skidded over the rain slick surface.
2. Many people protested when the drinking age was lowered from twenty-one to twenty.
3. Instead of an old Victorian, we settled for a modern split-level surrounded by maples.
4. One-quarter of the class signed up for the debate on U.S. foreign aid to Latin America.
5. At the end of *Macbeth*, the hero feels himself profoundly a-lone.

# 45

## Capital letters

In addition to the following rules, a good dictionary can often tell you when to use capital letters.

**45a** Capitalize proper nouns and words derived from them; do not capitalize common nouns.

Proper nouns are the names of specific persons, places, and things. All other nouns are common nouns. The following types of words are usually capitalized: names for the deity, religions, religious followers, sacred books; words of family relationship used as names; particular places; nationalities and their languages, races, tribes; educational institutions, departments, degrees, particular courses; government departments, organizations, political parties; and historical movements, periods, events, documents.

| PROPER NOUNS | COMMON NOUNS |
|---|---|
| God (used as a name) | a god |
| Book of Jeremiah | a book |
| Grandmother Bishop | my grandmother |
| Father (used as a name) | my father |
| Lake Superior | a picturesque lake |
| the Capital Center | a center for advanced studies |
| the South | a southern state |
| Japan, a Japanese garden | an ornamental garden |
| University of Wisconsin | a good university |
| Geology 101 | geology |
| Environmental Protection Agency | a federal agency |
| Phi Kappa Psi | a fraternity |
| a Democrat | an independent |
| the Enlightenment | the eighteenth century |
| the Declaration of Independence | a treaty |

Months, holidays, and days of the week are treated as proper nouns; the seasons and numbers of the days of the month are not.

> Our academic year begins on a Tuesday in early September, right after Labor Day.

> My mother's birthday is in early summer, on the thirteenth of June.

Names of school subjects are capitalized only if they are derived from the names of countries.

> This semester Austin is taking math, geography, geology, French, and English.

**CAUTION:** Do not capitalize common nouns to make them seem important: *Our company is presently hiring computer programmers* (not *Company, Computer Programmers*).

**45b**  Capitalize titles when they precede proper names but usually not when they follow proper names or are used alone.

> Professor Margaret Barnes; Dr. Harold Stevens; John Scott Williams, Jr.; Ms. Anne Tilton, LL.D.

> District Attorney Marshall was reprimanded for badgering the witness.

> The district attorney was elected for a two-year term.

**45c**  Capitalize the first, last, and all major words in titles of works such as books, articles, and songs. Do not capitalize articles (*a, an, the*) or prepositions of fewer than five letters unless they are the first or last word of a title. Capitalize any word after a colon in a title; capitalize the second part of a hyphenated word in a title if the second part is as important as the first part of the word.

> *The Country of the Pointed Firs*
> *The Impossible Theater: A Manifesto*
> *The F-Plan Diet*

Capitalize chapter titles and the titles of other major divisions of a work.

> "Work and Play" in Santayana's *The Nature of Beauty*

**45d**  Capitalize the first word of a sentence.

> When lightning struck the house, the chimney collapsed.

Capitalize the first word in every line of poetry unless the poet uses a different convention.

When I consider everything that grows
Holds in perfection but a little moment                — *Shakespeare*

it was the week        that
i felt the city's narrow breezes rush about
me                                                                            — *Don L. Lee*

**45e** Capitalize the first word of a quoted sentence unless it is blended into the sentence that introduces it.

> In *Time* magazine Robert Hughes writes, "There are only about sixty Watteau paintings on whose authenticity all experts agree."

> Russell Baker has written that in our country "it is sport that is the opiate of the masses."

If a quoted sentence is interrupted, do not capitalize the first word after the interruption.

> "If you wanted to go out," he said sharply, "you should have told me."

**NOTE:** In a quotation, capitalize all words capitalized by the author.

**45f** Do not capitalize the first word after a colon unless it begins an independent clause, in which case capitalization is optional.

> Most of the bar's patrons can be divided into two groups: the occasional after-work socializers and the nothing-to-go-home-to regulars.

> This we are forced to conclude: the [or The] federal government is needed to protect the rights of minorities.

**45g** Capitalize abbreviations for the departments and agencies of government, other organizations, and corporations; capitalize trade names and the call letters of radio and television stations.

EPA, FBI, OPEC, IBM
Xerox, WCRB, WOR-TV

## EXERCISE 45–1

Edit the following sentences to correct errors in capitalization. Some sentences are correct. Example:

On our trip to the West we visited the *g̶*rand *c̶*anyon and the *g̶*reat *s̶*alt *d̶*esert.

a. District attorney Johnson was disgusted when the jurors turned in a not guilty verdict after only one hour of deliberation.

b. *The World according to Garp* is a strange novel and an even stranger film.

c. W. C. Fields's epitaph reads, "On the whole, I'd rather be in Philadelphia."

d. Refugees from central America are finding it more and more difficult to cross the rio Grande into the United States.

e. I want to take Environmental Biology 103, one other Biology course, and one English course.

1. "Forbidding people things they like or think they might enjoy," contends Gore Vidal, "Only makes them want those things all the more."

2. Whenever my brother took us to the movies, he gave us three choices: A brainless beach party flick, a foreign fluff film, or a blood-and-lust adventure movie.

3. In our family, aunt Stevens was notorious for her biting tongue.

4. Historians have described Robert E. Lee as the aristocratic south personified.

5. My brother is a Doctor and my sister-in-law is a Lawyer.

# 46

## Manuscript preparation

By following standard guidelines in preparing manuscripts, a writer fulfills the reader's expectations about how a paper should look. Decisions about where to put the title, where to number the pages, and how much margin to leave become easier for the writer, and the paper is more legible for the reader. If your instructor provides formal guidelines, follow them; otherwise, use the guidelines given in this section.

### Materials

For a typed paper use $8\frac{1}{2}'' \times 11''$, 20-pound typing paper, not onionskin. Some instructors allow erasable or corrasable bond, but ink smears easily on this coated paper, so you should probably avoid it. Use a fresh ribbon, and clean the typewriter keys before you begin. Use Liquid Paper or some other white correction fluid to eliminate errors completely. Allow the liquid to dry and then type over the error. Do not type hyphens, $x$'s, or slashes through a mistake, and do not strike over a mistake without first erasing it or whiting it out. Some instructors will accept a line through the mistake with the correction neatly written or typed above. Use a caret (∧) to indicate where the correction should be inserted. Make the finished page as neat and legible as possible. If a mistake is substantial (more than one line of type), retype the page.

For handwritten papers use $8\frac{1}{2}'' \times 11''$, wide-ruled white paper, and write on only one side of the sheet. Do not use legal-size paper or sheets torn from a notebook. Again, the aim is legibility and neatness. If your handwriting is difficult to read, make an effort to type the paper or have it typed. If you must submit a handwritten paper, make your handwriting as clear as possible. Most instructors ask students to skip one line between each line of writing. Use blue or black ink (not pencil) and be sure to use an ink eraser when correcting mistakes. Never scribble over mistakes. Rewrite the page if an error is substantial.

### Title and identification

Unless your instructor asks for one, you do not need a separate title page. Place your name, the instructor's name, the course number, and the date on separate lines, double-spacing between each line. Type this heading against the left margin about one inch from the top. Double-space after the heading and center the title of the paper in the width of the page. If the title has two or more lines, double-space between the lines and double-space after the title to begin the body of the paper. Capitalize the first and last words of the title and all other words except articles (*a, an, the*), conjunctions, and prepositions of fewer than five letters. Capitalize any word after a colon in the title. Do not underline the title or put it in quotation marks, and do not use a period after the title. If you mention another work in your title, underline the title of that work if it is a book, long poem, play, and so on, or enclose it in quotation marks if it is a poem, essay, short story, or other shorter work. (See 37d and 42a.)

### Margins, spacing, and indentation

Leave margins of one inch at the top, bottom, and sides of the paper. (The vertical line on ruled paper provides an ample left margin for handwritten papers.) Double-space between lines in a typewritten paper. For quotations of longer than four typed lines, indent each line ten spaces from the left margin. Double-space between the body of the paper and the quotation, and double-space the lines of the quotation. Such quotations set off from the text by spacing and indentation should not be enclosed in quotation marks.

### Pagination

Although the first page of the paper is counted as page 1, by convention it goes unnumbered. (If you have a separate title page, the title page is uncounted and unnumbered.) Number all other pages at the upper right-hand corner of the page, one-half inch below the top edge. Use Arabic numerals (2, 3, 4, and so on). Do not put a period after the number and do not enclose the number in parentheses.

If there are endnotes, begin them on a separate page after the text of the paper and continue to number these pages. Similarly, begin the list of works cited on a separate page and number these pages. If you include an outline, you can number the outline pages with small Roman numerals (i, ii, iii, iv, and so on).

### Miscellaneous

In typing the paper leave one space after words, commas, colons, semicolons, and between the dots in ellipses. Leave two spaces after periods, questions marks, and exclamation points. If you must break a word at the end of a line, be sure to find the correct syllable breaks in a dictionary.

### Proofreading

Misspelled words, incorrect hyphenation, and errors in grammar and punctuation detract from the overall effect of a paper; if there are too many of these errors, readers will lose patience. Your ideas deserve clear and correct expression. Proofread the final draft of the paper and then proofread it again.

# PART IX

## *Grammar Basics*

# 47

## Parts of speech

There are eight parts of speech: noun, pronoun, verb, adjective, adverb, preposition, conjunction, and interjection. Many words can function as more than one part of speech. For example, depending on its use in a sentence, the word *paint* can be a noun (*The paint is wet*) or a verb (*Please paint the ceiling next*).

## **47a** Nouns

As every schoolchild knows, a noun is the name of a person, place, or thing. In addition, grammarians describe a noun as follows:

> the kind of word that is often marked with an article (*a spoon, an apple, the newspaper*);

> the kind of word that can be pluralized (*one cat, two cats*) or made possessive (*the cat's paw*);

> the kind of word that when derived from another word typically takes one of these endings: play*er*, just*ice*, happi*ness*, divis*ion*, guid*ance*, refer*ence*, pave*ment*, child*hood*, king*dom*, agen*cy*, tour*ist*, sincer*ity*, censor*ship*;

> the kind of word that can fill one of these slots in a sentence: subject, direct object, indirect object, subject complement, object complement, and object of the preposition. (See 48a and 48c.)

Nouns, in other words, may be identified as much by their form and function as by their meaning.

Nouns may occasionally be used as adjectives modifying other nouns (*school* bus, the *city's* park). Because they have a split personality, nouns used in this manner may be called *noun/adjectives.*

## EXERCISE 47 – 1

Underline the nouns (and noun/adjectives) in the following sentences. Example:

Pride is at the bottom of all great mistakes.

a. The cat in gloves catches no mice.
b. Repetition does not transform a lie into truth.
c. Our national flower is the concrete cloverleaf.
d. The ultimate censorship is the flick of the dial.
e. Figures won't lie, but liars will figure.

1. Conservatism is the worship of dead revolutions.
2. The winds and the waves are always on the side of the ablest navigators.
3. You can't make a silk purse out of a sow's ear.
4. A scalded dog fears even cold water.
5. Prejudice is the child of ignorance.

## 47b Pronouns

There are thousands of nouns, and new ones come into the language every year. This is not true of pronouns, which number about one hundred and are extremely resistant to change. Most of the pronouns in English are listed in this section.

A pronoun is a word used for a noun. A pronoun usually substitutes for a specific noun, known as its *antecedent.*

When Susan opened the door, *she* pretended surprise.

The noun *Susan* is the antecedent of the pronoun *she.*

Although most pronouns function as substitutes for nouns, some can function as adjectives modifying nouns.

*This* new car was *my* birthday present.

*This* modifies the noun *car*, and *my* modifies the noun *present*. Because they have the form of a pronoun and the function of an adjective, such pronouns may be called *pronoun/adjectives*.

Pronouns are classified as personal, possessive, intensive or reflexive, relative, interrogative, demonstrative, and indefinite.

*Personal pronouns* refer to specific persons or things. They are singular or plural in form, and they always function as noun equivalents.

**SINGULAR PERSONAL PRONOUNS**   I, me, you, he, him, she, her, it

**PLURAL PERSONAL PRONOUNS**   we, us, you, they, them

*Possessive pronouns* indicate ownership. Like personal pronouns, they are singular or plural in form.

**SINGULAR POSSESSIVE PRONOUNS**   my, mine, your, yours, his, her, hers, its

**PLURAL POSSESSIVE PRONOUNS**   our, ours, your, yours, their, theirs

Some of these possessive pronouns function as adjectives modifying nouns: *my, your, his, her, its, our, their.*

*Intensive pronouns* emphasize a noun or another pronoun (The congresswoman *herself* met us at the door). *Reflexive pronouns*, which have the same form as intensive pronouns, name a receiver of an action identical with the doer of the action (Paula cut *herself*). Intensive and reflexive pronouns are singular or plural in form.

**SINGULAR INTENSIVE AND REFLEXIVE PRONOUNS**   myself, yourself, himself, herself, itself

**PLURAL INTENSIVE AND REFLEXIVE PRONOUNS**   ourselves, yourselves, themselves

*Relative pronouns* introduce subordinate clauses functioning as adjectives (The man *who robbed us* was never caught). In addition to introducing the clause, the relative pronoun, in this case *who*, points back to the noun or pronoun that the clause modifies (*man*). (See 49b.)

**RELATIVE PRONOUNS**   who, whom, whose, which, that

*Interrogative pronouns* introduce questions (*Who* is expected to win the election?).

**INTERROGATIVE PRONOUNS**   who, whom, whose, which, what

*Demonstrative pronouns* are used to identify nouns. Frequently they function as adjectives (*This* chair is my favorite), but they may also function as noun equivalents (*This* is my favorite chair).

**DEMONSTRATIVE PRONOUNS**   this, that, these, those

*Indefinite pronouns* are used for general rather than specific references. Some are always singular (*everyone, each, none*); others are always plural (*all, both, many*). Most indefinite pronouns function as noun equivalents, but some can also function as adjectives.

| | | | | |
|---|---|---|---|---|
| all | anything | everyone | nobody | several |
| another | both | everything | none | some |
| any | each | few | no one | somebody |
| anybody | either | many | nothing | someone |
| anyone | everybody | neither | one | something |

EXERCISE 47 – 2

Underline the pronouns (and pronoun/adjectives) in the following sentences. Example:

**Beware of persons <u>who</u> are praised by <u>everyone</u>.**

a. Admonish your friends in private; praise them in public.
b. Nothing is permanent except change.
c. I have written some poetry that I myself don't understand.
d. A skeptic is a person who would ask God for his I.D.
e. This novel is not to be tossed lightly aside, but to be hurled with great force.

1. The louder he talked of his honor, the faster we counted our spoons.
2. God made us, but we admire ourselves.
3. We will never have friends if we expect to find them without fault.
4. If a man bites a dog, that is news.
5. Anyone who serves God for money will serve the devil for better wages.

# 47c  Verbs

The verb in a sentence usually expresses action (*jump, think*) or being (*is, become*). It is composed of a main verb and any helping verbs used with the main verb.

There are twenty-three helping verbs in English. Nine of them, called "modals," function only as helping verbs, never as main verbs: *can, will, shall, should, could, would, may, might, must.* The other helping verbs may be either helping verbs or main verbs: *have, has, had; do, does, did; be, am, is, are, was, were, being, been.*

Helping verbs never follow their main verbs; when they are present, they always come first:

A marriage *is* not *built* in a day.

Even God *has been defended* with nonsense.

Notice that words can intervene between the helping and the main verb (*is* not *built*) and that a main verb can have more than one helping verb (*has been defended*).

The main verb of a sentence will always be the kind of word that would change form if put into these slots:

| | |
|---|---|
| **INFINITIVE FORM** | Today I (*walk, ride*). |
| **PAST-TENSE FORM** | Yesterday I (*walked, rode*). |
| **PAST PARTICIPLE** | I have (*walked, ridden*) many times before. |
| **PRESENT PARTICIPLE** | I am (*walking, riding*) right now. |
| **-S FORM** | He/she/it (*walks, rides*) regularly. |

If both the past-tense and past-participle forms of a verb end in *-ed*, the verb is regular (*walked, walked*). Otherwise, the verb is irregular (*rode, ridden*) (see 30). The verb *be* has eight forms instead of the usual five: *be, am, is, are, was, were, being, been.*

Helping verbs combine with the various forms of main verbs to create tenses. Tenses indicate the time of the action in relation to the time of speaking or writing.

The present tense is used primarily for actions occurring at the time of speaking or for actions occurring regularly. The past tense is used for actions completed in the past. The future tense is used for actions that will occur in the future. Of these three simple tenses, only the future requires a helping verb.

**PRESENT TENSE**

| SINGULAR | | PLURAL | |
|---|---|---|---|
| I | walk, ride, am | we | walk, ride, are |
| you | walk, ride, are | you | walk, ride, are |
| he/she/it | walks, rides, is | they | walk, ride, are |

**PAST TENSE**

| SINGULAR | | PLURAL | |
|---|---|---|---|
| I | walked, rode, was | we | walked, rode, were |
| you | walked, rode, were | you | walked, rode, were |
| he/she/it | walked, rode, was | they | walked, rode, were |

**FUTURE TENSE**

I, you, he/she/it, we, they   will walk, ride, be

More complex time relations are indicated by the perfect and progressive tenses. A verb in one of the perfect tenses expresses an action that was or will be completed at the time of another action. A verb in a progressive tense expresses an action that is continuing.

**PRESENT PERFECT**

| I, you, we, they | have walked, ridden, been |
|---|---|
| he/she/it | has walked, ridden, been |

**PAST PERFECT**

I, you, he/she/it, we, they   had walked, ridden, been

**FUTURE PERFECT**

I, you, he/she/it, we, they   will have walked, ridden, been

**PRESENT PROGRESSIVE**

| I | am walking, riding, being |
|---|---|
| he/she/it | is walking, riding, being |
| you, we, they | are walking, riding, being |

**PAST PROGRESSIVE**

| I, he/she/it | was walking, riding, being |
|---|---|
| you, we, they | were walking, riding, being |

**FUTURE PROGRESSIVE**

I, you, he/she/it, we, they   will be walking, riding, being

EXERCISE 47–3

Underline the verbs in the following sentences, including helping verbs. Example:

> **Throw a lucky man into the sea, and he will emerge with a**
>
> **fish in his mouth.**

a. Great persons have not commonly been great scholars.
b. Without the spice of guilt, can sin be fully savored?
c. There are many paths to the top of the mountain, but the view is always the same.
d. Birds of a feather flock together.
e. Don't scald your tongue in other people's broth.

1. The king can do no wrong.
2. The road to hell is usually paved with good intentions.
3. Clothe an idea in words, and it loses its freedom of movement.
4. Life can only be understood backwards, but it must be lived forwards.
5. He has every attribute of a dog except loyalty.

## 47d Adjectives

An adjective is a word used to modify, or describe, a noun or pronoun. An adjective usually answers one of these questions: Which one? What kind of? How many?

> the *lame* elephant [Which elephant?]
>
> *rare, valuable, old* stamps [What kind of stamps?]
>
> *sixteen* candles [How many candles?]

Grammarians also define adjectives according to their form and their typical position in a sentence, as follows:

the kind of word that usually comes before a noun in a noun phrase (a *frisky* puppy, an *amiable young* man);

the kind of word that can follow a linking verb and describe the subject (the ship was *unsinkable;* talk is *cheap*) (see 48c);

the kind of word that when derived from another part of speech typically takes one of these endings: wonder*ful*, courte*ous*, luck*y*, fool*ish*, pleasur*able*, colon*ial*, defen*sible*, urg*ent*, help*less*, disgust*ing*, friend*ly*, spectacul*ar*, secret*ive*.

The three articles — *a, an,* and *the* — are also classified as adjectives.

## 47e Adverbs

An adverb is a word used to modify, or qualify, a verb (or verbal), an adjective, or another adverb. It usually answers one of these questions: When? Where? How? Why? Under what conditions? To what degree?

Pull *gently* at a weak rope. [Pull how?]

Read the best books *first*. [Read the best books when?]

Adverbs that modify a verb are also defined according to their form and their typical positions in a sentence, as follows:

the kind of word that can appear nearly anywhere in a sentence and is often movable (he *sometimes* jogged after work; *sometimes* he jogged after work);

the kind of word that when derived from an adjective typically takes an *-ly* ending (nice, nice*ly;* profound, profound*ly*).

Adverbs modifying adjectives or other adverbs usually intensify or limit the intensity of the word they modify.

The *least* plain sister is the family beauty.

Hope is a *very* thin diet.

Adverbs modifying adjectives and other adverbs are not movable. We can't say "plain *least* sister" or "*very* hope is a thin diet."

The negators *not* and *never* are classified as adverbs. A word such as *cannot* contains a helping verb, *can*, and an adverb, *not*.

## EXERCISE 47 – 4

Underline the adjectives and circle the adverbs in the following sentences. If a word is a noun or pronoun in form but an adjective in function, treat it as an adjective. Also treat the articles *a, an,* and *the* as adjectives. Example:

A little sincerity is a dangerous thing, and a great deal of it

is (absolutely) fatal.

a. Useless laws weaken necessary ones.
b. The American public is wonderfully tolerant.
c. People think too historically.
d. Problems are opportunities in work clothes.
e. Sleep faster. We need the pillows.

1. We cannot be too careful in the choice of our enemies.
2. A wild goose never laid a tame egg.
3. Money will buy a pretty good dog, but it will not buy the wag of its tail.
4. Loquacious people seldom have much sense.
5. An old quarrel can be easily revived.

# **47f** Prepositions

A preposition is a word placed before a noun or pronoun to form a phrase modifying another word in the sentence. The prepositional phrase always functions as an adjective or as an adverb.

The road *to ruin* is always kept *in good repair.*

*To ruin* functions as an adjective, modifying the noun *road; in good repair* functions as an adverb, modifying the verb *is kept.*

Prepositional phrases functioning as adjectives usually answer one of the adjective questions: Which one? What kind of? And they always appear immediately following the word they modify. (See 49a.)

Prepositional phrases functioning as adverbs usually answer one of the adverb questions: When? Where? How? Why? Under what conditions? To what degree? Prepositional phrases modifying verbs may appear nearly anywhere in the sentence, and they are often movable. (See 49a.)

There are a limited number of prepositions in English. The most common ones are included in the following list:

| | | | | |
|---|---|---|---|---|
| about | beside | from | outside | toward |
| above | besides | in | over | under |
| across | between | inside | past | underneath |
| after | beyond | into | plus | unlike |
| against | but | like | regarding | until |
| along | by | near | respecting | unto |
| among | concerning | next | round | up |
| around | considering | of | since | upon |
| as | despite | off | than | with |
| at | down | on | through | without |
| before | during | onto | throughout | |
| behind | except | opposite | till | |
| below | for | out | to | |

Sometimes a preposition is more than one word long. *Along with, as well as, in addition to, next to,* and *up to* are common examples.

# 47g Conjunctions

Conjunctions join words, phrases, or clauses, and they indicate the relation between the elements joined.

A coordinating conjunction is used to connect grammatically equal elements. The coordinating conjunctions are *and, but, or, nor, for, so,* and *yet.*

> Poverty is the parent of revolution *and* crime.

> Admire a little ship, *but* put your cargo in a big one.

*And* connects two nouns; *but* connects two independent clauses.

Correlative conjunctions come in pairs: *either . . . or; neither . . . nor; not only . . . but also; whether . . . or; both . . . and.* Like coordinating conjunctions, they connect grammatically equal elements.

> *Either* Jack Sprat *or* his wife could eat no fat.

A subordinating conjunction introduces a subordinate clause and indicates its relation to the rest of the sentence. (See 49b.) The most common subordinating conjunctions are *after, although, as, as if, because, before, in order that, if, since, so that, though, till, unless, until, when,* and *while.*

> *If* triangles had a god, it would have three sides.

A conjunctive adverb may be used with a semicolon to connect independent clauses; it usually serves as a transition between the clauses. The most common conjunctive adverbs are *consequently, finally, furthermore, however, moreover, nevertheless, similarly, then, therefore,* and *thus.*

> When we want to murder a tiger, we call it sport; *however,* when the tiger wants to murder us, we call it ferocity.

## 47h   Interjections

An interjection is a word used to express surprise or emotion (*Oh! Hey! Wow!*).

# 48

## Parts of sentences

Most English sentences flow from subject to verb to any objects or complements. The vast majority of sentences conform to one of these five patterns:

    subject / verb
    subject / verb / subject complement
    subject / verb / direct object
    subject / verb / indirect object / direct object
    subject / verb / direct object / object complement

Adverbial modifiers, words or word groups qualifying the meaning of the verb, may be added to any of these patterns, and they may appear nearly anywhere — before the subject, between the subject and the verb, between the verb and an object or complement, or at the very end.

*Predicate* is the grammatical term given to everything except the subject. The predicate of a sentence includes its verb(s), any objects or complements, and any adverbial modifiers.

## 48a  Subjects

The subject of a sentence usually names who or what the sentence is about. The complete subject is composed of a simple subject, always a noun or pronoun, plus any words or word groups modifying the simple subject. To find the complete subject, ask Who? or What?, insert the verb, and finish the question. The answer is the complete subject.

┌── COMPLETE SUBJECT ──┐
The purity of a revolution usually lasts about two weeks.

Who or what lasts about two weeks? *The purity of a revolution.*

┌──────── COMPLETE SUBJECT ────────┐
Historical books that contain no lies are extremely tedious.

Who or what are extremely tedious? *Historical books that contain no lies.*

COMPLETE
SUBJECT
┌──────┐
In every country the sun rises in the morning.

Who or what rises in the morning? *The sun.* Notice that *in every country the sun* is not a sensible answer to the question. *In every country* is an adverbial modifier modifying the verb *rises.* Since sentences frequently open with such modifiers, it is not safe to assume that the subject must always appear first.

To find the simple subject, strip away all modifiers in the complete subject. This includes single-word modifiers such as *the* and *historical*, phrases such as *of a revolution*, and subordinate clauses such as *that contain no lies*.

The ⌐SS⌐ purity *of a revolution* usually lasts about two weeks.

Historical ⌐SS⌐ books *that contain no lies* are extremely tedious.

In every country *the* ⌐SS⌐ *sun* rises in the morning.

A sentence may have a compound subject containing two or more simple subjects joined with a coordinating conjunction such as *and, but,* or *or.*

*Much* ⌐ SS ⌐ *industry and little* ⌐ SS ⌐ *conscience* make us rich.

Occasionally a verb's subject is understood but not present in the sentence. In imperative sentences, those giving advice or commands, the subject is understood to be *you.*

[*You*] Hitch your wagon to a star.

Although the subject ordinarily comes before the verb, occasionally it does not. When a sentence begins with *there is* or *there are* (or *there was* or *there were*), the subject follows the verb. The word *there* is an expletive in such constructions, an empty word serving merely to get the sentence started.

There is *no* ⌐ SS ⌐ *substitute for victory.*

Occasionally a writer will invert a sentence for effect.

┌ ss ┐
Happy is *the nation that has no history.*

*Happy* is an adjective, so it cannot be the subject. Turn this sentence around and its structure becomes obvious: *The nation that has no history is happy.*

In questions, the subject frequently appears in an unusual position, sandwiched between parts of the verb.

┌ss┐
Do *married men* make the best husbands?

Turn the question into a statement, and the words will appear in their usual order: *Married men do make the best husbands.* (*Do make* is the verb.)

## EXERCISE 48–1

In the following sentences, underline the complete subject and write ss above the simple subject(s). If the subject is an understood *you*, insert it in parentheses. Example:

*ss*
**A little inaccuracy** **sometimes saves many explanations.**

 a. A spoiled child never loves its mother.
 b. To some lawyers, all facts are created equal.
 c. Love your enemies.
 d. There is nothing new under the sun.
 e. Does hope really spring eternal in the human breast?

 1. Habit is overcome by habit.
 2. The gardens of kindness never fade.
 3. The dog with the bone is always in danger.
 4. Fools and their money are soon parted.
 5. In golden pots are hidden the most deadly poisons.

## **48b** Verbs

Section 47c explains how to find the verb of a sentence, which consists of a main verb possibly preceded by one or more helping verbs. A sentence's verb is classified as linking, intransitive, or transitive, depending on the kinds of objects or complements the verb can (or cannot) take.

### *Linking verbs*

Linking verbs link the subject to a subject complement, a word or word group that completes the meaning of the subject by renaming or describing it. If the subject complement *renames* the subject, it will be a noun or noun equivalent.

```
 ┌──────────── s ────────────┐ ┌─v─┐ ┌─sc─┐
 The handwriting on the wall may be a forgery.
```

If the subject complement *describes* the subject, it will be an adjective or adjective equivalent.

```
 s  v  sc
 Love is blind.
```

Whenever they appear as main verbs (rather than helping verbs), the forms of *be* — *be, am, is, are, was, were, being,* and *been* — are nearly always linking. In the preceding sentences, for example, the main verbs are *be* and *is.*

Verbs such as *appear, become, feel, grow, look, make, seem, smell, sound,* and *taste* are sometimes linking, depending on the sense of the sentence.

```
 ┌─s─┐ ┌─v─┐ ┌─sc─┐
 At the touch of love, everyone becomes a poet.
 ┌─s──┐ ┌─v─┐ ┌sc┐
 At first sight, original art often looks ugly.
```

When you suspect that a verb such as *becomes* or *looks* is linking, check to see if the word or words following it rename or describe the subject. In the sample sentences, *a poet* renames *everyone* and *ugly* describes *art*.

### Intransitive verbs

If a verb is not linking, it is either transitive or intransitive, depending on whether it can take a direct object to receive its action. Intransitive verbs cannot take direct objects. Their pattern is always subject/verb.

```
 ┌ S ┐ ┌ V ┐
Money talks.
 ┌── S ──┐      ┌V┐
Revolutions never go backward.
```

Nothing receives the actions of talking and going in these sentences, so the verbs are intransitive. Notice that such verbs may or may not be followed by adverbial modifiers. In the second sentence, *backward* is an adverb.

### Transitive verbs

A transitive verb takes a direct object, a word or word group that names a receiver of the action.

```
 ┌S┐ ┌─V─┐ ┌─DO─┐
Love will find a way.
```

In such sentences, the subject and verb alone will seem incomplete. Once we have read "Love will find," for example, we want to know the rest: Love will find what? The answer to the question What? (or Whom?) is the direct object.

Transitive verbs usually appear in the active voice, with the subject doing the action and a direct object receiving the action. Sentences with such a pattern can be transformed into the passive voice, with the subject receiving the action instead.

> **ACTIVE VOICE**   Love will find a way.
>
> **PASSIVE VOICE**   A way will be found by love.

What was once the direct object (*a way*) has become the subject in the passive voice transformation, and the original subject appears in a prepositional phrase beginning with the word *by*. This phrase is frequently omitted in passive constructions.

> **PASSIVE VOICE**   A way will be found.

Verbs in the passive voice can be identified by their form alone. The main verb is always a past participle such as *found* (see 47c), and a form of *be* (*be, am, is, are, was, were, being, been*) always appears immediately before it (*will be found, had been found, was found*) unless adverbs intervene (*was never found*).

## EXERCISE 48–2

Underline the verbs in the following sentences. Then label the verbs as linking, transitive, or intransitive. Example:

> *trans.*                          *link.*
> We <u>enjoyed</u> the ballet, but the tickets <u>were</u> too expensive.

a. That bedspread is a family heirloom.
b. Roy pounded on the door, but nobody responded.
c. I can see a silver maple from my study.
d. Paul was reading at the kitchen table.
e. Your fig tree is thriving, but mine looks nearly dead.

1. Church bells pealed in celebration.
2. Bill replaced the shutters.
3. Those pears were delicious.

4. Maria grows several varieties of roses.
5. We invited twenty children to the party, and nearly all came.
6. The Smiths were unlucky, but they remained optimistic.
7. Sandra sold an antique back scratcher to my mother.
8. Garlic is a member of the lily family.
9. We drove to New Market in our new truck.
10. The child is being difficult, but normally he is good-natured.

## 48c Objects and complements

In addition to subjects and verbs, many sentences contain objects or complements. Linking verbs take subject complements, and transitive verbs take direct objects (see 48b). In addition, transitive verbs sometimes take indirect objects or object complements.

### Subject complements

A subject complement completes the meaning of the subject by either renaming or describing it.

The simple subject complement will always be a noun (or pronoun) or an adjective (sometimes called a *predicate noun* or *predicate adjective*). When it is a noun or pronoun such as *bucket*, the complete subject complement renames the subject (*a bucket of ashes* renames *history*). When it is an adjective such as *wisest*, the subject complement describes the subject (*wisest thoughts*).

Subject complements appear only with linking verbs. If the main verb is a form of *be* (*be, am, is, are, was, were, being, been*), the verb is probably linking. Verbs such as *appear, become, feel, grow, look, make, prove, seem, smell, sound,* and *taste* are sometimes linking and sometimes not. (See 48b.)

### Direct objects

A direct object, which occurs only with transitive verbs (see 48b), completes the meaning of the verb by naming the receiver of the action.

```
      ┌────── S ──────┐  ┌─ V ─┐  ┌────────── DO ──────────┐
      The little snake  studies  the ways of the big serpent.
```

The simple direct object will always be a noun or pronoun (such as *ways*). To find the complete direct object, read the subject and verb and then ask What? or Whom? The little snake studies what? *The ways of the big serpent.*

The questions What? and Whom? are not, however, a foolproof test for direct objects, because subject complements can also answer the questions. Consider, for example, this pair of sentences.

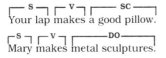

```
      ┌─ S ─┐ ┌─ V ─┐ ┌──── SC ────┐
      Your lap makes a good pillow.
      ┌ S ┐ ┌ V ┐ ┌────DO────┐
      Mary makes metal sculptures.
```

*A good pillow* and *metal sculptures* both answer the question What? But *a good pillow* is a subject complement because it renames the subject, and *metal sculptures* is a direct object because it receives the action of the verb. The verb *makes* is linking in the first sentence, transitive in the second.

### Indirect objects

An indirect object, which always appears before a direct object, tells to whom or for whom the action of the sentence is done.

```
  S    V   IO ┌DO┐    S ┌─ V ─┐ IO  ┌─DO─┐
```
You show me a hero, and I will write you a tragedy.

The simple indirect object will always be a noun or pronoun. To test for an indirect object, insert the word *to* or *for* before the word or word group in question. If the sentence makes sense, the word or word group is an indirect object.

You show [to] me a hero, and I will write [for] you a tragedy.

An indirect object may be turned into a prepositional phrase using *to* or *for*: *You show a hero to me, and I will write a tragedy for you.*

Only certain transitive verbs take indirect objects. Common examples are *give, ask, bring, find, get, lend, offer, pay, promise, read, send, show, teach, tell, throw,* and *write.*

### Object complements

An object complement always follows a direct object, completing its meaning by renaming it or describing it.

```
┌─S─┐   ┌V┐ ┌─DO─┐ ┌────── OC ──────────┐
```
People now call a spade an agricultural implement.
```
┌─S─┐ ┌─ V ─┐ ┌───── DO ─────┐ ┌─OC─┐
```
Love makes all hard hearts gentle.

When the object complement *renames* the direct object, it will be a noun or pronoun (such as *implement*). When it *describes* the direct object, it will be an adjective (such as *gentle*).

### EXERCISE 48–3

Label any subject complements, direct objects, indirect objects, or object complements in the following sentences. If an object or complement consists of more than one word, bracket and label all of it. Example:

10 ┌─*DO*─┐ ┌─*DO*─┐
**Fate gives us our relatives, but we choose our friends.**

a. Victory has a hundred fathers, but defeat is an orphan.
b. One misfortune always carries another on its back.
c. Lock your door and keep your neighbors honest.
d. All work and no play make Jack a dull boy.
e. Lizzie Borden gave her father forty whacks.

1. Good medicine always tastes bitter.
2. Ask me no questions, and I will tell you no lies.
3. The mob has many heads but no brains.
4. Some folk want their luck buttered.
5. Every bird likes its own nest best.

# 49

## Subordinate word groups

Subordinate word groups include prepositional phrases, subordinate clauses, verbal phrases, appositives, and absolutes. Not all of these word groups are subordinate in quite the same way. Some are subordinate because they are modifiers; others function as noun equivalents, not as modifiers.

## 49a Prepositional phrases

A prepositional phrase begins with a preposition such as *at, by, for, from, in, of, on, to,* or *with* (47f) and ends with a noun or noun equivalent: *on the table, for him, with great fanfare.* The noun or noun equivalent is known as the *object of the preposition.*

Prepositional phrases function either as adjectives modifying a noun or pronoun or as adverbs usually modifying a verb, occasionally qualifying an adjective or another adverb. When functioning as an adjective, a prepositional phrase always appears immediately following the noun or pronoun it modifies:

Variety is the spice *of life.*

Adjective phrases usually answer one or both of the questions Which one? What kind of? If we ask Which spice? or What kind of spice? we get a sensible answer: the spice *of life.*

Adverbial prepositional phrases that modify the verb can appear nearly anywhere in a sentence.

Do not judge a tree *by its bark.*

Tyranny will *in time* lead to revolution.

*To the ant,* a few drops of rain is a flood.

Adverbial word groups usually answer one of these questions: When? Where? How? Why? Under what conditions?

Do not judge a tree *how? By its bark.*

Tyranny will lead to revolution *when? In time.*

A few drops of rain is a flood *under what conditions? To the ant.*

If a prepositional phrase is movable, you can be certain that it is adverbial, for adjectival prepositional phrases are wedded to the words they modify. At least some of the time, adverbials can be moved to other positions in the sentence.

*By their fruits* you shall know them.

You shall know them *by their fruits.*

**EXERCISE 49 – 1**

Underline the prepositional phrases in the following sentences. Be prepared to explain the function of each phrase. Example:

> **By a private door, God enters into every individual.**

a. Laughter is a tranquilizer with no side effects.
b. Fish and visitors smell in three days.
c. The great enemy of clear language is insincerity.
d. Wall Street begins in a graveyard and ends in a river.
e. You can stroke people with words.

1. A pleasant companion reduces the length of the journey.
2. A society of sheep produces a government of wolves.
3. Some people feel with their heads and think with their hearts.
4. In love and war, all is fair.
5. To my embarrassment, I was born in bed with a lady.

# **49b** Subordinate clauses

Subordinate clauses are patterned like sentences, having subjects and verbs and sometimes objects or complements. But they function within sentences as adjectives, adverbs, or nouns. They cannot stand alone as complete sentences.

### *Adjective clauses*

Like other word groups functioning as adjectives, adjective clauses modify nouns or pronouns. An adjective clause nearly always appears immediately following the noun or pronoun it modifies.

The arrow *that has left the bow* never returns.

Relatives are persons *who live too near and die too seldom.*

To test whether a subordinate clause functions as an adjective, ask the adjective questions: Which one? What kind of? The answer should make sense. Which arrow? The arrow *that has left the bow.* What kind of persons? Persons *who live too near and die too seldom.*

Most adjective clauses begin with a relative pronoun (*who, whom, whose, which,* or *that*), which marks them as grammatically subordinate. In addition to introducing the clause, the relative pronoun points back to the noun that the clause modifies.

The fur *that warms a monarch* once warmed a bear.

Occasionally an adjective clause will be introduced by a relative adverb, usually *when, where,* or *why.*

Home is the place *where you slip in the bathtub and break your neck.*

The parts of an adjective clause are often arranged as in sentences (subject/verb/object or complement), as in the following example.

                                S    V    DO
We often forgive the people *who bore us.*

Frequently, however, the object or complement appears first, out of its normal order:

                           DO    S    V
We rarely forgive those *whom we bore.*

To determine the subject of a clause, ask Who? or What? and insert the verb. Don't be surprised if the answer is an echo, as in the first adjective clause above: Who bore us? *Who.* To find any objects or complements, read the subject and the verb and then ask Who? Whom? or What? Again, be prepared for a possible echo, as in the second adjective clause above: We bore whom? *Whom.*

### Adverb clauses

Adverb clauses usually modify verbs, in which case they may appear nearly anywhere in a sentence — at the beginning, at the end, or somewhere in the middle. Like other adverbial word groups, they tell when, where, why, under what conditions, or to what degree an action occurred.

*When the well is dry*, we know the worth of water.

Venice would be a fine city *if it were only drained.*

When do we know the worth of water? *When the well is dry.* Under what conditions would Venice be a fine city? *If it were only drained.*

Unlike adjective clauses, adverb clauses are frequently movable. In the sentences above, for example, the adverb clauses can be moved without affecting the meaning of the sentences.

We know the worth of water *when the well is dry.*

*If it were only drained*, Venice would be a fine city.

Adverb clauses always begin with a subordinating conjunction such as *although, because, before, if, unless, when, where,* or *while* (47g). Subordinating conjunctions introduce clauses and express their relation to the rest of the sentence.

### Noun clauses

Because they do not function as modifiers, noun clauses are not subordinate in the same sense as are adjective and adverb clauses. They are called subordinate only because they cannot stand alone: They must function within another sentence pattern, always as nouns.

A noun clause functions just like a single-word noun, usually as a subject, subject complement, direct object, or object of a preposition.

┌─────── S ───────┐
*Whoever gossips to you* will gossip of you.
       ┌─────── DO ───────┐
We never forget *that we buried the hatchet.*

A noun clause usually begins with one of the following subordinating conjunctions: *who, whom, that, what, how, when, where, whether.* The subordinating conjunction may or may not play a significant role in the clause. In the sentences above, for example, *whoever* is the subject of its clause, but *that* does not perform a function in its clause.

As with adjective clauses, the parts of a noun clause may appear out of their normal order (subject/verb/object).

        DO  S  V
Talent is *what you possess.*

The parts of a noun clause may also appear in normal order.

       S     V    DO
Genius is *what possesses you.*

## EXERCISE 49–2

Underline the subordinate clauses in the following sentences. Be prepared to explain the function of each clause. Example:

<u>When the insects take over the world</u>, we hope <u>that they will remember our picnics with gratitude.</u>

a. Though you live near a forest, do not waste firewood.
b. Beware of the person who is praised by everyone.
c. What is whispered is heard all over town.
d. The dog that trots finds the bone.
e. A fraud is not perfect unless it is practiced on clever persons.

1. What history teaches us is that people have never learned anything from it.
2. Dig a well before you are thirsty.
3. Whoever named it necking was a poor judge of anatomy.
4. If you were born lucky, even your rooster will lay eggs.
5. Modern poverty is not the poverty that was blessed in the Sermon on the Mount.

# **49c** Verbal phrases

A verbal is a verb form that does not function as the verb of a clause. Verbals include infinitives (the word *to* plus the dictionary form of the verb), present participles (the *-ing* form of the verb), and past participles (the form of the verb that can follow *have*, often ending in *-ed* or *-en*) (see 47c).

| INFINITIVE | PRESENT PARTICIPLE | PAST PARTICIPLE |
|---|---|---|
| to dream | dreaming | dreamed |
| to choose | choosing | chosen |
| to build | building | built |
| to grow | growing | grown |

Instead of functioning as the verb of a clause, a verbal or a verbal phrase functions as an adjective, a noun, or an adverb.

| | |
|---|---|
| **ADJECTIVE** | *Stolen* grapes are especially sweet. |
| **NOUN** | Continual *dripping* wears away a stone. |
| **ADVERB** | Were we born *to suffer?* |

Verbals can take objects, complements, and modifiers to form verbal phrases; the phrases ordinarily lack subjects.

> *Living well* is the best revenge.

> Governments exist *to protect the rights of minorities.*

The verbal *living* is followed by an adverb modifier, *well;* the verbal *to protect* is followed by a direct object, *the rights of minorities.*

Like single-word verbals, verbal phrases function as adjectives, nouns, or adverbs. In the sentences above, for example, *living well* functions as a noun to fill the subject slot of the sentence, and *to protect the rights of minorities* functions as an adverb, answering the question Why?

Verbal phrases are ordinarily classified as participles, gerunds, and infinitives. This classification is based partly on form (whether the verbal is a present participle, a past participle, or an infinitive) and partly on function (whether the whole phrase functions as an adjective, a noun, or an adverb).

### Participial phrases

Participial phrases always function as adjectives. Their verbals are either present participles, always ending in *-ing,* or past participles, frequently ending in *-ed* or *-en* but often appearing in irregular forms (see 30).

Participial phrases frequently appear immediately following the noun or pronoun they modify.

Congress shall make no law *abridging the freedom of speech or of the press.*

Truth *kept in the dark* will never save the world.

Unlike other adjectival word groups, however, which must always follow the noun or pronoun they modify, participial phrases are often movable. Frequently they precede the word they modify.

*Being a philosopher,* I have a problem for every solution.

They may also appear at some distance from the word they modify.

History is something that never happened, *written by someone who wasn't there.*

### Gerund phrases

Gerund phrases are built around present participles (verb forms ending in *-ing*), and they always function as nouns: usually as subjects, subject complements, direct objects, or objects of a preposition.

       S
*Justifying a fault* doubles it.

       SC
The secret of education is *respecting the pupil.*

       DO
Kleptomaniacs can't help *helping themselves.*

       OBJ OF PREP
The hen is an egg's way of *producing another egg.*

### Infinitive phrases

Infinitive phrases, always constructed around the *to* form of the verb (*to call, to drink*), can function as nouns, as adjectives, or as adverbs.

When functioning as a noun, an infinitive phrase may appear in almost any noun slot, usually as a subject, subject complement, or direct object.

```
      ┌──── S ────┐
```
*To side with truth* is noble.
```
      ┌────────── DO ──────────┐
```
Never try *to leap a chasm in two jumps.*

Infinitive phrases functioning as adjectives usually appear immediately following the noun or pronoun they modify.

We do not have the right *to abandon the poor.*

The infinitive phrase limits the meaning of the noun *right.* Which right? *The right to abandon the poor.*

Adverbial infinitive phrases usually qualify the meaning of the verb, telling when, where, how, why, under what conditions, or to what degree an action occurred.

He cut off his nose *to spite his face.*

Here the phrase explains why: Why did he cut off his nose? *To spite his face.*

### EXERCISE 49–3

Underline the verbal phrases in the sentences below. Be prepared to explain the function of each phrase. Example:

**Fate tried <u>to conceal him</u> by <u>naming him Smith.</u>**

a. The best substitute for experience is being sixteen.
b. Vows made in storms are forgotten in calms.
c. To help a friend is to give ourselves pleasure.

d. Beware of Greeks bearing gifts.
e. Every genius is considerably helped by being dead.

1. The thing generally raised on city land is taxes.
2. To make a crooked stick straight, we bend it the contrary way.
3. He has the gall of a shoplifter returning an item for a refund.
4. Do you want to be a writer? Then write.
5. Crossing a one-way street, a pessimist looks both ways.

## 49d Appositive phrases

Though strictly speaking they are not subordinate word groups, appositive phrases function somewhat as adjectives do, to describe nouns or pronouns. Instead of modifying nouns or pronouns, however, appositive phrases rename them. In form they are nouns or noun equivalents.

Appositive phrases are said to be "in apposition" to the nouns or pronouns that they follow.

> Politicians, *acrobats at heart*, can sit on a fence and yet keep both ears to the ground.

> Psychoanalysis, *a fraud practiced on the rich*, is the disease it pretends to cure.

*Acrobats at heart* is in apposition to *politicians; a fraud practiced on the rich* is in apposition to *psychoanalysis*.

## 49e Absolute phrases

An absolute phrase is subordinate to a whole clause or sentence, not just to one word, and it may appear nearly anywhere in the sentence. In form it consists of a noun or noun equivalent and a participial phrase.

> *His words dipped in honey*, the senator mesmerized the crowd.

The senator, *his words dipped in honey*, mesmerized the crowd.

The senator mesmerized the crowd, *his words dipped in honey*.

# 50

## Types of sentences

Depending on the number and type of clauses they contain, sentences are classified as simple, compound, complex, or compound-complex.

Clauses come in two varieties: independent and subordinate. An independent clause is a full sentence pattern that does not function within another sentence pattern: It contains a subject and verb plus any objects, complements, and modifiers of that verb, and it either stands alone or could stand alone. A subordinate clause is a full sentence pattern that functions within a sentence as an adjective, an adverb, or a noun but that cannot stand alone as a complete sentence. (See 49b.)

## 50a  Simple sentences

A simple sentence is one independent clause with no subordinate clauses.

```
┌──────── INDEPENDENT CLAUSE ────────┐
Without music, life would be a mistake.
```

This sentence contains a subject (*life*), a verb (*would be*), a complement (*a mistake*), and an adverbial modifier (*without music*).

A simple sentence may contain compound elements — a compound subject, verb, or object, for example — but it does not contain more than one full sentence pattern. The following sentence is simple because its two verbs (*enters* and *spreads*) share the same subject.

```
┌───────────── INDEPENDENT CLAUSE ─────────────┐
Evil enters like a needle and spreads like an oak.
```

## 50b   Compound sentences

A compound sentence is composed of two or more independent clauses with no subordinate clauses. The independent clauses are joined with a comma and a coordinating conjunction (*and, but, or, nor, for, so, yet*) or sometimes with a semicolon.

```
┌─ INDEPENDENT CLAUSE ─┐   ┌──── INDEPENDENT CLAUSE ────┐
One arrow is easily broken, but you can't break a bundle of ten.
┌──────────INDEPENDENT CLAUSE──────────┐ ┌─INDEPENDENT─┐
We are born brave, trusting, and greedy; most of us have
┌─── CLAUSE───┐
remained greedy.
```

## 50c   Complex sentences

A complex sentence is composed of one independent clause with one or more subordinate clauses. See 49b.

```
                SUBORDINATE
              ┌─ CLAUSE ─┐
ADJECTIVE   They that sow in tears shall reap in joy.
```

ADVERB  ┌SUBORDINATE CLAUSE┐

If you scatter thorns, don't go barefoot.

NOUN  ┌────── SUBORDINATE CLAUSE ──────┐

What the scientists have in their briefcases is terrifying.

## 50d Compound-complex sentences

A compound-complex sentence contains at least two independent clauses and at least one subordinate clause. The following sentence contains two full sentence patterns that can stand alone.

┌INDEPENDENT CLAUSE┐  ┌── INDEPENDENT CLAUSE──┐

Tell me what you eat, and I will tell you what you are.

And each independent clause contains a subordinate clause, making the sentence both compound and complex.

┌──── IND CL ────┐  ┌──── IND CL ────┐
┌ SUB CL ┐  ┌ SUB CL ┐

Tell me what you eat, and I will tell you what you are.

## EXERCISE 50–1

Identify the following sentences as simple, compound, complex, or compound-complex. Be prepared to identify the subordinate clauses and classify them according to their function: adjective, adverb, or noun. (See 49b.) Example:

My folks didn't come over on the Mayflower; they were there

to meet the boat. *compound*

a. The poet is a liar who always speaks the truth.
b. Love your enemies; it will drive them nuts.

c. No one can blow and swallow at the same time.
d. If you don't go to other people's funerals, they won't go to yours.
e. People who sleep like a baby usually don't have one.

1. We often give our enemies the means for our own destruction.
2. Those who write clearly have readers; those who write obscurely have commentators.
3. The impersonal hand of government can never replace the helping hand of a neighbor.
4. Human action can be modified to some extent, but human nature cannot be changed.
5. What has been fashionable once will become fashionable again.

# PART X

# *Special Types of Writing*

# 51

## Research papers

The requirements of academic research papers vary among the thousands of professors who assign them, but they have one thing in common. Professors want students to *think*, not to go on a treasure hunt for good quotations. Most professors want their students to conduct research the same way they themselves do: to explore an idea in a systematic way, to interpret what they read, to form a thesis, and to support that thesis with valid and well-documented evidence.

## **51a**  Choose a suitable topic.

A good topic fits the assignment, takes you to a variety of sources, and allows you to support a conclusion. Topics that don't meet these requirements are not suitable for college research papers. You should avoid how-to subjects (such as how to install solar panels or how to use the NEC 3550 Spinwriter printer with Wordstar software) because they give you no opportunity to use a variety of sources or to support a conclusion. But you can argue that the U.S. government should or should not give tax breaks to homeowners who install solar panels or explain why the Osborne computer company filed for bankruptcy in 1983 even though it made an excellent and popular computer.

A current news event (such as a terrorist kidnapping) is a poor choice of topic because all of the sources will report the same facts and speculations and because most newspaper and magazine accounts are only a few pages long. A better topic would be an investigation into the background or cause of a news event because this calls for interpretation. Remember that you are not just collecting information. You are investigating evidence to support an opinion, a judgment, your approval or disapproval of a proposal, your interpretation of a poem, or the feasibility of a project.

## 51b Explore your library.

Before you begin looking for books and articles, walk around the library to find out what it's like. Most libraries prepare maps and location guides, descriptions of special reference services, and practical advice for conducting research. Many conduct orientation programs or have cassette walking tours or slide-cassette shows. Find out whether the stacks are open or closed and whether some books, periodicals, U.S. government documents, or reference materials are located in special rooms or even in other buildings.

Is there a traditional card catalog in rows of drawers, or are the library's holdings listed on microfiche or microfilm or on-line computer? Does the library store periodicals older than a certain date on microfilm or microfiche? Does the library own films, videotapes, slide-sound sets, records, or floppy disks, and where are they cataloged?

Is there a computer search service? For research on a very specialized topic or for a comprehensive listing of all available sources, at some libraries you can buy time for a computer to search one or more of the hundreds of computer databases available.

The library staff is more useful than any equipment. Librarians are information specialists who can save you time by helping you define what you are looking for and then telling you where to find it. Librarians, especially those in college and university libraries, are educators. Feel free to tell them about your information needs, not just to ask where to find the encyclopedias.

**51c**  Follow a search strategy.

A search strategy matches your need for specific information to the reference tools that contain the information. A reference librarian can help you devise a strategy for your specific assignment.

If you are investigating a topic new to you, stay away from the card catalog for a while. A good search strategy moves from general reference works, such as encyclopedias and the *Library of Congress Subject Headings*, to specific books (located through the card catalog) and specific magazine and newspaper articles (located through periodical indexes).

But if your topic is already very specific, you can skip some steps in the general investigative process and go straight to the single reference tool you need — for example, to the *Nursing Index* for articles on postoperative group counseling of heart patients.

### Encyclopedias

Begin by reading some background information in both general and specialized encyclopedias. Encyclopedia articles introduce your topic to you, give you a sense of how broad or narrow it is, and usually end with a bibliography of books for further reading. In your preliminary reading, look for areas in which experts take different positions or where there are changing trends, attitudes, beliefs, or circumstances; your finished paper could demonstrate your support for one of the positions or explain the causes or effects of the changes.

You probably will not use the information from general encyclopedias directly in your finished paper because you will find more specific information during your search. Specialized encyclopedias cover topics in much more detail and are therefore more likely to be cited in your finished paper. Here is a short list of the most widely used general and specialized encyclopedias, as well as other general reference works.

**GENERAL ENCYCLOPEDIAS**

*Academic American Encyclopedia.* 21 vols. Princeton, NJ: Arête Publishing Co., 1983. Short articles on current topics; updated by yearbook.

*Encyclopedia Americana.* 30 vols. New York: Americana Corporation, 1981. General emphasis on United States; revised continuously; current events yearbook.

*The New Encyclopaedia Britannica.* 30 vols. Chicago: Encyclopaedia Britannica, 1980. In three parts: *Propaedia,* a 1-volume "Outline of Knowledge"; 10-volume *Micropaedia* with brief entries; 19-volume *Macropaedia* of long articles, with bibliographies. Updated annually by yearbook.

**SPECIALIZED ENCYCLOPEDIAS**

*Encyclopedia of Bioethics.* 4 vols. New York: Free Press, 1982. Articles on the positions taken on life, death, and health in the areas of technology and human values in many fields.

*Encyclopedia of Crime and Justice.* 5 vols. New York: Macmillan, 1983. Articles covering crime and society in many fields.

*The Encyclopedia of Philosophy.* 4 vols. New York: Free Press, 1973. Articles on ancient, medieval, and modern philosophy; also related topics in other fields such as mathematics, ethics, and religion.

*International Encyclopedia of the Social Sciences.* 8 vols. plus supplement. New York: Free Press, 1977. Articles in the fields of anthropology, economics, education, geography, history, law, political science, psychology, and sociology.

*McGraw-Hill Encyclopedia of Science and Technology: An International Reference Work.* 15 vols. New York: McGraw-Hill, 1982. Articles in all fields of science and technology; updated by yearbook.

**BIOGRAPHICAL REFERENCES**

*Contemporary Authors.* Detroit: Gale, 1962 – 1984. This series is subtitled "A Bio-Bibliographical Guide to Current Writers in Fiction, General Nonfiction, Poetry, Journalism, Drama, Motion Pictures, Television, and Other Fields."

*Current Biography.* New York: H. W. Wilson, 1946 to date. Articles on contemporary figures in all fields.

*Dictionary of American Biography.* 16 vols. plus supplements. New York: Scribner's, 1927 – 1984. Historical figures since 1776.

*Notable American Women, 1607 – 1950.* Cambridge, MA: The Belknap Press of Harvard Univ. Press, 1974. (With supplement: *Notable American Women: The Modern Period,* 1980.)

**ATLASES**

*Historical Atlas of the World.* Chicago: Rand McNally, 1981.

*Rand McNally Cosmopolitan World Atlas.* Chicago: Rand McNally, 1978.

**ALMANACS AND YEARBOOKS**

*Facts on File Yearbook.* New York: Person's Index, Facts on File, 1940 to date. Covers dates, events, and personalities in the news.

*The World Almanac and Book of Facts.* New York: World Almanac, 1868 to date. Data on people, places, events, even postal zip codes and sports facts.

## The Library of Congress Subject Headings

*The Library of Congress Subject Headings* (*LCSH*) is a reference work that tells you how your subject is organized and lists the headings under which you are likely to find information. It consists of two large red volumes usually placed by the card catalog. Though its listings are keyed to the Library of Congress system for classifying books, used in many libraries, it can be useful even if your library uses the Dewey decimal system, since many of the headings will be the same. The headings are also likely to be similar to those used in magazine and newspaper indexes.

**WHAT THE LCSH TELLS YOU**

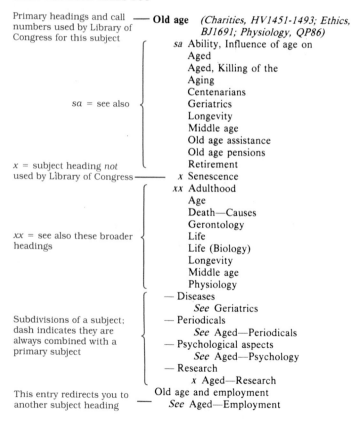

Primary headings and call numbers used by Library of Congress for this subject — **Old age**  *(Charities, HV1451-1493; Ethics, BJ1691; Physiology, QP86)*

*sa* = see also

- *sa* Ability, Influence of age on
- Aged
- Aged, Killing of the
- Aging
- Centenarians
- Geriatrics
- Longevity
- Middle age
- Old age assistance
- Old age pensions
- Retirement

*x* = subject heading *not* used by Library of Congress — *x* Senescence

*xx* = see also these broader headings

- *xx* Adulthood
- Age
- Death—Causes
- Gerontology
- Life
- Life (Biology)
- Longevity
- Middle age
- Physiology

Subdivisions of a subject; dash indicates they are always combined with a primary subject

- — Diseases
  - *See* Geriatrics
- — Periodicals
  - *See* Aged—Periodicals
- — Psychological aspects
  - *See* Aged—Psychology
- — Research
  - *x* Aged—Research

This entry redirects you to another subject heading

- Old age and employment
  - *See* Aged—Employment

If you are interested in researching senior citizens, for example, you would be frustrated by going directly to the card catalog and discovering nothing under "senior citizens." But by looking up "senior citizens" in *LCSH*, you would be referred to "aged," which covers two entire pages with subheadings. By looking up just one heading, "old age," you would learn that twenty-three different headings are used for books on the subject. From that one look into *LCSH*, you may be able to restrict your topic, and you can discover other subject categories that might offer possibilities for research.

### The card catalog

The subject headings in *LCSH* will tell you where to look in the card catalog for the books your library owns on a particular topic. The catalog lists books alphabetically by author's name, title of the book, and subject. The cards in the catalog drawer (or on microfiche or displayed on the computer terminal) will look like the example on page 311, though the top line might list an author or title instead of the subject.

If you know what to look for on the card, you can immediately select or reject a book, and you can use the "tracings," lists of related headings, to lead you to more books. Keep the following points in mind as you look through the subject file for books most relevant to your topic.

Check the date to see when the book was published. For some topics, only the most recent books may be useful.

Check to see if the book has an index for easy reference.

Check to see if the book contains a bibliography to suggest more books.

Check the tracings, lists of other places to look in the card catalog.

If the book looks useful, write on a bibliography card the call number, author, title, publishing information, and subject heading (see 51d).

**WHAT THE CARD CATALOG TELLS YOU**

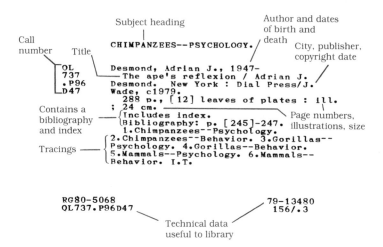

Subject heading

Author and dates
of birth and
death

City, publisher,
copyright date

Call
number      Title

CHIMPANZEES--PSYCHOLOGY.

QL
737
.P96
D47

Desmond, Adrian J., 1947-
The ape's reflexion / Adrian J.
Desmond.  New York : Dial Press/J.
Wade, c1979.
    288 p., [12] leaves of plates : ill.
; 24 cm.
{Includes index.
{Bibliography: p. [245]-247.
    1.Chimpanzees--Psychology.
{2.Chimpanzees--Behavior. 3.Gorillas--
{Psychology. 4.Gorillas--Behavior.
{5.Mammals--Psychology. 6.Mammals--
{Behavior. I.T.

Contains a
bibliography
and index

Page numbers,
illustrations, size

Tracings

RG80-5068
QL737.P96D47

79-13480
156/.3

Technical data
useful to library

## Periodical indexes

Periodicals are publications issued at regular intervals: specialized scholarly and technical journals, general magazines,
newsletters, and weekly and daily newspapers. Articles in periodicals are useful reference sources because they contain
more up-to-date information and news than books and because they often discuss a specific aspect of a subject in some
detail.

Depending on how specialized your purpose is, use either
a general index or a specialized index to track down useful
articles. General indexes list articles in general magazines
such as *Time, Popular Mechanics, Science, Fortune,* and
*Psychology Today.* To locate articles in technical and scholarly journals such as *Computer World* and *Communication
Quarterly,* you'll need to turn to a specialized index.

An entry from a typical periodical index—*Readers' Guide
to Periodical Literature*—is shown on the next page.

**WHAT THE READERS' GUIDE TELLS YOU**

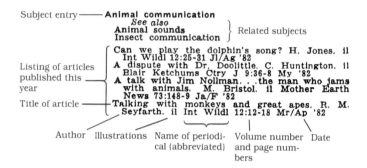

Subject entry —— **Animal communication**
*See also*
**Animal sounds** } Related subjects
**Insect communication**

Listing of articles published this year

Title of article

**Can we play the dolphin's song?** H. Jones. il Int Wildl 12:25-31 Jl/Ag '82
**A dispute with Dr. Doolittle.** C. Huntington. il Blair Ketchums Ctry J 9:36-8 My '82
**A talk with Jim Nollman. . .the man who jams with animals.** M. Bristol. il Mother Earth News 73:148-9 Ja/F '82
**Talking with monkeys and great apes.** R. M. Seyfarth. il Int Wildl 12:12-18 Mr/Ap '82

Author    Illustrations   Name of periodical (abbreviated)   Volume number and page numbers   Date

If your assignment requires scholarly or scientific articles, you can find specialized indexes easily in the card catalog. Look up the general subject and find cards giving the subheadings "Abstracts" and "Periodicals and Indexes" (for example, "Biology — Periodicals and Indexes"). The card catalog will provide the title and call number for the index, usually with REF as the top line, indicating that you will find it in the reference room. The librarian also can help you locate specialized indexes.

The general and specialized indexes most commonly used by undergraduates and businesspeople are listed below.

**GENERAL PERIODICAL INDEXES**

*Magazine Index.* Menlo Park, CA: Information Access Corp., 1979 to date. A microfilm machine that indexes twice as many articles as *Readers' Guide;* it cumulates the last five years into one index, and it is updated monthly.

*National Newspaper Index.* Menlo Park, CA: Information Access Corp., 1979 to date. A microfilm compilation of articles in five newspapers: the *New York Times,* the *Christian Science Monitor,* the *Wall Street Journal,* the *Washington Post,* and the *Los Angeles Times.*

*Newsbank.* New Canaan, CT: Newsbank Inc., 1970 to date. Over one hundred city newspapers are indexed, and the articles are included on a microfiche machine, so you can read articles while seated at the machine (unlike the *New York Times Index*, which refers you to articles you have to read on another microfilm machine).

*New York Times Index.* New York: The New York Times Co./Bowker, 1913 to date. Lists all the articles printed in the *New York Times* — an excellent source of condensed and recent information. There are similar indexes for other major newspapers, such as the *Washington Post*, the *Wall Street Journal*, and *The Times* (London).

*Readers' Guide to Periodical Literature.* New York: H.W. Wilson, 1900 to date. Check the latest annual volumes, the latest quarterly cumulation, and the latest months to get the most up-to-date articles.

**SPECIALIZED PERIODICAL INDEXES**

*Applied Science and Technology Index.* New York: H.W. Wilson, 1958 to date. Formerly *Industrial Arts Index*, 1913–1957.

*Biography Index.* New York: H.W. Wilson, 1946 to date.

*Biological and Agricultural Index.* New York: H.W. Wilson, 1964 to date. Formerly *Agricultural Index*, 1916–1964.

*Business Index.* Los Altos, CA: Information Access Corp., 1979 to date.

*Business Periodicals Index.* New York: H.W. Wilson, 1958 to date. Formerly *Industrial Arts Index*, 1913–1957.

*Education Index.* New York: H.W. Wilson, 1929 to date.

*General Science Index.* New York: H.W. Wilson, 1978 to date.

*Humanities Index.* New York: H.W. Wilson, 1974 to date. Formerly *International Index*, 1907–1965, and *Social Sciences and Humanities Index*, 1965–1974.

*Public Affairs Information Service Bulletin.* New York: Public Affairs Information Service, 1915 to date.

*Social Sciences Index.* New York: H.W. Wilson, 1974 to date. Formerly *International Index*, 1907–1965, and *Social Sciences and Humanities Index*, 1965–1974.

*United States Government Publications, Monthly Catalog.* Washington, DC: Government Printing Office, 1895 to date.

## **51d** Prepare bibliography cards.

The titles you have discovered in your search through the card catalog, bibliographies in other books, and indexes should all be listed on separate 3″ × 5″ cards. For books, take down carefully and completely the following information:

Call number

All authors

Title and subtitle

Publishing information: city, publishing company, edition (if not the first), and date

For periodical articles you need this information:

Title of magazine or journal

All authors of the article

Title and subtitle of the article

Date, volume, issue, and page numbers

On the card write personal comments about the content after you have examined the book or article — even those sources you reject. (Later you will write more specific notes on note cards; see 51f.) Researchers almost always get better ideas halfway through an outline or first draft and change their minds about their topic. As your purpose narrows, be ready to go back to one of the sources you first rejected.

**SAMPLE BIBLIOGRAPHY CARD**

> QL776. D38   1978
>
> Davis, Flora. *Eloquent Animals: A Study in Animal Communication: How Chimps Lie, Whales Sing and Slime Molds Pass the message Along.* New York: Coward, McCann & Geoghegan, 1978.
>
> − only first 6 chapters on apes and chimps.
> − discusses what grammar is pages 24–26.
> − interesting anecdotes, interviews.

**51e**   Evaluate sources for relevance and reliability.

Even after you have narrowed your topic, your search for useful titles will supply you with many more books and articles than you have time to read. But you can often judge both the relevance and the reliability of a source without even reading it.

You might reject a book with an irrelevant subtitle or a too-old date, or you might select one by a well-known expert in the field. Reading the table of contents of a book may uncover a relevant chapter or two; the index at the back of the book as well as the preface and introduction can indicate the coverage of the book. Periodical articles often express their purpose and coverage in the first several paragraphs. Sometimes you have to read only one paragraph to either reject an irrelevant article or decide to read the whole piece.

You can also estimate the reliability of a source before you read it. Reading book reviews will tell you whether a book was well received by experts when it was published—an especially important strategy if your paper draws on only one or two books to establish its arguments. *Book Review Digest* is a good general survey of book reviews. *Book Review Index* covers fiction and books in the humanities and social sciences; *Technical Book Review Index* covers reviews in scientific and technical fields. Biographical directories in many different fields list the publications of the better-known practitioners; checking these will help establish the credentials of an author. A magazine publisher's reputation for checking facts closely and for objectivity can be discovered in *Magazines for Libraries*, a guide to the reputations of more than 6,500 magazines.

The preliminary judgments you make about the relevance and reliability of your sources need to be confirmed as you read them closely. After you've obtained the same background information in two different books, for example, you can skip background sections. After you've noticed the same interpretation of a poem in three articles, you should start looking for different views. If you discover only popular journalistic presentations of your subject in general magazines, seek out scholarly or technical discussions by experts.

Your best guide to the reliability of what you read is your own critical intelligence. Are all the author's assertions proved with valid evidence? Does the author present research data and not just a few anecdotes or emotional examples? Are the sources clearly documented? Is expert judgment cited? Does the author avoid logical fallacies and emotional language? (See logic in argumentative essays, 52.)

### Primary and secondary sources

Research usually requires a reading of both primary and secondary sources. A primary source is an original piece of writing—a novel, poem, play, speech, diary, legislative bill, court case, laboratory study, field research, or eyewitness account.

A secondary source is a book or article about the primary document. For example, in Karen Shaw's sample research paper at the end of this chapter, Flora Davis's book *Eloquent Animals* is a secondary source for information about Washoe, a chimpanzee who was taught sign language; a primary source was an article in a scientific journal by psychologists Allen and Beatrice Gardner, the chimp's trainers.

You should use primary sources as much as possible. Naturally, you can better evaluate what the secondary sources say if you have first read the primary source and are familiar with it. Reading the primary source will establish your credibility as a thorough researcher and an independent thinker.

## 51f  Take notes accurately and efficiently.

At the note-taking stage, you are reacting to what you read, critically evaluating the ideas and evidence and at the same time tentatively planning what future use you will make of this material in your paper. Be careful not to oversimplify a complex argument or to distort an author's position. If you take notes accurately, without plagiarizing, you will discover later that some of your rough draft has already been written — on your note cards.

You may take notes in any way that suits you, as long as they are accurate, but the following suggestions may help you make the most efficient use of your time. Have nearby a stack of blank, white cards ($4'' \times 6''$ is customary). Write one note on each card so you can reshuffle the cards in different orders later as you arrange the paragraphs of your paper. Put the last name of the author of your source in the upper right corner of the card, and put a subject label in the upper left corner. If you have read enough to form a preliminary outline, use the subdivisions of the outline as subject headings on your cards.

Next decide the most helpful way to preserve the information in your source: summarizing a long paragraph in a few words, paraphrasing the source in your own words, quoting word for word an especially effective sentence or passage, or writing a personal note to yourself about the source's relevance. Label each card as summary, paraphrase, quote, or personal.

*Note cards that summarize*

Summarizing is the best kind of preliminary note taking, because it is fastest. Later, you can write detailed notes about specific pages if you have to use the information there to support a point. A note card can summarize a paragraph, a graph or chart, a section, a chapter, an article, an entire book — whatever you judge to be significant at that stage of your investigation. Be sure to write the note in your own words without echoing the title or introductory paragraph of the source. If you do use especially apt phrases from the source, put them in quotation marks.

Using grammar        Summary              Davis

Chapter 2 "The Washoe Project" (pp. 17-27)
Describes experiments by Gardners with
chimp named Washoe. They never used human
language around her; taught her ASL. Washoe
connected ASL signs in combinations,
invented new signs (like _bib_). Signs to
herself when no one is around. Linguists
claim her combining signs is not real grammar
because Washoe demonstrates no meaningful
syntax. Project ends after 4 years.

## Note cards that paraphrase

Like a summary, a paraphrase is written in your own words, but whereas a summary reports significant information in fewer words than the source, a paraphrase retells the information in roughly the same number of words.

Be certain that you paraphrase in your own voice. If you retain occasional choice phrases from the source, put quotation marks around them so that you'll know later which phrases are your own.

---

Using grammar    Paraphrase        Davis

Chapter 6 "The Lana Project" (pp 64-72)

p. 67. says "greatest breakthrough" was on day
Lana learned how to ask for names of objects.
(Compared to Helen Keller's dramatic scene in
Miracle Worker.)

p. 68. Lana figures out how to use key for
"name-of" to ask for name of objects she
doesn't know. Example of "creative use of
language."

---

## Note cards that quote

Copy the exact words of the source only for special purposes: to use a writer's especially vivid or expressive wording, to allow an expert to explain a complex matter clearly, or to let critics of an opinion object in their own words. If you find yourself quoting a great deal in your notes, you are unwisely postponing important decisions about content, relevance, and reliability until the draft-writing stage.

When you quote, be sure to copy the words of your source exactly (including punctuation and capitalization) and to put quotation marks around the quoted material.

---

*Using grammar*        *Quote*        *Davis*

*p. 47 Nim had "a vocabulary of ninety to ninety-five signs and that to date, he had strung them together in 4700 combinations of from two to five signs. The number of combinations was increasing much faster than his vocabulary was."*

---

### Personal note cards

At unexpected moments in your reading, you will experience the lucky accidents typical of the creative process: flashes of insight, connections with other reading, sharp questions, a more restricted topic, ways to set up the arguments of two opposing positions, a vivid scenario. Write these inspirations down before you forget them. (An example of such a note card is at the top of the next page.)

### Avoiding plagiarism while taking notes

You will discover that it is amazingly easy to borrow too much language from a source as you take notes. Do not allow this to happen. You are guilty of plagiarism if you half-copy the author's sentences — either by mixing the author's well-chosen phrases with your own without quotation marks or

Cueing          Personal          Terrace

*Terrace probably correct in saying
claims by Gardners & others go too far.
I probably would like to believe apes
can use language but should maybe
change my thesis. Back off. Read Davis
again — this time more critically.*

by plugging your synonyms into the author's sentence structures.

Plagiarism, whether it occurs deliberately or unintentionally, is considered cheating. Half-copying a source is *never* acceptable — even if you name the source in the paper — because half-copying does not make clear *exactly* which language is from the source and which is your own.

Section 51i discusses plagiarism fully, but you should be aware of it at the note-taking stage as well; distinguishing between your own and the source's material in your notes will help you avoid unintentional plagiarism later.

## **51g** Form a tentative thesis and plan its development.

Writers of long research papers who begin their rough drafts before first formulating a tentative thesis and sketching a plan of development usually regret skipping this step. A look through your note cards will probably suggest many different ways to present your material. Decide on one main point and one specific organization before you start writing the first draft or you will flounder among the possibilities. Part I of this handbook presents advice on generating ideas, focusing on a thesis or main point, and arranging support.

In some fields, readers expect specific arrangements and formats, such as in proposals, technical and lab reports, field research, feasibility studies, and critiques. Obviously, it is a good idea to follow the format expected by readers.

Whether you have the freedom to organize the whole paper or only some sections, consider your options. Before committing yourself to a detailed outline, experiment with alternatives. Shuffle and reshuffle your note cards to get a feeling for the possibilities. Formulate a preliminary thesis and then plan a way to arrange your material in stages through a convincing argument. Rather than dividing your subject into static subdivisions, see the main body of your paper as a line of thought that moves step by step. What should be presented and analyzed first? Second? What is the most important reason or evidence to save for the end? In an argumentative paper it is usually better to present the case for the other side first, followed by your refutation of the other side combined with the presentation of your own case.

While you are designing a preliminary outline, you may see weak spots in the development of your ideas. At this point you may need to go back to some of your sources for essential information.

Furthermore, as you decide which sources to use at various places in your preliminary outline, you may notice that you are using the same source for most of your major ideas. Avoid overusing one source. It gives readers the impression that you have not done a thorough job of research.

Outlines can be topic or sentence outlines, whichever best suits the subject matter. Topic outlines are written in phrases, not sentences with subjects and verbs. Sentence outlines are, of course, written in sentences. The chief advantage of sentence outlines is that they force you to make statements about the topics, not just to name the topics — that is, to make decisions about your focus and the validity of your assertions. Often the sentences of the sentence outline become the topic sentences of paragraphs in the rough draft. In general, the more decisions about content that you can make before starting the rough draft, the faster you can write.

Instructors who want a preview of a long paper sometimes require that a final outline accompany the final paper. For that reason the content and emphasis of the final outline should match those of the final paper. The final outline should be in conventional style. Put the title and thesis at the top. Put specific information in headings and subheadings; don't just write "Introduction" or "First reason" or "Example from Smith's article" or "Significance of the problem."

Use parallel structure to express parallel ideas. That is, use the same grammatical patterns for headings and subheadings at the same level. Use all noun phrases or all verb phrases or all sentences. Outlines are expected to follow this standard format: Roman numerals at the margin for the major headings, capital letters, indented, for the next level, then Arabic numbers, and then small letters if there is a fourth level. See 1d and Karen Shaw's final outline on pages 350 – 351 for more discussion and an example of outlining.


## **51h** Write a first draft.

With a restricted thesis and purpose, a clear sense of what the assignment requires, a stack of note cards in your own words, and a fairly detailed preliminary outline, you are ready to write a first rough draft. Keep it rough and keep it moving. Don't let your wish for perfect sentences stall you at this stage. First write down your ideas and their supporting details; polish your sentences later. Writing rapidly usually produces a more natural, individual voice and helps you avoid echoing your sources.

A chatty, breezy voice is usually not welcome in academic papers, but neither is a stuffy, pretentious style or a timid, unsure one. If you believe in your main point and are interested in your information, try to communicate that sense of conviction. Some writers find that they convey their tone more intensely if they imagine as they write that they are talking to a group of people or explaining their ideas to a television interviewer. To sound natural, Karen Shaw pretended that she was the guest lecturer in a psychology class.

Many researchers find that writing only from their outlines (rather than directly from their note cards) allows them to write in their own voices without mimicking the style of their sources. In writing their first draft they will refer only briefly to their note cards, postponing an extensive filling out of their paragraphs until after they have produced a skeleton first draft. Other writers prefer to work closely with their note cards, filling out paragraphs with source information as they continue through their paper. Whichever method you prefer, it is crucial that your sentences be in your own words and not half-copied from your sources.

### Writing your introduction

In a research paper that refers to many other writers, it is especially important to establish your own voice in the introduction. Your opening paragraphs introduce you as well as your ideas to the reader.

One or two paragraphs are usually enough introduction for most papers in undergraduate courses. If you are writing about a subject new to you, you may be tempted to give the readers too much background, probably because you assume that since you needed to learn it, so will they. Most readers don't want much background; they want you to get right to your point.

You will be wise to reduce a too-long introduction later when you polish the draft. Your first-draft sentences may be wordy until you get warmed up and start writing more concisely. Your sense of proportion may be clearer after you have finished your paper, and it will lead you to slim down a top-heavy introduction. Also, after the entire paper has been written, you may recognize the need to move parts of a long introduction to more important places in the main body.

Readers are accustomed to seeing the thesis statement at the very beginning or very end of the introduction. The advantage of beginning with the thesis is that your readers can immediately grasp your purpose. The advantage of delaying the thesis statement is that you will have the opportunity for closer focus as you lead up to your thesis. Before you state your thesis, you may want to establish the importance of your topic, then review various attitudes toward it, and finally point to your view in your thesis.

In addition to stating the thesis and showing its importance, an introduction should hook the readers. Sometimes you can connect your topic to something recently in the news or bring your readers up to date about changing ideas. Other strategies are to present a puzzling problem or to open with a startling statistic. Karen Shaw's sample paper begins with a series of vivid examples leading up to her thesis.

### Avoiding excessive quotations

It is tempting to insert many long quotations in your paper and to use your own words only for connecting passages. This is an especially strong temptation if you feel that the authors of your sources are better writers than you are. But do not quote excessively. Long series of quotations give readers the impression that you cannot think for yourself.

The advice given earlier about note taking is relevant here: Use direct quotes only when the source is particularly clear or expressive or when it is important to let the debaters of an issue explain their positions in their own words. Except for this infrequent need for direct quotes, use your own words for summaries and paraphrases of your sources and to explain your own ideas.

**51i** Do not plagiarize: Cite all sources; use quotation marks for all quoted material.

Your research paper is a collaboration between you and the sources you have read. To be fair and ethical, acknowledge your borrowing of other writers' ideas, facts, and words. To borrow without acknowledgment is plagiarism, whether deliberate or accidental.

Unintended plagiarism ruins a writer's reputation just as much as outright cheating. The academic, business, and legal communities take plagiarism very seriously. Universities have been known to withdraw graduate degrees from students who have plagiarized. Professional writers sue for (and get) thousands of dollars when they discover that someone has plagiarized their work.

You must document anything specific that you have read and used in your paper: direct quotes; paraphrases of sentences; summaries of paragraphs or chapters; tables, graphs, and diagrams that you copy or construct yourself from specific information. The only exception is common knowledge or general information that appears in most sources because it is indeed commonly or generally known. For example, the current population of the United States is common knowledge in such fields as sociology and economics; Freud's theory of the importance of the subconscious is general information. If you are new to a topic and are not sure about what is considered common knowledge, ask someone with expertise. When in doubt, cite the source.

Two different acts are considered plagiarism: (1) to borrow someone's ideas, information, or style without citing the source, and (2) to cite the source but borrow choice words and sentence structure without using quotation marks to indicate the borrowing. It isn't enough to name the source; you must quote the source exactly in quotation marks or you must paraphrase its meaning completely in your own words.

When you paraphrase, you still need to name the source. You can mix your source's especially apt phrases with your own words only if you put quotation marks around the source's phrases—a practice that makes your sentences legal but rather odd-looking unless you use transitional signals very skillfully (see 51j). You document sources to acknowledge the sources' information, not to give yourself the chance to steal their wording. The following is an example of plagiarizing an author's wording, even though the source is cited.

**ORIGINAL VERSION**
If the existence of a signing ape was unsettling for linguists, it was also startling news for animal behaviorists.

**UNACCEPTABLE BORROWING OF WORDS, ALTHOUGH SOURCE IS CITED**

An ape who knew sign language unsettled linguists and

startled animal behaviorists (Davis 26).

Notice that "unsettling for linguists" and "startling news for animal behaviorists" have been barely changed.

It is also considered plagiarizing to borrow the source's sentence structure but to substitute your own synonyms, even though the source is cited, as illustrated below.

**UNACCEPTABLE BORROWING OF STRUCTURE, ALTHOUGH SOURCE IS CITED**

If the presence of a sign-language-using chimp was dis-

turbing for scientists studying language, it was also

surprising to scientists studying animals (Davis 26).

If your transitional signal and documentation make it very clear that you are presenting something you have read, you may use without quotation marks the necessary general words but not the author's particularly striking phrases.

The advice given about avoiding plagiarism at the note-taking stage (51f) is even more important to follow at the draft-writing stage. It is dangerously easy for your memory to restore unconsciously the source's original wording to your paraphrased rough draft when you polish it later. Your only precaution is to double-check potential unconscious plagiarizing by comparing your draft with your note cards—or, better yet, with the original—before typing the finished version of your paper.

In summary, to avoid plagiarism

1. identify the source precisely, and
2. either paraphrase the source in your own words or copy the author's words exactly, using quotation marks.

## 51j Cite sources using a consistent system.

The various academic disciplines use their own editorial styles, both for citations and for the list of works cited. The style used in this chapter is that of the Modern Language Association in the *MLA Handbook for Writers of Research Papers* (2nd ed., 1984).

The preferred MLA format is the in-text citation, given in parentheses in the text of the paper itself, but the *MLA Handbook* also presents footnoting as an acceptable alternative. Both formats are discussed in this section.

### In-text citations

In-text citations are handled through a combination of signal phrases and parenthetical references. A signal phrase indicates that something taken from a source is about to be used; usually it includes the author's name. The parenthetical reference includes at least a page number.

As Flora Davis puts it, "If the existence of a signing ape was unsettling for linguists, it was also startling news for animal behaviorists" (26).

The signal phrase — *As Flora Davis puts it* — provides the name of the author, and the parenthetical citation gives the page number where the quoted sentence may be found. By looking up the author's last name in the list of works cited at the end of the paper, readers will find complete information about the work's title, publisher, and date.

Citations in parentheses should be as concise as possible but complete enough so that readers can track down the source in the list of works cited, where works are listed under the author's last name. The general rules are as follows:

1. Do not repeat within parentheses anything already mentioned in the signal phrase.
2. Name the author within the parentheses if the signal phrase does not.
3. If there are two or more sources by the same author (or by authors with the same last name), either mention the title in the signal phrase or use an abbreviated form of the title in the parentheses.

The procedure is the same whether you are summarizing, paraphrasing, or citing direct quotations, though the punctuation will of course differ depending on the need for quotation marks.

**QUOTATION: AUTHOR NAMED IN SIGNAL PHRASE, PAGE NUMBER IN PARENTHESES**

According to Flora Davis, a chimp at the Yerkes Primate Research Center "has combined words into new sentences that she was never taught" (67).

**PARAPHRASE: AUTHOR NAMED IN SIGNAL PHRASE, PAGE NUMBER IN PARENTHESES**

As reported in Flora Davis's <u>Eloquent Animals</u>, Lana, a chimp at the Yerkes Primate Research Center, has created new sentences in sequences she had not been trained by her instructors to produce (67).

**AUTHOR AND PAGE NUMBER IN PARENTHESES**

Lana, a chimp at the Yerkes Primate Research Center, "has combined words into new sentences that she was never taught" (Davis 67).

**SHORT TITLE AND PAGE NUMBER IN PARENTHESES**

According to Flora Davis, a chimp at the Yerkes Primate Research Center "has combined words into new sentences that she was never taught" (<u>Animals</u> 67).

**AUTHOR, SHORT TITLE, AND PAGE NUMBER IN PARENTHESES**

Lana, a chimp at the Yerkes Primate Research Center, "has combined words into new sentences that she was never taught" (Davis, <u>Animals</u> 67).

If the author is not known, name the title that is listed in the works cited. The title may appear either in the signal phrase or in the parentheses.

In a recent interview, "A Talk with Gary Hart," Hart said that the U.S. should rely on economic

```
assistance rather than military aid to influence
Central America (32).
```

```
In a recent interview Gary Hart said that the U.S. should
rely on economic assistance rather than military aid to
influence Central America ("A Talk with Gary Hart" 32).
```

If your source has two or three authors, name them in the signal phrase or include them in the parenthetical reference:

### A WORK WITH TWO OR MORE AUTHORS

```
Patterson and Linden agree that the gorilla Koko
acquired language more slowly than a normal speaking
child, but they also point out that there wasn't
a great difference between Koko and deaf children
in learning signs (83-90).
```

If your source has more than three authors, include only the first author's name followed by "et al." in the signal phrase or in the parenthetical reference.

```
The study was extended for two years, and only after
results were duplicated on both coasts did the authors
publish their results (Doe et al. 137).
```

If you use more than one volume of a multivolume work, you must indicate which volume you are referring to in the parenthetical citation of the work:

**A MULTIVOLUME WORK**

Terman's studies of gifted children reveal a pattern

of accelerated language acquisition (2:279).

If you use only one volume of a multivolume work, this volume
will be listed in the bibliography at the end of the paper. A
parenthetical reference to the work need only include the author and page number in the signal phrase or in the citation.

In citing a government document or a work with a corporate author, try to include the name of the author in the
signal phrase introducing the reference:

**A GOVERNMENT DOCUMENT OR WORK WITH A CORPORATE
AUTHOR**

In Tax Guide for Small Business the Internal Revenue

Service warns businesses that deductions for "lavish

and extravagant" entertainment are not allowed (43).

In citing literary sources, include information that will
enable your readers to find the passage in various editions of
the work (since novels, plays, and poems are often available
in many editions). For a novel put the page first, followed by
information on the part or chapter in which the passage can
be found.

**A NOVEL**

Fitzgerald's narrator captures Gatsby in a moment of

isolation: "A sudden emptiness seemed to flow now from

the windows and the great doors, endowing with complete

isolation the figure of the host" (56; ch. 3).

For a verse play, list the act, scene, and line numbers in the parenthetical citation.

**A PLAY**

In his famous advice to the players, Hamlet defines the

purpose of theater, "whose end, both at the first and

now, was and is, to hold, as 'twere, the mirror up to

nature" (III.ii.21-23).

For a poem, cite the part (if there are a number of parts) and the line numbers.

**A POEM**

When Homer's Odysseus came to the hall of Circe, he

found his men "mild/in her soft spell, fed on her drug

of evil" (X.209-11).

You may want to cite several sources for one point, or you may want to summarize two or more sources in one paragraph. The following example covers both cases.

**PARENTHETICAL CITATION OF TWO OR MORE WORKS**

With intensive training, the apes in this study learned

over 200 signs or signals (Desmond 229; Linden 173).

You can also use an endnote to cite several works that support a single point.

Researchers who use the in-text citation system for documenting sources may also use footnotes or endnotes for one of two purposes:

1. to provide additional information that might interrupt the flow of the paper yet is important enough to include;
2. to refer readers to sources not included in the list of works cited or to evaluate a source.

Footnotes appear at the foot of the page, endnotes at the end of the paper. They are numbered consecutively throughout the paper. The text of the paper contains a raised Arabic numeral that corresponds to the number of the note.

**TEXT**

The apes' achievements cannot be explained away as the

simple results of conditioning or unconscious cueing by

trainers.[1]

**NOTE**

   [1] For a discussion of the cueing of animals, see

Wade, 1349-51.

The use of notes to add information or to refer readers to sources not listed in the works cited should not be confused with the use of notes as an alternative to in-text citations. That alternative system is discussed below.

*Footnotes or endnotes (an alternative system)*

Until 1984 the *MLA Handbook* recommended footnotes or endnotes instead of in-text citations. Though the current *MLA Handbook* treats in-text citations as its preferred style, it also lists the traditional notes as an acceptable alternative.

Notes provide complete publishing information, making it unnecessary for readers to turn to the list of works cited in order to track down a source. In form, notes are considerably more complex than in-text citations. The examples below cover the formats that are most frequently encountered.

The first time you cite a source in your paper, you should give the full publication information for that work — author's name, title, publisher, date — as well as the page number of the specific information you are referring to.

**BASIC FORMAT FOR A BOOK**

<sup>1</sup> Flora Davis, <u>Eloquent Animals: A Study in Animal Communication</u> (New York: Coward, 1978) 68.

**A WORK WITH TWO OR MORE AUTHORS**

<sup>2</sup> Roger Fisher and William Ury, <u>Getting to Yes: Negotiating Agreement Without Giving In</u> (Boston: Houghton, 1981) 108–15.

Name the authors in the order presented on the title page. The names of three authors are separated by commas: *Thomas Smith, Sharon Jones, and Harry Brown.* For four or more authors use only the first author followed by "et al.": *Jane Doe et al.* Cite multiple authors or articles the same way as authors of books.

**A MULTIVOLUME WORK**

<sup>3</sup> Curt von Westernhagen, <u>Wagner: A Biography</u>, trans. Mary Whittale, 2 vols. (Cambridge: Cambridge UP, 1978) 2: 378.

The citation is for page 378 in volume 2. Note the format for naming translators.

**A PAMPHLET**

[4] Maryland Commission for Women, <u>How to Translate</u>
<u>Volunteer Skills into Employment Credentials</u> (Baltimore:
MD Commission for Women, 1979) 15.

**ANONYMOUS AUTHOR**

[5] <u>How to Translate Volunteer Skills into Employment</u>
<u>Credentials</u> (Baltimore: MD Commission for Women, 1979) 6.

**ARTICLE OR ESSAY IN A COLLECTION**

[6] John P. Brennan and Michael C. Downs, "Anarchism
and Utopian Tradition in <u>The Dispossessed</u>," <u>Ursula K.</u>
<u>LeGuin,</u> ed. Joseph D. Olander and Martin Harry Green-
berg, Writers of the 21st Century Series (New York:
Taplinger, 1979) 118.

**ARTICLE IN A MONTHLY MAGAZINE WITH SEPARATE**
**PAGINATION**

[7] Wanda L. Lorenz, "Problem Areas in Accounting for
Income Taxes," <u>The Practical Accountant</u> Feb. 1984: 70.

See pages 344 – 345 for the difference between a monthly
magazine and a journal with continuous pagination.

**ARTICLE IN A JOURNAL WITH CONTINUOUS PAGINATION**

[8] Mary L. Otto, "Child Abuse: Group Treatment for
Parents," <u>Personnel and Guidance Journal</u> 62 (1984): 336.

Leave out the abbreviations for volume and page when citing journals.

**ARTICLE IN A WEEKLY MAGAZINE**

   [9] Matt Clark, "Medicine: A Brave New World,"

Newsweek 5 Mar. 1984: 64-76.

**UNSIGNED ARTICLE IN A DAILY NEWSPAPER**

   [10] "Market Leaks: Illegal Insider Trading Seems

to Be on Rise; Ethical Issues Muddled," Wall Street

Journal 2 Mar. 1984, sec. 1: 1.

**SIGNED ARTICLE IN AN ENCYCLOPEDIA**

   [11] Mark S. Frankel, "Human Experimentation: Social

and Professional Control," Encyclopedia of Bioethics,

1978 ed.

**PERSONAL OR TELEPHONE INTERVIEW**

   [12] Lloyd Shaw, personal interview, 21 June 1984.

Subsequent references to a work that has already been cited in a note can be given in shortened form. You need to give only enough information for the reader to be able to identify which work you are referring to. Usually the author's last name and a page number are all you need. The abbreviations *ibid.* and *op. cit.* are no longer used.

   [13] Davis 49.

   [14] Smith, Jones, and Brown 17.

If you are using more than one work by one author or two works by authors with the same last name, cite the author's last name and a shortened title.

[15] Davis, <u>Intuitions</u> 53.

[16] Davis, <u>Animals</u> 48–50.

If you are referring to a work by an anonymous author, use a shortened form of the title.

[17] <u>Volunteer Skills</u> 6.

**51k** Handle ellipses, brackets, and long quotations correctly.

After revising your draft for content, style, and correct grammar and punctuation, save enough time to prepare the correct formats for certain kinds of quotations requiring special handling. Examining Karen Shaw's sample paper on pages 348 – 380 and reading the comments on the pages opposite the essay will show you how to handle other technical details such as the size of the four margins, the place for page numbers, and the format of the title page.

*Ellipses*

Sometimes you will not wish to quote all of your source's words. Whenever you interrupt a quotation to leave out words, whether you leave out a single word or several sentences, use three periods (with spaces between) to indicate you have left out words. What remains must be grammatically complete.

**ORIGINAL SOURCE**
Scientists like Patterson stress the need for an exceptionally close personal relationship between instructor and subject — like the bond between small children and their teachers.

**ELLIPSES TO SHOW OMISSIONS**

```
According to Robert Seyfarth, "scientists . . . stress

the need for an exceptionally close personal rela-

tionship between instructor and subject . . ." (15).
```

The first ellipsis mark (after *scientists*) indicates the omission of *like Patterson*. The second ellipsis mark (after *subject*) indicates the omission of part of the original sentence: — *like the bond between small children and their teachers.* If the writer had included *like the bond between small children and their teachers*, an ellipsis mark would not be needed at the end of the sentence because omitting the rest of the paragraph does not require an ellipsis mark.

Notice that the parenthetical citation is inserted after the three ellipsis periods and before the period at the end of the sentence. If you had *no* parenthetical citation following the last ellipsis, you would use four periods: a combination of three ellipsis periods and the end-of-sentence period.

Never use an ellipsis to distort the meaning of your source.

## Brackets

Use square brackets to indicate that you have altered a quotation by adding words of your own within the quotation marks. You use them to explain a confusing reference or to keep a sentence grammatical.

```
Robert Seyfarth reports that "Premack [a scientist at

the University of Pennsylvania] taught a seven-year-

old chimpanzee, Sarah, that the word for 'apple' was

a small, plastic triangle" (13).
```

If your typewriter has no brackets, ink them in by hand. Brackets and ellipsis marks are also discussed in 39.

## Long quotations

When you quote more than four typed lines, help your reader more easily spot the long quotation by indenting it ten spaces, without using quotation marks. This form displays your source's words more obviously than two tiny, widely separated quotation marks. The quotation should be double-spaced. Long quotations should be introduced by informative comments as well as by a signal phrase.

> Desmond describes how Washoe, when the Gardners
> returned her to an ape colony in Oklahoma, tried
> signing to the other apes:
>
> > One particularly memorable day, a snake
> > spread terror through the castaways on the
> > ape island, and all but one fled in panic.
> > This male sat absorbed, staring intently at
> > the serpent. Then Washoe was seen running
> > over signing to him "come, hurry up." (42)

Notice that at the end of a block quotation the parenthetical citation goes outside the final period.

## **511** Prepare a bibliography of works cited.

If you are using parenthetical citations within the text of your paper, you'll need to prepare a bibliography of works cited that gives full publishing information for each of the works you cite. (If you are using footnotes to document your paper, you may or may not need to prepare such a bibliography — ask your instructor.) All sources mentioned in your paper (and only those sources) should be listed alphabetically at the end of your paper. Sources not actually cited should not be listed — even though you read them. Start on a new page and title your list "Works Cited." The bibliography at the end of Karen Shaw's paper on page 380 will show you how to handle some of the technical details: how to alphabetize the list, how to indent, and so on. The following models illustrate the form of the bibliographic entries.

### BASIC FORMAT FOR A BOOK

Davis, Flora.  <u>Eloquent Animals: A Study in Animal</u>

    <u>Communication</u>.  New York: Coward, 1978.

This information is taken from the title page of the book, not from the outside cover. The complete name of the publisher (Coward, McCann & Geoghegan, Inc.) is not given; use a shortened form instead. The date given is the copyright date found on the reverse side of the book's title page.

### A WORK WITH TWO OR MORE AUTHORS

Fisher, Roger, and William Ury.  <u>Getting to Yes:</u>

    <u>Negotiating Agreement Without Giving In</u>.  Boston:

    Houghton, 1981.

Name the authors in the order in which they are presented on the title page; reverse the name of only the first author. The names of three authors are separated by commas: *Smith, Thomas, Sharon Jones, and Harry Brown.* For four or more authors, cite only the first one, followed by "et al." (the Latin abbreviation for "and others"): *Doe, Jane, et al.* The procedure for citing multiple authors of articles in periodicals is the same as for citing multiple authors of books.

### TWO WORKS BY THE SAME AUTHOR

Davis, Flora.  <u>Eloquent Animals: A Study in Animal Com-

munication</u>.  New York: Coward, 1978.

---.  <u>Inside Intuition: What We Know About Nonverbal

Communication</u>.  New York: McGraw, 1973.

List the titles in alphabetical order, not chronological order. Use three hyphens and a period instead of repeating the author's name.

### A LATER EDITION

<u>The Chicago Manual of Style</u>.  13th ed.  Chicago: U of

Chicago P, 1982.

The number of the edition immediately follows the title of the book.

### A MULTIVOLUME WORK

Westernhagen, Curt von.  <u>Wagner: A Biography</u>.  Trans.

Mary Whittale.  2 vols.  Cambridge: Cambridge UP,

1978.  Vol. 2.

This entry cites only volume 2. If you had cited the entire set, you would end your bibliographical entry after the date, leaving off the "Vol. 2."

Notice that Cambridge UP (without periods) is the abbreviation for Cambridge University Press. Notice also the format for naming the translator of a book.

**A TRANSLATION**

Tolstoy, Leo.  Anna Karenina.  Trans. Constance Garnett.

Indianapolis: Bobbs, 1978.

**BOOK WITH AN EDITOR**

Lenneberg, Eric H., and Elizabeth Lenneberg, eds.

Foundations of Language Development: A Multi-

disciplinary Approach.  New York: Academic, 1975.

Reverse the name of only the first editor.

**AN ESSAY FROM A REPRINTED COLLECTION**

Abrams, M. H.  "English Romanticism: The Spirit of the

Age."  Romanticism Reconsidered.  Ed. Northrop Frye.

New York: Columbia UP, 1963.  63–88.  Rpt. in Roman-

ticism and Consciousness: Essays in Criticism.  Ed.

Harold Bloom.  New York: Norton, 1970.  90–119.

**A PAMPHLET**

Maryland Commission for Women.  How to Translate

Volunteer Skills into Employment Credentials.

Baltimore: MD Commission for Women, 1979.

You may abbreviate the publisher rather than repeat the same information given in naming the author. An alternative way of handling works when the title page attributes authorship to an agency or corporation and not to a person is to consider the author to be anonymous, beginning the bibliographical entry with the title, as the following entry illustrates.

**ANONYMOUS AUTHOR**

How to Translate Volunteer Skills into Employment Cre-

dentials. Baltimore: MD Commission for Women,

1979.

Place anonymous works alphabetically according to the first word of the title.

**ARTICLE OR ESSAY IN A COLLECTION**

Brennan, John P., and Michael C. Downs. "Anarchism and

Utopian Tradition in The Dispossessed." Ursula

K. LeGuin. Ed. Joseph D. Olander and Martin Harry

Greenberg. Writers of the 21st Century Series.

New York: Taplinger, 1979. 116-52.

The names of the two editors are given in normal order. Notice that this model also shows how to identify books that are part of a series.

**ARTICLE IN A MONTHLY MAGAZINE WITH SEPARATE PAGINATION**

Lorenz, Wanda L. "Problem Areas in Accounting for

Income Taxes." The Practical Accountant Feb.

1984: 69-77.

The month is abbreviated. The article appeared in volume 17, issue number 2, but the word *volume* or *vol.* or the number 17 is not used because the year identifies it clearly. The issue number is not given because the month identifies it clearly. The volume and issue are not given *only* when each new issue starts with page 1. Contrast this entry with the next one.

**ARTICLE IN A JOURNAL WITH CONTINUOUS PAGINATION**

Otto, Mary L. "Child Abuse: Group Treatment for

   Parents." <u>Personnel and Guidance Journal</u> 62

   (1984): 336-38.

Many professional journals continue page numbers throughout the year rather than start each new issue with page 1. In these journals, interested readers can easily find the article you cite if you supply only the year and volume number. They will not need to know that the article was in issue number 6 in February; they can just turn to page 336 in the library's bound volume 62 or microfilm roll.

**ARTICLE IN A WEEKLY MAGAZINE**

Clark, Matt. "Medicine: A Brave New World." <u>Newsweek</u>

   5 Mar. 1984: 64-70.

Articles in news magazines are often written with the assistance of other reporters; cite only the principal author.

**UNSIGNED ARTICLE IN A DAILY NEWSPAPER**

"Market Leaks: Illegal Insider Trading Seems to Be on

   Rise; Ethical Issues Muddled." <u>Wall Street Journal</u>

   2 Mar. 1984: sec. 1: 1.

### SIGNED ARTICLE IN AN ENCYCLOPEDIA

Frankel, Mark S. "Human Experimentation: Social and

Professional Control." Encyclopedia of Bioethics

(1978).

Volume and page numbers are not given for encyclopedia articles because the entries are arranged alphabetically and therefore are easy to locate without them.

### A BOOK REVIEW

Yardley, Jonathan. Rev. of Presidents and the Press:

The Nixon Legacy, by Joseph C. Spear. Washington

Post National Weekly Edition 30 July 1984: 36.

### GOVERNMENT DOCUMENT

United States. Internal Revenue Service. Tax Guide

for Small Business. Publication 334. Washington:

GPO, 1983.

### FILMS AND TELEVISION PROGRAMS

North by Northwest. Dir. Alfred Hitchcock. With Cary

Grant. MGM, 1959.

### PLAY

Mother Courage. By Bertolt Brecht. Dir. Timothy Mayer.

With Linda Hunt. Boston Shakespeare Company

Theater, Boston. 20 Jan. 1984.

**RECORDING**

Handel, George Frederick. <u>Messiah</u>. With Elizabeth
Harwood, Janet Baker, Paul Esswood, Robert Tear,
and Raimund Herincz. Cond. Charles Mackerras.
English Chamber Orch. and The Ambrosian Singers.
Angel, R 67-2682, 1967.

**COMPUTER SOFTWARE**

<u>Childpace</u>. Computer software. Computerose, 1984.
Commodore 64, disk.

**PERSONAL OR TELEPHONE INTERVIEW**

Shaw, Lloyd. Personal interview. 21 Mar. 1984.

Somewhere Between the Word and the Sentence:

The Great Apes and the Acquisition of Language

1

By Karen Shaw

English 101, Section 30

Dr. Barshay

April 12, 1985

1. *Title page format.* Because an outline is included with this paper, Shaw uses a separate title page. She types the title about one-third down the page. One inch below the title Shaw types *By* and then her name, and one inch below that she types information required by her instructor, including the name and section number of the course, her instructor's name, and the date. Each item is on a separate line, double-spaced. All the information is centered between the left and right margins.

### Pages 350–351

2. *Outline format.* Some instructors ask that an outline be included with the paper. In that case, a separate title page is required. Place the outline between the title page and the text. If the outline consists of more than one page, number the pages with small Roman numerals at the top right-hand corner, beginning with *ii.* Leave the first page of the outline unnumbered.
3. *Outline content.* Shaw begins the outline with her thesis statement. It is a two-part thesis, stating that the greater apes have language abilities but then suggesting that these abilities are limited. The outline has two major divisions corresponding to the two parts of the thesis. Each subdivision in an outline should relate directly to its main division. Parallel phrasing should be used for parallel levels in the outline.

Outline

Thesis: The great apes resemble humans in language
abilities more than researchers once believed,
but it is doubtful whether apes can combine
symbols in grammatical patterns.

I. The great apes have demonstrated significant
language skills.

    A. Chimpanzees and gorillas have acquired
large vocabularies in American sign language
and in two artificial languages.

        1. In sign language, chimpanzee Washoe
learned 160 signs, gorilla Koko possibly
as many as 600.

        2. In artificial languages, Sarah learned
130 symbols, Lana 109.

    B. Despite charges that they are merely respond-
ing to their trainers' cues, apes have used
signs spontaneously.

        1. They have performed well in experiments
that eliminate the possibility of cueing.

        2. They initiate conversations with other
apes.

ii

    C. Apes appear to use their language skills creatively, though this is a matter of some dispute.

        1. They have invented creative names.

        2. They have been known to swear, lie, and possibly even joke.

II. It has not yet been demonstrated that apes can combine signs in grammatical patterns to form sentences.

    A. The apes' sequences of signs are often confusing and repetitious.

    B. Lana's manipulation of stock sentences could be the result of conditioning.

    C. The Gardners' example is inconclusive.

    D. Even Patterson does not claim that her apes grasp grammar.

**51**   *Sample research paper*

Somewhere Between the Word and the Sentence:     4

The Great Apes and the Acquisition of Language     5

   Choosing from among the eighty signs in American     6
sign language that she had learned, a chimpanzee
named Lucy selected three and signaled to her trainer,
"Roger tickle Lucy." When Roger failed to respond to
her request and signaled instead, "No, Lucy tickle
Roger," the chimpanzee jumped onto his lap and began
to tickle him (Desmond 43-44). One afternoon, Koko
the gorilla, who was often bored with language
lessons, stubbornly and repeatedly signaled "red"
when asked the color of a white towel. She did this
even though she had correctly identified the color
white many times before. At last the gorilla produced "a minute speck of red lint that had been     7
clinging to the towel" (Patterson and Linden 80-81).
In Atlanta a chimpanzee named Lana was taught to

4. *Title.* The first part of Shaw's title is an evocative phrase introducing an idea that will be clarified at the end of the paper. The subtitle is an explicit description of her topic.
5. *Paper format.* The title is centered between the left and right margins, about two inches from the top of the page. The text begins four spaces below the title. Number all pages with Arabic numerals at the upper right-hand corner, about a half-inch from the top. The text is double-spaced (including quotations, notes, and bibliography). There should be a margin of one inch at the top and bottom and on both sides. The beginning of each paragraph is indented five spaces from the left margin. Block quotations are indented ten spaces from the left margin.
6. *Introduction.* Karen Shaw decided to open her paper with three vivid examples that provide an overview of her subject. She relies on fascinating examples throughout the paper to keep her readers interested in the subject. Shaw decided not to use signal phrases such as "As Adrian Desmond points out" to introduce the first three examples, thinking that such phrases would interrupt the narrative flow of the paragraph. The names of the authors of her references therefore appear in parentheses, along with the page numbers on which she found the material. Complete bibliographical information for these references is provided in the list of works cited at the end of the paper.
7. *Incorporating quotations into the text.* Shaw skillfully integrates the language of the quotations into her own style in these opening examples.

communicate on a computerized keyboard by pressing
keys marked with symbols representing words. Though
it took Lana "two weeks and 1600 tries" before she
understood the symbol for "name of," once she learned
it she quickly began to ask for the things she wanted
by name (Davis 67).

These and hundreds of similar scenes played out
over the past fifteen years make it clear that the
great apes (chimpanzees, gorillas, and orangutans)
resemble humans in language abilities more than had
previously been believed. Just how far that resem-
blance extends, however, is a matter of some controversy. Researchers agree that apes have acquired
large vocabularies, but they differ sharply in interpreting the uses to which these vocabularies have
been put. On balance, the evidence suggests--despite    8
the opinions of some skeptics--that apes have used
symbols spontaneously and creatively. It has not yet   9
been demonstrated, however, that they can combine
symbols in even rudimentary grammatical patterns.

Though apes lack the vocal ability to produce
human sounds, they have acquired fairly large

8. *Location of thesis.* Shaw's thesis appears at the end of the second paragraph. Shaw needs two sentences to express her thesis because her conclusions about the ape experiments are complex. Notice that the thesis sentences survey the organization of the paper, preparing readers for its two main parts and even for some of its subparts.

9. *Focusing the thesis.* The thesis of the paper is not as dramatic as Shaw thought it would be when she began the paper. Having seen several television shows and read a number of popular articles before fully researching her subject, Shaw was at first convinced that apes could learn a rudimentary grammar. As she read more widely, she began to doubt her preliminary thesis and even considered making the thesis a negative one. On completing her reading, however, Shaw decided that the evidence for the apes' abilities was most convincing, even though not as firmly established as she had once thought. Students writing research papers should be willing to change their minds but should not be afraid to challenge authorities.

vocabularies in American sign language, or Ameslan,
and in two artificial languages. Washoe, an African-
born chimpanzee trained by psychologists Allen and        10
Beatrice Gardner from 1966 to 1970, learned 160 signs
in Ameslan. Washoe began to learn signs by spontaneously imitating the Gardners, who used only sign
language in her presence, but she learned more rapidly
when the Gardners took her hands and molded the signs
with them. To determine when Washoe truly knew a sign,
the Gardners applied a rigid criterion: The sign had      11
to be used "spontaneously and appropriately at least
once on each of 15 days" (300).                           12

The largest Ameslan vocabulary claimed for an
ape, 600 signs, is that of Francine Patterson's
gorilla Koko, who has lived with Patterson since 1972.
This figure is based on a simple count, not on the
Gardners' strict criterion. But Patterson has also
kept records showing that Koko has mastered nearly
200 signs as measured by the Gardners' criterion
(Patterson and Linden 83-84).                             13

The first ape to acquire a vocabulary in an
artificial language was Sarah, a chimpanzee trained

10. *Primary sources.* The Gardners are an important primary source, so Shaw introduces them fully, giving their complete names and describing them as the psychologists who trained Washoe. Later in the paper, she calls them by their last names because at that point readers will be familiar with them.

11. *Author included in signal phrase.* The name of the authors appears in a signal phrase, so the parentheses contain only the page number.

12. *Importance of statistics and other numerical evidence.* Shaw uses statistics throughout to support her assertions. Here she provides a concrete explanation of what the Gardners mean by a rigid criterion.

13. *Multiple authors in a parenthetical reference.* When there are two or three authors of a book or article, include all the names in the parenthetical reference. When there are more than three authors, include only the first author's name followed by "et al."

by psychologist David Premack in the late 1960s.
Sarah learned 130 "words" in a language of plastic          14
tokens, each representing a different word or word
combination in English.   In the early 1970s, another
chimp, Lana, learned 109 symbols in Yerkish, an artificial language on a computerized keyboard developed
by psychologist Duane Rumbaugh.

    In spite of claims made for Washoe, Koko, and
others, however, there is still skepticism about
whether the apes really learn signs or whether they
merely imitate or respond to the cues of their
trainers.[1]   Psychologist H. S. Terrace, the chief          15
trainer of a chimp named Nim, is one of the most
formidable of the skeptics because he was once a be-
liever.   Ultimately Terrace concluded that most of
Nim's, Washoe's, and Koko's signs were responses to
deliberate or nondeliberate cues given by trainers
immediately before the ape signed (Terrace et al.
899).

    Although Terrace may be correct in asserting          16
that a high percentage of the apes' signs have been
in response to cues, he and other critics have not

14. *Undisputed and common knowledge.* The vocabularies of the apes were mentioned in more than two general sources and they did not seem to be a matter of dispute, so Shaw did not provide citations for them. In the earlier paragraph about Koko's vocabulary, however, a citation was needed because those statistics have been challenged.

15. *Use of endnotes.* The number at the end of this sentence refers to a note at the end of the paper. Shaw's rough draft contained a long discussion of cueing and the subtle ways it can occur, but the material had to be cut because Shaw was losing her focus on the thesis. She preserved a short passage by putting it in the note.

16. *Addressing opposing arguments.* Shaw wisely addresses her opponents' arguments throughout the paper, showing that she knows both sides and that she believes her arguments stand up against the opposition. Here she counters Terrace's conclusion and offers evidence from concrete experiments to support her assertion.

demonstrated that all of them are.  The Gardners and
other researchers have performed elaborate double-
blind experiments that prevent any possibility of
cueing, and the apes have performed well in such
tests.[2]  But perhaps the most convincing evidence is     17
that the apes have used the signs spontaneously among
themselves, even without a trainer present.

When the Gardners returned Washoe to an ape
colony in Oklahoma, she desperately signaled to humans
from whom she was separated by a moat, and from the
start she signed to the other apes:

> Frustrated by lack of conversationalists,     18
> she [Washoe] even tried talking to dogs.
> . . . One particularly memorable day, a
> snake spread terror through . . . the ape
> island, and all but one fled in panic.
> This male sat absorbed, staring intently at
> the serpent.  Then Washoe was seen running
> over signing to him, "come, hurry up."
> (Desmond 42)

Patterson's gorillas Koko and Michael sign to
one another, with Michael occasionally using signs

17. *Use of endnotes.* This note leads readers to a source not listed in the works cited. Shaw does not have the space to discuss the double-blind experiments but thinks some readers may want to read about them.

18. *Indented quotations, ellipses, and brackets.* Quotations longer than four typed lines should be double-spaced and indented ten spaces from the left margin. Quotation marks should not be used when a quotation is indented. It is a sacred rule of research that material should be quoted *exactly* as it appears in a source, including misspellings. Often, however, it is necessary to insert or omit material in a quoted passage. Brackets are used to insert words not in the original source, in this case the name Washoe. Bracketed information often clarifies the quotation or makes it fit grammatically within the text. Ellipsis dots indicate that words have been deleted. The first ellipsis in the quotation consists of a period indicating the end of a sentence and three dots. The second ellipsis appears within a sentence, so it consists simply of three dots.

that he could have learned only from Koko. "Even more intriguing," writes Patterson, "is his variation of the <u>tickle</u> sign depending on whom he is conversing with" (Patterson and Linden 176). One of the most dramatic instances of one ape signing to another occurred in 1976, when Washoe had a baby. Though the baby chimp lived for only a few hours, Washoe signed to it before it died (Davis 42).

In addition to showing that apes learn signs and use them spontaneously, the studies suggest a third important conclusion: Apes can use language, or something like it, creatively. Though creative uses of language are difficult to prove, there is considerable evidence that apes have invented creative names and that they have used signs to swear, lie, and perhaps even joke.

One incident in particular has become a rallying point for those who feel too much has been claimed for the apes, however. Chimpanzee Washoe, who knew the signs for "water" and "bird," once signed "water bird" when in the presence of a swan. H. S. Terrace legitimately points out that although Washoe's answer

19. *Documentation of paraphrased material.* Shaw para-
    phrases the story of Washoe's baby instead of quoting
    Davis's account of the incident. But she still documents
    her source in a parenthetical reference.
20. *Use of summary as a transition.* Here Shaw summarizes
    the points she has made so far about the apes' language
    ability; the summary is an effective transition to the next
    part of her discussion.
21. *Acknowledging the opposition.* By presenting Terrace's
    interpretation of the "water bird" example, Shaw proves
    herself to be a fair researcher who listens to reasonable
    arguments even when they go against her own bias. In
    the next paragraph Shaw counters Terrace's conclusions
    with other examples of creative names that cannot be so
    easily explained away.

may seem creative, there is "no basis for concluding
that Washoe was characterizing the swan as a 'bird
that inhabits water.'" Washoe may simply have been
"identifying correctly a body of water and a bird, in
that order" (Terrace et al. 895).

Other examples are not so easily explained away.
For instance, Lana once described a cucumber as
"banana which-is green" (Davis 67). The Gardners'
Lucy is reported to have called an onion "cry fruit"
and a radish "cry hurt food" (Desmond 40). And
Patterson's Koko has a long list of creative names
to her credit:

22

> "elephant baby" to describe a Pinocchio
> doll
>
> "finger bracelet" to describe a ring
>
> "white tiger" to describe a toy zebra
>
> "red corn drink" to describe pomegranate
> seeds
>
> "bottle match" to describe a cigarette
> lighter
>
> "eye hat" to describe a mask (Patterson
> and Linden 146)

22. *Effective use of evidence.* Shaw draws upon many different sources for evocative examples of creative names. Each example or series of examples is followed by a parenthetical reference to its source.

If Terrace's analysis of the "water bird" example
were applied to these examples, it would not hold.
Surely Koko did not see first an elephant and then a
baby before signing "elephant baby"--or a bottle and
a match before signing "bottle match."

Apes who invent names are not simply learning by
rote. They are adapting language for their own purposes, including swearing, lying, and possibly playing
jokes.

Among Koko's swear words are "rotten," "stupid,"    23
"stinker," "nut," "bird," "devil," "toilet," and
"dirty." According to Patterson, "the word dirty,
which Koko first used at about age three, and which
we use to refer to her feces, became one of Koko's
favorite insults. Under extreme provocation she will
combine dirty with toilet to make her meaning ines-
capable" (Patterson and Linden 39). Washoe also
turned the word dirty into a swear word without
prompting (Davis 34). So, apparently, did Nim,
though his own trainer, Terrace, refuses to be convinced. He argues that at times Nim used the sign
dirty to signal a need to go to the bathroom when

23. *Effective use of evidence.* In this paragraph, Shaw offers two different interpretations of the apes' use of the word *dirty.* She engages the reader, inviting him or her to decide which interpretation makes the most sense. Shaw's larger point is that apes use language for their own purposes, and both interpretations (apes cursing or apes manipulating their teachers with language) support that assertion.

what he really wanted was to be removed from an unpleasant situation. In other words, Nim's "presumed cursing" was simply a clever technique to manipulate his teachers (Terrace 154).

Terrace clearly believes, as do other researchers, 24 that apes are capable of lying. In fact, Terrace's argument that Nim's "dirty" is not a swear word is based on his assumption that it is a lie--Nim's false claim that he needs to use the toilet. Both Lucy and Koko have been reported to lie (Desmond 201), and Lucy has been clever enough to see through the lies of her trainers (Desmond 102). Ted Crail points out that lies "fall within that part of language which is 'half art.' Lies are different from memorization or mimicking. They call for a conclusion on the animal's part that it would not like to get caught or that it would like to talk you out of something" (137).

Whether apes can joke is highly debatable. 25 Francine Patterson is convinced that Koko both appreciates jokes and jokes back in turn with her trainers. Patterson claims that many of the apparent "mistakes" made by Koko in her lessons are really attempts to

24. *Transition through repetition.* By continuing to refer to Terrace, Shaw makes a smooth transition to the next paragraph and to the next point about the ape's creative use of language.

25. *Development of an idea.* Shaw develops this paragraph through narration. The story about Koko follows the topic sentence describing Patterson's belief that apes can joke. Notice how Shaw develops her argument logically and coherently. For example, on page 6 Shaw states that there is evidence that apes invent creative names, swear, lie, and joke. In the next three pages she expands on each part of this assertion in order. She offers examples of creative naming, swearing, lying, and joking, and she interprets these examples using both sides of the argument about apes' language ability. She seems to have mastered the evidence, and she has a clear sense of how to develop a coherent argument.

inject variety into boring classroom drills. For
example, when one trainer asked Koko where she wanted
to put some apple juice, Koko replied first "nose,"
then "eye," and then "ear." The trainer retorted,
"Okay, here it goes in your ear." Koko laughed,
signed "drink," and opened her mouth, showing that
she knew very well where the drink belonged (Patterson and Linden 142-43). Patterson is well aware that
many scientists find her anecdotal evidence of humor
unconvincing, but she doubts whether an experiment
that would satisfy them could be designed for such a
subjective activity as joking (Patterson and Linden
207).

Though the great apes have demonstrated signifi-    26
cant language skills, the question remains whether
they can combine signs in grammatical patterns to
form sentences. All human languages have a grammar,
a system through which relations among words are con-
veyed. H. S. Terrace's description of grammar echoes    27
that of linguist Noam Chomsky, after whom his chimp
Nim was named:

26. *Restating the thesis as a transition.* Shaw shifts smoothly to the second part of her thesis by restating it. The last section of the paper, beginning with this paragraph, corresponds to the second half of Shaw's outline — II.A–D.
27. *Use of definition.* Shaw introduces this next section of the paper by defining *grammar.* The definition is a good strategy; if grammar is what distinguishes human beings from other species, then readers must have a clear understanding of what that distinction is.

Unlike words, most sentences cannot be learned individually. Psychologists, psycholinguists, and linguists are in general agreement that using a human language indicates knowledge of a grammar. How else can one account for a child's ultimate ability to create an indeterminate number of meaningful sentences from a finite number of words? (Terrace et al. 891)

It is true that apes have strung together various signs (for instance, "Roger tickle Lucy"), but the sequences are often confusing and repetitious. Nim's series of sixteen signs is a case in point: "give orange me give eat orange me eat orange give me eat orange give me you" (Terrace et al. 895).

28

Lana, the chimpanzee who communicates in an artificial language, can tap out about six stock sentences. For example, she might punch "please," then a name, then a verb (such as "tickle" or "groom"), and then Lana. Such "sentences," however, could be conditioned responses involving little or no understanding of grammar.

28. *Repeated reference.* The phrase *"Roger tickle Lucy"* is
    not only a good example of how apes string together vari-
    ous signs; it also refers the reader back to the beginning
    of the paper where the phrase was first introduced. The
    repeated reference helps unify the paper.

The Gardners were impressed by Washoe's multi-sign sequences, seeing in them the beginnings of some grasp of grammar, but these findings have been disputed. In one frequently cited filmed sequence, Washoe's teacher placed a baby doll in a cup. Washoe signed "baby in baby in my drink," a series of signs that seemed to make grammatical sense. Terrace points out, however, that Washoe had previously been drilled in similar patterns and that the teacher had pointed to the objects (Terrace et al. 898).

Of all the apes, it is Patterson's Koko and Michael for whom the most is claimed, but even Patterson in her book The Education of Koko does not make large claims for her apes' grasp of grammar. Many of Michael and Koko's short sequences make sense, but whether one can conclude much from the longer sequences seems doubtful. For instance, when Michael was asked what "bird" meant, he signed the following: "Bird good cat chase eat red trouble cat eat bird." Patterson believes that Michael had seen a cat catch a bird and was trying to describe the scene (Patterson and Linden 173). It is certainly possible but,

29. *Heavy reliance on one source.* Shaw relies heavily on Terrace throughout the paper; this is acceptable because Terrace is one of the foremost authorities on the subject and also because Shaw uses many other sources as well. A thesis that can be supported by only one main source should not be pursued.

as Patterson herself would probably admit, hardly
proved.

The best summation of the current state of ape
language studies comes from biologist Robert Seyfarth,   30
who writes that the line separating humans from other
animals "remains hazily drawn, somewhere between the
word and the sentence" (18). Apes have acquired large   31
vocabularies and they have used their "words" spontaneously and creatively. But it is still to be discovered if they can create a complex sentence with
their vocabularies to say, for instance, "If I refuse
to eat this green banana, will I still be allowed to
watch the Bonzo rerun on television?"

30. *Revision.* The first draft of the paper included a long discussion of Seyfarth's studies of monkeys in the wild. Shaw wisely eliminated this discussion because it introduced a new kind of evidence (all the other examples involve apes learning language from human beings).
31. *Conclusion.* Shaw's conclusion summarizes the whole argument and satisfies the reader's desire to know where she stands on the issue of the apes' ability to learn language. Here the evocative phrase used for the title is seen in context; this phrase provides a memorable statement of Shaw's final position.

Notes      32

[1] The most famous example of cueing involves a      33
horse named Clever Hans whose owner sincerely thought
the horse could solve mathematical problems, tapping
out the answers with his foot. It was demonstrated
that the horse was in fact responding to the involun-
tary jerks of the owner's head at the point when the
correct number of taps had been reached.

[2] For a description of the Gardners' double-blind      34
experiments, see Thomas A. Sebeok and Jean Umiker-
Sebeok, "Performing Animals: Secrets of the Trade,"
Psychology Today Nov. 1979: 78-91.

32. *Format of endnotes.* Begin the endnotes on a separate page. Type the heading *Notes* one inch from the top of the page and center it between the left and right margins. Begin the notes two spaces below the heading. Double-space them and indent the first line of each note five spaces from the left margin. The number of the note (corresponding to the number used in the text) should be raised slightly above the note and separated from it by one space. The number should not be followed by a period or enclosed in parentheses.

33. *Use of endnotes.* The first note includes important information that Shaw wanted to make available to the reader but that does not belong in the text. Notice how Shaw relies on the strategy she has used successfully throughout the paper: She explains cueing by offering an example.

34. *Format of reference to a work.* Unlike in the list of works cited, the authors' names are in normal order.

Works Cited    35

Crail, Ted. <u>Apetalk and Whalespeak</u>. Los Angeles:    36
    Tarcher, 1981.

Davis, Flora. <u>Eloquent Animals: A Study in Animal</u>
    <u>Communication</u>. New York: Coward, 1978.

Desmond, Adrian. <u>The Ape's Reflexion</u>. New York:
    Dial, 1979.

Gardner, R. Allen, and Beatrice T. Gardner. "Com-    37
    parative Psychology and Language Acquisition."    38
    <u>Annals of the New York Academy of Sciences</u> 309
    (1978): 37-76. Rpt. in <u>Speaking of Apes</u>. Ed.
    Thomas A. Sebeok and Jean Umiker-Sebeok. New
    York: Plenum, 1980.

Patterson, Francine, and Eugene Linden. <u>The Educa-</u>
    <u>tion of Koko</u>. New York: Holt, 1981.

Seyfarth, Robert M. "Talking with Monkeys and Great
    Apes." <u>International Wildlife</u> Mar.-Apr. 1982:
    13-18.

Terrace, H. S. <u>Nim</u>. New York: Knopf, 1979.

Terrace, H. S., et al. "Can an Ape Create a    39
    Sentence?" <u>Science</u> 206 (1979): 891-902.    40

35. *Format of the list of works cited.* Begin the list of works cited on a separate page. Type the heading *Works Cited* one inch from the top of the page, centered between the left and right margins and followed by two lines of space. Double-space the entries, with the first line of each entry beginning at the left margin; indent subsequent lines in an entry five spaces from the left margin. Begin each entry with the author's name (or names), giving the first author's name in inverted order and any additional names in normal order. Alphabetize the entire list. Anonymous works should be alphabetized by the title of the work.

36. *Work by a single author.*

37. *Work by two or three authors.* For a work with two or three authors, invert the name of the first author and give subsequent authors' names in normal order.

38. *Work reprinted in another collection.*

39. *Work by more than three authors.* Only the first author's name is included, in inverted form, followed by "et al." If Terrace alone had written both the previous book and this one, this second entry would begin with three hyphens in place of the author's name, followed by a period. But because Terrace has coauthors for the second book, his name must be given again in full.

40. *Article in a journal with continuous pagination throughout the annual volume.*

# 52

---

## Logic in argumentative essays

---

Nearly all writing involves persuasion. When you produce an essay or term paper for a class or a memo, business letter, research report, or magazine article for a job, part of your task is persuading readers to agree with your premises and conclusions. Choosing your evidence carefully is essential. Equally important is knowing how to organize and present data so that readers can follow your reasoning and accept your interpretation of the evidence. An effective argument depends not only on facts but on logic.

How can you use logic to help you make your case? First, you should be familiar with the two main methods of argument: inductive and deductive reasoning. Second, you should be aware of the most common mistakes writers make in moving from data or assumptions to a conclusion; these are known as the *logical fallacies.*

**52a**　Be aware of the differences between inductive and deductive reasoning.

Inductive reasoning consists of gathering evidence and then interpreting it. When you reason inductively, you move from the specific (an array of facts) to the general (a conclusion drawn from those facts).

> According to our survey, 434 of the 500 households questioned say they would like to subscribe to cable television. Assuming our sample is representative, most households in our city would subscribe if cable were available.

Inductive reasoning underlies most positions we hold and most decisions we make. If a friend tells you that Anne Tyler is her favorite novelist, the implication is that she has read novels by many different writers, including Tyler, and has drawn her general conclusion from these specific experiences. When you are looking for a new stereo system, your first step is to gather data: You might ask your friends how they like their stereos or look up recent articles comparing different systems or listen to demonstration models in a showroom. From these data you might conclude that Company *X* makes reliable stereos, with good sound, at a reasonable price.

The validity of a conclusion reached by inductive reasoning depends on how accurately the specific cases tested represent the population being generalized about. If a salesperson tells you that the Soundmaster TX3 is the best stereo system in your price range, you would want to know how many other brands he or she is familiar with before you accept the conclusion. Although it would be impractical to listen to every stereo system manufactured, you probably would try to collect information on at least four or five different makes and models before you decide which one to buy.

Similarly, when you use inductive reasoning in your writing, be sure the evidence you present is sufficient to justify your conclusion. You should draw your data from a variety of sources — direct observation, personal experience, interviews, magazine articles, books, government documents, collaborative reports, and so on. Your sources, in turn, should collectively have considered a range of specific cases broad enough to represent the whole population to which your conclusion applies.

Deductive reasoning begins with an observation or assumption, brings in a fact relevant to the assumption, and draws a conclusion. When you reason deductively, you move from the general to the specific.

Most teenagers rate MTV as their favorite cable television channel. Our city has a high proportion of teenage residents. Therefore many people in our city would watch MTV if it were available.

Deductive reasoning is often known as *if . . . then* thinking. The three steps in this logical strategy can often be expressed as a *syllogism:*

1. Anything that increases radiation in the environment is dangerous to public health. [major premise]
2. Nuclear reactors increase radiation in the environment. [minor premise]
3. Nuclear reactors are dangerous to public health. [conclusion]

The major premise of a syllogism is usually a generalization, often one arrived at inductively. The minor premise is often a specific fact. The conclusion follows from applying the general rule to the specific case.

Many deductive arguments do not state one of the premises but rather leave the reader to infer it. In the example above, the conclusion would still sound plausible without the major premise: *Nuclear reactors increase radiation in the environment; therefore, they are dangerous to public health.* A careful reader, however, will see the missing part and question the whole argument if this premise is debatable.

In writing, both inductive and deductive reasoning are essential. Inductive reasoning is usually a larger-scale process, valuable for pulling together evidence on which the writer can base the main premises of his or her argument. Deductive reasoning then can be used to fine-tune these premises into a conclusion.

## 52b Avoid logical fallacies.

When you draw conclusions inductively from data or deductively from premises, your reasoning as well as your conclusions should be persuasive to your audience. Keep in mind as you write that your goal is to win over neutral or skeptical readers, not just to impress those who already agree with you.

Faulty reasoning is one of the most common weaknesses in writing. An error in logic — known as a *logical fallacy* — creates a weak spot in an argument that critics can use to discredit the writer's position. Always check your writing carefully to guard against logical fallacies.

### Hasty generalization

When you make a statement based on data, be sure your conclusion is justified by the information you have presented. A hasty generalization is a conclusion based on insufficient evidence or unrepresentative evidence.

> Drug-related fatalities in the city of Metropolis have doubled in the past three years. More Americans than ever before are dying from drug abuse.

Data from one city do not justify a conclusion about the whole United States.

Many hasty generalizations contain words like *all, every, always,* and *never,* when *most, many, usually,* or *seldom* would be more accurate. Go over your writing carefully for such blanket statements and make sure that you have enough data to verify your position or that you qualify the statement.

### Oversimplification

Oversimplification, like hasty generalization, is a form of jumping to conclusions.

> Senator Quagmire voted against building a nuclear power plant in this area and in favor of raising the gasoline tax. If he is reelected, look forward to higher utility rates.

The conclusion is based on the assumptions that Senator Quagmire favors policies that would cause utility rates to go up and that he has enough clout to push these policies through Congress.

### Either . . . or fallacy

The *either . . . or* fallacy consists of the suggestion that only two alternatives exist when in fact there are more. This logical error may result from a conclusion based on insufficient data or from faulty deductive reasoning.

> You can't get a decent job after college unless you know how to operate a computer.

Many occupations do not require knowledge of computers.

### Non sequitur

A *non sequitur* is a conclusion that does not follow logically from preceding statements.

> Several large corporations and government agencies use lie-detector tests in screening job applicants. Our admissions department should make lie-detector tests part of students' application process.

Data on the use of lie-detector tests by other organizations have no bearing on the value of those tests for a college admissions department.

### Post hoc

Careless thinkers often assume that because one event follows another, the first is the cause of the second. This common fallacy is known as *post hoc*, from the Latin *post hoc, ergo propter hoc*, meaning "after this, therefore because of this." Like a non sequitur, it is a leap to an unjustified conclusion.

> Governor Smoot is committed to civil rights. Since he took office, employment among minorities in Metropolis alone has increased by seven percent.

Unless the writer can show that Governor Smoot's policies are responsible for this increase, the reader is unlikely to agree that the governor increased employment.

### False analogy

Analogies can be helpful for pointing out similarities between two situations. No two situations, however, are identical. If you imply that *A* will turn out like *B* because *A* has some of the same characteristics as *B*, your readers are likely to look immediately for the dissimilarities you have ignored. This fallacy is often called false analogy.

> If we can put humans on the moon, why can't we find a cure for the common cold?

The space program faces different challenges and has different sources of support than do medical researchers.

### Circular reasoning and begging the question

Suppose you went to see a doctor about a rash you had suddenly developed. "I have a rash," you say to the doctor. "What's the problem?" The doctor answers, "You have allergitis." You ask, "What's that?" The doctor answers, "It's a rash." This is an example of circular reasoning: No real information has been introduced; by a trick of semantics you have wound up back where you started.

Circular reasoning is also known as begging the question because it involves ducking the issue instead of arguing it with evidence and logic. The writer may state a premise as if it were already proved, or, as in the preceding example, use the definition of a term as if it brought new information into the argument.

> Faculty and administrators should not be permitted to come to student council meetings because student council meetings should be for students only.

The writer has given no reason for this position, only a repetition of the premise.

> Women who have abortions should be prosecuted the same as any other murderers.

The writer has ducked the central issue — is abortion murder? — by stating it as if it were true by definition.

### Appeals to emotions

Many of the arguments we see in the media strive to win our sympathy rather than our intelligent agreement. A TV commercial suggesting that you will be thin, tan, and sexy if you drink a certain diet beverage is making a pitch to emotions. So is a political speech that recommends electing John D'Eau because he is a devoted husband and father who fought for our nation in World War II. Addressing an audience's ideals, hopes, or fears instead of their capacity to think can be a successful tactic, but its impact is usually limited. Emotional appeals may fade from mind unless they are repeated, and they are often easy for a well-prepared opponent to refute. The writer who supports his or her argument with sound evidence has a better chance of winning the reader's long-lasting agreement.

One of the most common types of emotional appeal is the argument *ad hominem,* or "to the man," in which the person making an argument, rather than the argument itself, is attacked or defended.

> The Republican members of the panel made a strong case for their tax package. They had obviously rehearsed their presentation and spoke with much more assurance than their Democratic opponents, who kept dropping their note cards and glancing at the time clock.

The strength of the case for the tax package depends on what was said, not how it was said.

In checking your own and other people's writing for errors of logic, you will find that logical fallacies are frequently not so clear-cut that a casual reader can spot them immediately. Often they show up in combination. To recognize such fallacies in your own writing takes discipline, but it can be done if you train yourself to become a skeptical and demanding reader—the kind of person who measures all claims against the evidence.

## EXERCISE 52–1

Identify the logical fallacy or fallacies in the following statements.

a. It's never wise to buy the first used car you look at because finding a good used car takes time.

b. Soliciting money to save whales and baby seals is irresponsible when thousands of human beings can't afford food and shelter.

c. The board of selectmen should not have issued a permit for the jazz festival. Attracting so many outsiders into town will mean traffic jams, a strain on water and sewage facilities, and destruction of property.

d. It used to be possible to feed a family of four on $30 a week before the oil crisis of the mid-1970s drove up consumer prices.

e. As was agreed by all four faculty members I interviewed, tenure is one of the foremost issues at colleges and universities today.

1. If the president had learned the lesson of Vietnam, he would realize that sending U.S. troops into a foreign country can only end in disaster.

2. Although Ms. Bell's observations about Constable's iconography are impressive, one wonders if a critic born and educated in Australia can do full justice to the painter's intimacy with the English landscape.

3. If you're not part of the solution, you're part of the problem.

4. Those who oppose spraying paraquat on marijuana plants because it is hazardous to the health of anyone who smokes the poisoned marijuana should remember that marijuana wouldn't be illegal if it weren't hazardous to health.

5. It's no wonder today's elementary school children are hooked on video games: Their parents grew up glued to TV screens.

6. Governor Leroy should realize that if he carries out his plan to spend half a million dollars on a new governor's mansion, the taxpayers of this state will rise in full-scale revolt.

7. Most Americans never heard of blues musician Robert Johnson until the Rolling Stones recorded his song "Love in Vain" or of Sonny Boy Williamson until the Who recorded "Eyesight to the Blind." Can't we appreciate our own music unless the British introduce it to us?

8. If professional sports teams didn't pay athletes such high salaries, we wouldn't have so many kids breaking their legs at hockey and basketball camps.

9. The Russians have teams of scientific researchers studying parapsychological phenomena such as ESP. Our secretary of defense should see how foolish it is for the Pentagon to invest billions of dollars in nuclear weapons and leave America's vast parapsychological resources untapped.

10. Michael Jackson's impact on popular music is comparable to that of other major figures in the past — Buddy Holly, the Beatles, Bob Dylan — in that he both epitomizes the ideals of a particular period and pushes the musical scene in new directions. Jackson is a better musician, however, because he doesn't smoke, drink, or use drugs.

# 53

## Business letters and résumés

## 53a Business letters

In writing a business letter be direct, clear, and courteous, but do not hesitate to be firm if the situation calls for it. State your purpose or request at the beginning of the letter and include only pertinent information in the body. Follow conventions of form and usage, and avoid spelling errors.

Business letters usually follow one of three patterns: full block, block, and semiblock. In full block form, letterhead stationery, giving the return address of the writer (or of the writer's company), is used. Every element of the letter (including date, inside address, salutation, body, close, and signature) is typed flush with the left margin. In block form, the return address of the writer, the close, and the signature are moved to the right. Paragraphs are not indented but begin flush with the left margin. In semiblock form, considered the least formal of the three patterns, the return address, close, and signature are moved to the right, and the beginning of each paragraph is indented five spaces from the left margin.

Type business letters on letterhead stationery or on unlined paper that is at least $5\frac{1}{2}'' \times 8\frac{1}{2}''$. Type on only one side of the paper, single-spacing the body of the letter and double-spacing between paragraphs. The sample letter on the next page, in block form, illustrates the proper placement of each part of a business letter. The return address is followed by the date. (Note that the writer's name is not part of this heading.) The inside address includes the full name, title, and complete address of the person to whom the letter is written. (This information is repeated as the address on the envelope.) The inside address is typed flush left, a few lines below the return address heading. The salutation, or greeting, is typed two lines below the inside address. A colon follows the salutation, and the body of the letter begins two lines below the greeting.

In the salutation use *Ms.* if you are writing to a woman whose title or marital status you do not know or if you are writing to a woman who prefers this form of address. If you are not writing to a particular person, you can use the salutation *Dear Sir or Madam* or you can address the company itself—*Dear Solar Technology.*

In block form the close is lined up with the return address and typed two lines below the end of the letter. Common closes are *Yours truly, Very truly yours,* or *Sincerely.* (Note that only

Return
address { 293 Powderhouse Road
Somerville, MA   02143
March 12, 1985

Dr. Philip Brubaker
Director
Fairview School — Inside
937 Beech Street      address
Newton, MA   02165

Dr. Brubaker: — Salutation

I am applying for the summer internship you listed
with the Career Guidance Office at Tufts University.
I am a sophomore in the Early Childhood Education
program at Tufts.  Your job profile describing the
evaluation of courses as the heart of the job appealed
to me because I plan to make curriculum development
my major area of concentration.

As the enclosed résumé shows, I have taken upper-
level courses in child psychology and learning
disabilities, and I have had a great deal of field
experience working with young children.  For two        Body
years I served as a volunteer play supervisor with
the Somerville Department of Parks and Recreation.
My responsibilities were increased this past summer
when I was hired as playground coordinator.

In an independent study course, I developed an
experimental curriculum for an open classroom.  I
would be happy to send you a copy.  I am available
for an interview at almost any time and can be
reached at 628-7229.

I look forward to hearing from you.

Close — Sincerely,

*Janet Goodman*
Signature —
Janet Goodman

Enc.

the first word of the close is capitalized.) The name of the writer is typed four lines below the close, leaving room for the written signature between the close and the typed name. The name of the writer should not be prefaced by a title or followed by an abbreviation for a title or position. This information can be included in a separate line under the typed name (for example, *Director* or *Sales Manager*).

Other information can be included below the signature and flush with the left margin (for example: *Enc.*, indicating that something is enclosed with the letter; *cc: Mr. Theodore Jones*, indicating that a copy of the letter is being sent to Mr. Jones, a third party; or *JEF:njl*, indicating that JEF [the writer's initials] wrote the letter and njl typed it).

The name and return address of the writer is typed in the upper left-hand corner of the envelope. The addressee's name, title, and complete address are typed just right of the center of the envelope. The letter (which should be about the same width as the envelope) is folded in thirds.

## **53b** Résumés

An effective résumé presents relevant information in a clear and concise form. Every résumé should include name, address, and telephone number; a history of education and employment; a list of special interests or related activities; and information about how to obtain references. You may also include personal information such as date of birth or marital status, but such information is not necessary. Some résumés name the specific position desired. If you are applying for a number of different positions, you may find it more useful to name a broader employment goal.

In the education history, begin with the institution you are currently attending and work backward to your high school, listing degrees and dates of attendance. If you have won special honors, include them. In the employment history, again

RÉSUMÉ

Janet Goodman
293 Powderhouse Boulevard
Somerville, MA   02143
(617) 628-7229

Position Desired    Assistant kindergarten teacher

Education
1983 to present     Tufts University, Medford, MA. B.A.
                    in Early Childhood Education
                    expected May 1987.  Minor in
                    Psychology

1979-1983           Stoughton High School, Stoughton, MA

Experience
May-Sept. 1984      Playground Coordinator, Somerville
                    Parks Program, Somerville, MA.  Co-
                    ordinated daily activities at three
                    parks; supervised twelve volunteers;
                    evaluated programs.

Summer 1982, 1983   Volunteer play supervisor, Somer-
                    ville, MA.  Managed activities of
                    twenty children at a city park.

Related Interests   Volunteer tutoring in the Boston
and Activities      public schools; basketball; chil-
                    dren's theater.

References          Academic references available from
                    the Career Guidance Office at Tufts
                    University, Medford, MA   02155

                    Employment   Mr. Frank Simone
                    Reference    Somerville Parks Program
                                 497 Elm Street
                                 Somerville, MA   02144

                    Personal     Ms. Elizabeth Marks
                    Reference    271 Bigelow Street
                                 Cambridge, MA   02139

list your most recent job first and then work backward. Give the dates of employment and the company name and address. You can also list your supervisors. Describe your responsibilities, highlighting those tasks or skills related to the position you are seeking. In listing special interests, concentrate on those related to your employment goal. Instead of listing the names and addresses of references, you can state that references are available on request.

In a résumé, present yourself in the best possible light, but do not distort any of the facts about your experience or qualifications. Select details wisely and your résumé will be a valuable tool.

When you send your résumé, you should include a letter that tells what position you seek and where you learned about it. The letter should also summarize your education and past experience, relating them to the job you are applying for. You may want to highlight a specific qualification and refer the reader to your résumé for more information. End the letter with a suggestion for a meeting, and tell your prospective employer when you will be available.

(*Continued from page iv.*)

Barnaby Conrad III, from " 'Train of Kings, the King of Trains' Is Back on Track," *Smithsonian*, December 1983. Reprinted by permission of *Smithsonian*.

Earl Conrad, from *Harriet Tubman.* By permission of Paul S. Eriksson, Publisher.

James Crockett et al., from *The Time-Life Encyclopedia of Gardening.* © 1977 Time-Life Books Inc. Reprinted by permission of Time-Life Books Inc.

Thalassa Cruso, from *Making Things Grow Outdoors.* Copyright © 1971 by Thalassa Cruso. Reprinted by permission of Alfred A. Knopf, Inc.

Joan Didion, from "On Self-Respect," *Slouching Towards Bethlehem.* Copyright © 1961, 1968 by Joan Didion. Reprinted by permission of Farrar, Straus and Giroux, Inc.

Stephen Jay Gould, from "Were Dinosaurs Dumb?" *The Panda's Thumb, More Reflections in Natural History.* Copyright © 1980 by Stephen Jay Gould. Reprinted by permission of W. W. Norton & Company, Inc.

Hillary Hauser, from "Exploring a Sunken Realm in Australia," *National Geographic*, January 1984. Reprinted by permission of the National Geographic Society.

Richard Hofstadter, from *America at 1750: A Social Portrait.* Copyright © 1971 by Beatrice K. Hofstadter, executrix of the estate of Richard Hofstadter. Reprinted by permission of Alfred A. Knopf, Inc.

Margaret Mead, from "New Superstitions for Old," *A Way of Seeing.* Reprinted by permission of William Morrow & Company, Inc.

Saul K. Padover, from *Jefferson.* Copyright 1942, 1970 by Saul K. Padover. Reprinted by permission of Harcourt Brace Jovanovich, Inc.

*Readers Guide to Periodical Literature*, March 1982–February 1983, from entries under "Animal Communications." Copyright © 1982, 1983 by The H. W. Wilson Company. Material reproduced by permission of the publisher.

Arthur M. Schlesinger, Jr., from *The Age of Roosevelt: The Crisis of the Old Order.* Copyright © 1957 by Arthur M. Schlesinger, Jr. Reprinted by permission of Houghton Mifflin Company.

Lewis Thomas, from "On Societies as Organisms," *The Lives of a Cell.* Copyright © 1974 by Lewis Thomas. Originally appeared in *New England Journal of Medicine.* Reprinted by permission of Viking Penguin Inc.

James Thurber, from "University Days," *My Life and Hard Times.* Copyright © 1933, 1961 by James Thurber. Published by Harper & Row, Publishers, Inc. Reprinted by permission.

Olivia Vlahos, from *Human Beginnings.* Published by Viking Penguin Inc. Reprinted by permission of the author.

# Glossary of Usage

This glossary addresses an assortment of specific problems that do not fit neatly under more general headings. If an item is not listed here, consult the index. For irregular verbs (such as *sing, sang, sung*), see 30. For idiomatic use of prepositions, see section 18d.

**a, an**   Use *an* before a vowel sound, *a* before a consonant sound: *an apple, a peach*. Problems sometimes arise with words beginning with *h*. If the *h* is silent, the word begins with a vowel sound, so use *an: an hour, an heir, an honest senator, an honorable deed*. If the *h* is pronounced, the word begins with a consonant sound, so use *a: a hospital, a hymn, a historian, a hotel*.

**accept, except**   *Accept* is a verb meaning "to receive." *Except* is usually a preposition meaning "excluding." *I will accept all of the packages except that one. Except* is also a verb meaning "to exclude." *Please except that item from the list.*

**advice, advise**   *Advice* is a noun, *advise* a verb: *We advise you to follow John's advice.*

**affect, effect**   *Affect* is usually a verb meaning "influence." *Effect* is usually a noun meaning "result." *The drug did not affect the disease, and it had several adverse side effects. Effect* can also be a verb meaning "bring about": *Only the president can effect such a dramatic change.*

**aggravate**   *Aggravate* means "make worse or more troublesome": *Overgrazing aggravated the soil erosion.* In formal writing, avoid the colloquial use of *aggravate* to mean "annoy or irritate": *Her babbling annoyed* (not *aggravated*) *me.*

**agree to, agree with**   *Agree to* means "give consent." *Agree with* means "be in accord" or "come to an understanding": *He agrees with me about the need for change, but he won't agree to my plan.*

**ain't**   *Ain't* is nonstandard and should be avoided in formal English. Use *am not, are not (aren't),* or *is not (isn't): I am not* (not *ain't*) *going home for spring break.*

**all ready, already**   *All ready* means "completely prepared." *Already* means "previously." *Susan was all ready for the concert, but her friends had already left.*

**all right**   *All right* is always written as two words. *Alright* is nonstandard.

**all together, altogether**   *All together* means "everyone gathered." *Altogether* means "entirely." *We were not altogether certain that we could bring the family all together for the reunion.*

**allusion, illusion**   An *allusion* is an indirect reference. An *illusion* is a misconception or false impression. *Did you catch my allusion to Shakespeare? Mirrors give the room an illusion of depth.*

**a lot**   *A lot* is two words. Do not write *alot. We have had a lot of rain this spring.*

**A.M., P.M., a.m., p.m.**   Use these abbreviations with numerals: *6 P.M., 11 a.m.* Do not substitute them for the words *morning* or *evening: I worked until late in the evening* (not *p.m.*) *yesterday.*

**among, between**   Ordinarily, use *among* with three or more entities, *between* with two: *The prize was divided among several contestants. You have a choice between carrots and beans.*

**amount, number**   Use *amount* with quantities that cannot be counted; use *number* with those that can: *This recipe calls for a large amount of sugar. We have a large number of toads in our garden.*

**an**   See *a, an.*

**and etc.**   *Et cetera (etc.)* means "and so forth"; therefore, *and etc.* is redundant. See also *etc.*

**anymore**   Reserve *anymore* for negative contexts, where it means "any longer." *Moviegoers are rarely shocked anymore by profanity.* Do not use *anymore* in positive contexts. Use *now* or *nowadays* instead. *"Interest rates are so high nowadays* (not *anymore*) *that few people can afford to buy homes.*

**anyone, any one**   *Anyone,* an indefinite pronoun, means "any person at all." *Any one,* a pronoun preceded by the adjective *any,* refers to a particular person or thing in a group. *Anyone from Chicago may choose any one of the games on display.*

**anyplace**   *Anyplace* is informal for *anywhere.*

**anyways, anywheres**   *Anyways* and *anywheres* are nonstandard for *anyway* and *anywhere* and should be avoided in formal writing.

**as**   *As* is sometimes used to mean "because." But do not use it if there is any chance of ambiguity: *We canceled the picnic because* (not *as*) *it began raining.* The *as* here could mean "because" or "when."

**as,** like   See *like, as.*

**awful**   The adjective *awful* means "commanding awe." Colloquially it is used to mean "terrible" or "bad." The adverb *awfully* is sometimes used in conversation as an intensifier meaning "very": "I was *very* (not *awfully*) upset last night." In formal writing, avoid these colloquial uses.

**awhile, a while**   *Awhile* is an adverb; it can modify a verb, but it cannot be the object of a preposition such as *for.* The two-word form *a while* is a noun preceded by an article and therefore can be the object of a preposition. *Stay awhile. Stay for a while.*

**bad, badly**   *Bad* is an adjective, *badly* an adverb. (See 26.) *They felt bad about being late and ruining the surprise. Her arm hurt badly after she slid head-first into second base.*

**being as, being that**   *Being as* and *being that* are nonstandard expressions. Write *because* or *since* instead. *Because* (not *being as*) *I slept late, I had to skip breakfast.*

**beside, besides**   *Beside* is a preposition meaning "at the side of" or "next to." *Annie Oakley slept with her gun beside her bed. Besides* is a preposition meaning "except" or "in addition to." *No one besides Terrie can have that ice cream. Besides* is also an adverb meaning "in addition." *I'm not hungry; besides, I don't like ice cream.*

**between**   See *among, between.*

**bring, take**   Use *bring* when an object is being transported toward you, *take* when it is being moved away: *Please bring me a glass of water. Please take these flowers to Mr. Scott.*

**burst, bursted; bust, busted**   *Burst* is an irregular verb meaning "come open or fly apart suddenly or violently." The past-tense form *bursted* is nonstandard. *Bust* and *busted* are slang for *burst* and, along with *bursted,* should not be used in formal writing.

**can, may** The distinction between *can* and *may* is fading, but many careful writers still observe it in formal writing. *Can* is traditionally reserved for ability, *may* for permission. *Can you ski down the advanced slope without falling? May I help you?*

**capital, capitol** *Capital* refers to a city, *capitol* to a building where lawmakers meet. *Capital* also refers to wealth or resources. *The capitol has undergone extensive renovations. The residents of the state capital protested the development plans.*

**center around** *Center on* and *center in* are considered more logical than *center around*. *His talk centered on the global buildup of arms in the last five years.*

**climactic, climatic** *Climactic* is derived from *climax*, the point of greatest intensity in a series or progression of events. *Climatic* is derived from *climate* and refers to meteorological conditions. *The climactic period in the dinosaurs' reign was reached just before severe climatic conditions brought on an ice age.*

**compare to, compare with** *Compare to* means "represent as similar": *She compared him to a wild stallion. Compare with* means "examine the ways in which two things are similar:" *The study compared the language ability of apes with that of dolphins.*

**complement, compliment** *Complement* is a verb meaning "go with or complete." *Compliment* as a verb means "make a flattering remark"; as a noun it means "flattering remark." *Her skill at rushing the net complements his skill at volleying. Mother's flower arrangements receive many compliments.*

**conscience, conscious** *Conscience* is a noun meaning "moral principles." *Conscious* is an adjective meaning "aware or alert": *Let your conscience be your guide. Were you conscious of his love for you?*

**continual, continuous** *Continual* means "repeated regularly and frequently." *She grew weary of the continual telephone calls. Continuous* means "extended or prolonged without interruption." *The broken siren made a continuous wail.*

**could care less** *Could care less* is a nonstandard expression. Write *couldn't care less* instead. *He couldn't* (not *could*) *care less about his psychology final.*

**could of** *Of* is not a verb. Write *could have. We could* have (not *could of*) *had steak for dinner if we had remembered to take it out of the freezer.*

**criteria** *Criteria* is the plural of *criterion*, which means "a standard, rule, or test on which a judgment or decision can be based." *The only criterion for the scholarship is ability.*

**data** *Data* is the plural of *datum*, which means "a fact or proposition used to draw a conclusion." *The new data suggest* (not *suggests*) *that our theory is correct.* The singular form *datum* is rarely used.

**deal** Deal is a colloquial expression for "bargain," "business transaction," or "agreement": *We made a deal.* Avoid such colloquial use in formal writing.

**different from, different than** Ordinarily, write *different from: Your sense of style is different from Jim's.* However, *different than* is acceptable to avoid an awkward construction: *Please let me know if your plans are different than* (to avoid *from what*) *they were six weeks ago.*

**differ from, differ with** *Differ from* means "be unlike"; *differ with* means "disagree." *She differed with me about the wording of the agreement. My approach to the problem differed from hers.*

**disinterested, uninterested** *Disinterested* means "impartial, free from a selfish interest"; *uninterested* means "not interested." *She felt I was a disinterested observer. He was uninterested in anyone's opinion but his own.*

**don't** *Don't* is the contraction for *do not: I don't want any. Don't* should not be used as the contraction for *does not*, which is *doesn't. He doesn't* (not *don't*) *want any.* See also 28c.

**double negative** See 31e.

**due to** *Due to* should not be used as a preposition meaning "because of." *The trip was canceled because of* (not *due to*) *lack of interest. Due to* is acceptable as a subject complement and usually follows a form of the verb *be: His success was due to hard work.*

**effect** See *affect, effect.*

**enthused** Many people object to the use of *enthused* as an adjective. Use *enthusiastic* instead. *The children were enthusiastic* (not *enthused*) *about going to the circus.*

**-ess** Many people find the *-ess* suffix demeaning. Write *poet*, not *poetess; Jew*, not *Jewess; author*, not *authoress.*

**etc.** Avoid ending a list with *etc.* It is more emphatic to end with an example, and in most contexts readers will understand that the list is not exhaustive. When you don't wish to end with an example, *and so on* is more graceful than *etc.*

**everyone, every one** *Everyone* is an indefinite pronoun. *Every one*, a pronoun preceded by the adjective *every*, means "each individual or thing in a particular group." *Every one* is usually followed by *of*. *Everyone wanted to go. Every one of the missing books was found.*

**exam** *Exam* is informal for *examination*.

**except** See *accept, except*.

**expect** Avoid the colloquial use of *expect* to mean "believe, think, or suppose." *I think* (not *expect*) *it will rain tonight*.

**farther, further** *Farther* is used to describe distances: *Chicago is farther from Miami than I thought*. *Further* is used to suggest quantity or degree: *You extended the curfew further than you should have*.

**finalize** *Finalize* is jargon for "make final or complete," Avoid using it in formal writing.

**firstly** *Firstly* sounds pretentious, and it leads to the ungainly series *firstly, secondly, thirdly, fourthly*, and so on. Write *first, second, third*, and so on instead.

**flunk** *Flunk* is colloquial for *fail* and should be avoided in formal writing.

**folks** *Folks* is an informal expression for "parents" or "relatives" or for "people" in general. Use a more formal expression instead.

**further** See *farther, further*.

**get** *Get* has many colloquial uses. Avoid using *get* with the following meanings: "evoke an emotional response" (*That music always gets to me*); "annoy" (*After a while his sulking got to me*); "take revenge on" (*I got back at him by leaving the room*); "become" (*He got sick*); "start or begin" (*Let's get going*). Avoid using *have got to* in place of *must: I must* (not *have got to*) *finish this paper tonight*.

**good, well** *Good* is an adjective, *well* an adverb. See 26. *He hasn't felt good about his game since he sprained his wrist last season. She performed well on the uneven parallel bars*.

**hardly** Avoid expressions such as *can't hardly* and *not hardly*, which are considered double negatives. *I can* (not *can't*) *hardly describe my elation at getting the job*.

**has got, have got** *Got* is unnecessary and awkward in such constructions. It should be dropped. *We have* (not *have got*) *three days to prepare for the opening.*

**he** At one time it was acceptable to use *he* to mean "he or she." Today such usage offends many readers. See 22a for alternative constructions.

**hisself** *Hisself* is nonstandard. Use *himself.*

**hopefully** *Hopefully* means "in a hopeful manner": *We looked hopefully to the future.* Do not use *hopefully* in constructions such as the following: *Hopefully, your daughter will recover soon.* Tell readers who is doing the hoping: *I hope that your daughter will recover soon.*

**illusion** See *allusion, illusion.*

**imply, infer** *Imply* means "suggest or state indirectly"; *infer* means "draw a conclusion." *John implied that he knew all about computers, but the interviewer inferred that John was inexperienced.*

**in, into** *In* indicates location or condition; *into* indicates movement or a change in condition. *They found the lost letters in a box after moving into the house.* The colloquial use of *into* to mean "interested in" should be avoided. *I'm interested in* (not *into*) *mountain bikes.*

**in regards to** *In regards to* confuses two different phrases: *in regard to* and *as regards.* Use one or the other: *In regard to* (or *as regards*) *the contract, ignore the first clause.*

**irregardless** *Irregardless* is nonstandard. Use *regardless.*

**is when, is where** These mixed constructions are often incorrectly used in definitions: *A run-off election is a second election held to break a tie.* Not: *A run-off election is when a second election is held to break a tie.*

**its, it's** *Its* is a possessive pronoun; *it's* is a contracted form of *it is.* See 36c, 36e. *The dog licked its wound whenever its owner walked into the room. It's a perfect day to walk the twenty-mile trail.*

**kind(s)** *Kind* is a singular and should be treated as such throughout constructions in which it occurs. Don't write *These kind of chairs are rare.* Write instead *This kind of chair is rare. Kinds* is plural and should be used only when you mean more than one kind: *These kinds of chairs are rare.*

**kind of, sort of**   Avoid using *kind of* or *sort of* to mean "somewhat": *The movie was kind of boring.* Do not put *a* after either phrase: *That kind of* (not *kind of a*) *salesclerk annoys me.*

**learn, teach**   *Learn* means "gain knowledge"; *teach* means "impart knowledge." *I must teach* (not *learn*) *my sister to read.*

**lie, lay**   *Lie* is an irregular verb meaning "recline or rest on a surface." Its principal parts are *lie, lay, lain. Lay* is an irregular verb meaning "put or place." Its principal parts are *lay, laid, laid.* See 30c. *She has lain in the sun all day. He laid the books on the table.*

**like, as**   *Like* is a preposition, not a subordinating conjunction. It is followed by only a noun or a noun phrase. *As* is a subordinating conjunction that introduces a subordinate clause. In casual speech you may say "She looks *like* she hasn't slept" or "You don't know her *like* I do." But in formal writing, use *as: She looks as if she hasn't slept. You don't know her as I do.* See prepositions and subordinating conjunctions, 47f, 47g, 49b.

**likely, liable**   *Likely* means "plausible, in the realm of credibility"; *liable* means "legally obligated": *You're likely* (not *liable*) *to trip if you don't tie your shoelaces.*

**loan**   Some readers object to the use of *loan* as a verb. Use *lend* instead: *Please lend* (not *loan*) *me five dollars.*

**loose, lose**   *Loose* is an adjective meaning "not securely fastened." *Lose* is a verb meaning "misplace" or "not win." *Did you lose your only loose pair of work pants?*

**lots, lots of**   *Lots* and *lots of* are colloquial substitutes for *many, much,* or *a lot.* Avoid using them in formal writing.

**mankind**   Avoid *mankind* whenever possible. It offends many readers, who perceive it as excluding women. Use *humanity, humans, the human race,* or *humankind* instead.

**may**   See *can, may.*

**maybe, may be**   *Maybe* is an adverb meaning "possibly." *May be* is a verb phrase. *Maybe the sun will shine tomorrow. Tomorrow may be a brighter day.*

**may of, might of**   *May of* and *might of* are nonstandard expressions for *may have* and *might have. We may have* (not *may of*) *had too many cookies.*

**most**   *Most* is colloquial when used to mean "almost": *Almost* (not *most*) *everyone went to the parade.*

**must of** See *may of.*

**myself** *Myself* is a reflexive or intensive pronoun. See 47b. Reflexive: *I cut myself.* Intensive: *I will drive you myself.* Do not use *myself* in place of *I* or *me: He gave the flowers to Melinda and me* (not *myself*).

**nowheres** *Nowheres* is nonstandard for "nowhere." Avoid it in formal writing.

**number** See *amount, number.*

**off of** *Off* is sufficient. Drop *of. The ball rolled off* (not *off of*) *the table.*

**OK, O.K., okay** All three spellings are acceptable, but in formal speech and writing avoid these colloquial expressions for consent or approval.

**percent, per cent, percentage** *Percent* (also spelled *per cent*) and *percentage* refer to numbers and actual statistics. *Percent* is always preceded by a number and should be spelled out in formal writing (do not use %). *The candidate won 80 percent of the primary vote.* When preceded by *the, percentage* is singular: *The percentage of engineering students was high.* When preceded by *a, percentage* is either singular or plural depending on the number of the noun in the prepositional phrase that follows. Plural noun: *A small percentage of workers want to quit.* Singular: *A small percentage of the work force wants to quit.*

**phenomena** *Phenomena* is the plural of *phenomenon,* which means "an occurrence or fact that is directly perceptible by the senses." *Strange phenomena occur at all hours of the night in that house, but last night's phenomenon was the strangest of all.*

**principal, principle** *Principal* is a noun meaning "the head of a school or organization"; it is also an adjective meaning "most important." *Principle* is a noun meaning "an accepted rule of action." *The principal expelled her for three principal reasons. We believe in the principle of equal justice for all.*

**quote, quotation** *Quote* is a verb; *quotation* is a noun. Avoid using *quote* as a shortened form of the noun. *Her quotations* (not *quotes*) *from Shakespeare intrigued us.*

**raise, rise** *Raise* is a transitive verb meaning "move or cause to move upward." It takes a direct object. *I raised the shades. Rise* is an intransitive verb meaning "go up." It does not take a direct object. *Heat rises.*

**real, really**   *Real* is an adjective; *really* is an adverb. *Real* is sometimes used informally as an adverb, but avoid it in formal writing. *She was really* (not *real*) *angry.*

**reason is because**   Use a *that* clause after *reason: The reason I'm late is that* (not *because*) *my car broke down.*

**respectfully, respectively**   *Respectfully* means "showing or marked by respect." *He respectfully submitted his opinion to the judge. Respectively* means "each in the order designated or mentioned." *John, Tom, and Larry were a butcher, a baker, and a lawyer, respectively.*

**sensual, sensuous**   *Sensual* means "gratifying the physical senses," especially those associated with sexual pleasure. *Sensuous* means "pleasing to the senses," especially those involved in the experience of art, music, and nature. *The sensuous music and balmy air led the dancers to more sensual movements.*

**set, sit**   *Set* is an irregular verb meaning "put" or "place." Its principal parts are *set, set, set. Sit* is an irregular verb meaning "be seated." Its principal parts are *sit, sat, sat. She set the dough in a warm corner of the kitchen. The cat sat in the warmest part of the room, directly over the furnace.*

**shall, will**   *Shall* was once used as the helping verb with *I* or *we:* I *shall,* we *shall,* you *will,* he/she/it *will,* they *will.* Today, however, *will* is generally accepted even when the subject is *I* or *we.* The word *shall* occurs primarily in polite questions (*Shall I find you a pillow?*) and in legalistic sentences suggesting duty or obligation (*The applicant shall file form 1080 by December 31*).

**should of**   *Of* is not a verb. Write *should have. They should have* (not *should of*) *been home an hour ago.*

**since**   Do not use *since* to mean *because* if there is any chance of ambiguity: *Since we won the game, we have been celebrating with a pitcher of beer. Since* here could mean "because" or "from the time that."

**sit**   See *set, sit.*

**sometime, some time, sometimes**   *Sometime* is an adverb meaning "at an indefinite or unstated time": *I'll see you sometime soon. Some time* is an adjective, *some,* modifying a noun, *time,* and is spelled as two words to mean "a period of time": *I haven't lived there for some time. Sometimes* is an adverb meaning "at times, now and then": *Sometimes I run into him at the library.*

**sure and** *Sure and* is a nonstandard expression. Write *sure to* instead. *We were all taught to be sure to* (not *and*) *look both ways before crossing a street.*

**take** See *bring, take.*

**than, then** *Than* is a conjunction used in comparisons; *then* is an adverb denoting time. *That pizza is more than I can eat. Tom laughed, and then we recognized him.*

**that, which** Many writers reserve *that* for restrictive clauses, *which* for nonrestrictive clauses. See 32e.

**theirselves** *Theirselves* is nonstandard. Write *themselves* instead. *The two people were able to push the Volkswagen out of the way themselves* (not *theirselves*).

**there, their, they're** *There* is an adverb specifying place or an expletive. Adverb: *Sylvia is lying there unconscious.* Expletive: *There are two plums left. Their* is a possessive pronoun: *Fred and Jane finally washed their car. They're* is a contraction of *they are: They're later than usual today.*

**this kind** See *kind(s).*

**to, too, two** *To* is a preposition; *too* is an adverb; *two* is a number. *Too many of your shots slice to the left, but the last two were right on the mark.*

**toward, towards** *Toward* and *towards* are generally interchangeable, although *toward* is preferred.

**try and** *Try and* is a nonstandard expression. Write *try to* instead. *The teacher asked us all to try to* (not *and*) *write an original haiku.*

**unique** Avoid expressions such as *most unique, more straight, less perfect, very round.* Something is either unique or it isn't. It is illogical to suggest degrees of uniqueness. See 26f.

**use, utilize** *Utilize* means "make use of." It often sounds pretentious; in most cases *use* is sufficient: *I used* (not *utilized*) *the best workers to get the job done fast.*

**use to, suppose to** *Use to* and *suppose to* are nonstandard expressions. Use *used to* and *supposed to* instead. See 29.

**wait for, wait on** *Wait for* means "be in readiness for" or "await." *Wait on* means "serve." *We're only waiting for* (not *waiting on*) *Ruth before we can leave.*

**ways** *Ways* is colloquial when used to mean "distance": *The city is a long way* (not *ways*) *from here.*

**where**   Do not use *where* in place of *that. I heard that* (not *where*) *the crime rate is increasing.*

**which**   See *that, which.*

**while**   Avoid using *while* ambiguously: *While Gloria lost money in the slot machine, Tom won it at roulette.* Here *while* could mean "although" or "at the same time that."

**who, which**   Use *who* to refer to people, *which* to refer to things: *She was the guard who* (not *which*) *told me which stairway to use.*

**who's, whose**   *Who's* is a contraction of *who is; whose* is a possessive pronoun. *Who's ready for more popcorn? Whose coat is this?*

**will**   See *shall, will.*

**would of**   *Of* is not a verb. Write *would have. She would have* (not *would of*) *had a chance to play if she had arrived on time.*

**you**   In formal writing, avoid *you* in an indefinite sense meaning "anyone." See 3b. *Any spectator* (not *you*) *could tell by the way he caught the ball that his throw would be too late.*

**your, you're**   *Your* is a possessive pronoun; *you're* is a contraction of *you are. Is that your new motorcycle? You're on the list of finalists.*

# Answers to Lettered Exercises

## EXERCISE 8–1, page 59

Possible revisions:

a. After a couple of minutes went by, the teacher walked in smiling.
b. The secretary, deciding not to cooperate with Sue, sat all day and allowed her work to pile up.
c. Although Mary will graduate from high school in June, she has not yet decided on a college.
d. Some major companies exert an overwhelming influence on their employees by dictating where they must live, determining where their children should go to school, and deciding who their friends should be.
e. When we arrived at the Capital Center, to my dismay we had to pay $2.00 for parking.

## EXERCISE 8–2, page 62

Possible revisions:

a. This highly specialized medical training, called a "residency," usually takes four years to complete.
b. Lanie, who had polio at a young age, now walks with the help of braces.
c. When I presented the idea of job sharing to my supervisors, to my surprise they were delighted with the idea.

## EXERCISE 9–1, page 66

Possible revisions:

a. The board reported that their investments had done well in the first quarter but that they had since dropped in value.
b. The personnel officer told me that I would answer the phone, welcome visitors, distribute mail, and do some typing.
c. We couldn't decide whether to go to the concert or the movie.
d. The instructor taught us how to breathe and float. He (or she) also taught us the elementary backstroke, the crawl, and the dog paddle.

e. Nancy not only called the post office but checked with the neighbors to see if the package had come.

## EXERCISE 10–1, page 70

Possible revisions:

a. For many years Americans had trust in and affection for Walter Cronkite.
b. My brother's car was bigger than any of his friends' cars.
c. SETI (the Search for Extraterrestrial Intelligence) has excited and will continue to excite interest among space buffs.
d. Many people believe that the government is wasting money by monitoring outer space for signs of intelligent life.
e. The author uses the Sanchez family to provide an inside view of family life and to show what it means to grow up in a one-room apartment in Mexico City.

## EXERCISE 11–1, page 73

Possible revisions:

a. My instant reaction was anger and disappointment.
b. I first gave the books to the three who came in together.
c. People who are incapacitated or bedridden may have their meals delivered by a service known as "meals on wheels."
d. Being promoted without warning can be alarming.
e. Encouraging the players to excel may help them learn to overcome obstacles later in life.

## EXERCISE 12–1, page 76

Possible revisions:

a. Marie played almost the whole game, but she was taken out in the last ten minutes.
b. He wanted to buy only a single rose, not a dozen.
c. In the opinion of the press, our interest in the British royal family is sparked by royal weddings and births, but not by royal politics.
d. He promised at her deathbed never to remarry.
e. Each state would set into motion a program of recycling all reusable products.

## EXERCISE 12–2, page 78

Possible revisions:

a. By taking good care of myself, I avoided the flu and didn't miss a day of work this year.
b. To protest the arms buildup, demonstrators set bonfires throughout the park.
c. Feeling unprepared for the exam, she found the questions just as hard as she had expected them to be.

d. While still a beginner at tennis, the gifted young athlete was recruited for the Olympic team.

e. Commercials are especially irritating when I am watching my favorite series.

## EXERCISE 13–1, page 81

Possible revisions:

a. Before finally becoming fed up with the questions, she had answered the telephone survey for at least fifteen minutes.

b. Despite horrid weather, poor equipment, and long odds, the prospectors found gold.

c. Coming early in this century when evolutionary theory was in its infancy, the Piltdown Hoax had a profound effect on paleoanthropologists' thinking.

d. Jurors are encouraged to sift through the evidence carefully and thoroughly.

e. Dilapidated but lovely, with a gabled roof, a wide veranda, and a spreading oak in the back yard, the old house was a good buy.

## EXERCISE 14–1, page 85

Possible revisions:

a. One man collects the tickets and another searches the concert patrons for drugs.

b. Newspapers put the lurid details of an armed robbery on page 1 and relegate the warm, human interest stories to page G–10.

c. We waited in the emergency room for about an hour. Finally, the nurse came in and told us that we were in the wrong place.

d. We drove for eight hours until we reached the South Dakota Badlands. We could hardly believe the eeriness of the landscape at dusk.

e. The most successful weight-loss programs combine dieting with physical exercise. Dieters should not skip meals and expect to lose weight.

## EXERCISE 16–1, page 96

Possible revisions:

a. When visitors come, she just stares at the wall.

b. The colors of the reproductions were exact.

c. The race for the Democratic nomination is futile.

d. New Harmony, Indiana, was founded as a utopian community.

e. In Biology 10A a faculty tutor will assign you eight taped modules and clarify information on the tapes.

## EXERCISE 17–1, page 103

Possible revisions:

a. The military plans to destroy all vegetation with napalm.

b. Trips to exotic places are usual activities for the wealthy.

c. It is a widely held myth that middle-aged people can't change.

d. Please inform the publicity office of any newsworthy activities.
e. Dan's early work hours leave his afternoons free for errands and for helping the children with their homework.

## EXERCISE 18-3, page 113

a. I was so angry with the salesperson that I took his bag of samples and emptied it on the floor in front of him.
b. We plan to do the plastering a week from Tuesday.
c. Correct
d. "Your prejudice is no different from mine," she shouted.
e. The parade moved off the street and onto the beach as the tall ships sailed into the harbor.

## EXERCISE 18-4, page 114

Possible revisions:

a. He stormed into the room like a tornado.
b. Many of us are not persistent enough to make a change for the better.
c. When he heard about the accident, the color drained from his face.
d. Hours of long practice often make the difference between an excellent musician and a sloppy one.
e. I told him that he was taking a terrible risk when I heard that he intended to spy on the trustees' meeting.

## EXERCISE 19-1, page 119

Possible revisions:

a. My favorite athletes are those who combine exceptional physical talent with a tough mental attitude. I especially admire Larry Bird, Martina Navratilova, and Julius Erving.
b. While on a tour of Italy, Maria and Kathleen snuck away from their group to spend some quiet minutes with Leonardo da Vinci's *Last Supper,* a stunning fresco painted in the fifteenth century in a Milan monastery.
c. A tornado is a violent whirling wind that produces a funnel-shaped cloud and moves over land in a narrow path of destruction.
d. Correct
e. If the women of these desert tribes showed anger toward their husbands, they would be whipped in front of the whole village and shunned by the rest of the women.

## EXERCISE 20-1, page 124

Possible revisions:

a. The city had one public swimming pool that stayed packed with children all summer long.
b. Tom Baxter has been irritating me lately, so I avoid him when possible.
c. Why should we pay taxes to support public transportation? We prefer to save energy dollars by carpooling.
d. The kitchen was ordinarily the hub of activity; in the summer, though, it was nearly always empty.

## EXERCISE 20–2, page 125

Possible revisions:

a. Because the trail up Mount Finegold was declared impassable, we decided to return to our hotel a day early.
b. Correct
c. Last year's tomatoes, the best we'd ever grown, were plump, firm, and extraordinarily sweet.
d. Josie had all the equipment necessary for her first parachute jump; however, she forgot the required checklist and had to remain on the ground.

## EXERCISE 21–1, page 135

a. Subject: glass, verb: suits; b. Subject: gate and wall, verb: make; c. Subject: dangers, verb: are; d. Subject: Neither, verb: was; e. Subject: people, verb: are

## EXERCISE 21–2, page 135

a. Correct
b. Each of the furrows has been seeded.
c. At the back of the room are an aquarium and a terrarium.
d. Either Alice or Jan usually works the midnight shift.
e. Crystal chandeliers, polished floors, and a new oil painting have transformed Sandra's apartment.

## EXERCISE 22–1, page 140

Possible revisions:

a. Employees on extended leave may continue their life insurance.
b. Correct
c. The recruiter may tell the truth, but there is much that he or she chooses not to tell.
d. Parents who have been drinking or using drugs are more likely to abuse their children.
e. David lent his motorcycle to someone who allowed a friend to use it.

## EXERCISE 23–1, page 143

Possible revisions:

a. The detective removed the blood-stained shawl from the body and then photographed the body.
b. You should take advantage of the company's athletic facilities. The company offers squash and tennis courts, a small but adequate track, and several trampolines.
c. Abraham Lincoln was a man whose humble origins did not prevent him from rising to great prominence.
d. In her autobiography, Camilia revealed the story behind her short stay in prison.
e. The doctor told Jenny that she was worried about Jenny's mother's illness.

## EXERCISE 24–1, page 150

a. The most traumatic experience for her father and me occurred long after her operation.
b. Correct
c. The supervisor claimed that she was much more experienced than I.
d. At the drama festival, two actors, Christina and I, were selected to do the last scene of *King Lear.*
e. My father always tolerated our whispering after the lights were out.

## EXERCISE 25–1, page 153

a. Paula yelled that she would date whomever she wanted to date.
b. If asked who I think was the greatest American writer of the twentieth century, I would have difficulty choosing.
c. In his first production of *Hamlet,* whom did Laurence Olivier replace?
d. Correct
e. The elderly woman whom I was asked to take care of was a clever, delightful companion.

## EXERCISE 26–1, page 159

a. My mechanic showed me exactly where to wrap the wire firmly around the muffler.
b. I wanted the bike to be really safe in the truck.
c. Correct
d. My mother thinks that Carmen is the more pleasant of the twins.
e. Paula responded angrily, "That is the vilest joke I have ever heard."

## EXERCISE 27–1, page 163

a. Correct
b. Watson and Crick discovered the mechanism that controls inheritance in all life: the workings of the DNA molecule.
c. Marion would write more if she weren't distracted by a house full of children.

## EXERCISE 27–2, page 165

Possible revisions:

a. Parents do not use enough discretion in deciding which television programs their children may watch.
b. We noticed right away that the taxi driver had been exposed to Americans because he knew all the latest slang.
c. The members of the scout troop replaced the buttons, lengthened or shortened the hems, and cleaned and pressed all of the costumes.

## EXERCISE 28–1, page 172

a. Correct
b. Does he have enough energy to hold down two jobs while going to night school?

c. My days in this department have taught me to do what I'm told without question.

d. Our four older children play one or two instruments each.

e. Antoinette's skin is blotched and yellowish. She doesn't look at all healthy.

## EXERCISE 29–1, page 175

a. Correct

b. The troop had grown accustomed to expecting the worst.

c. That line of poetry can be expressed more dramatically.

d. Correct

e. How would you feel if your mother or a loved one had been a victim of a crime like this?

## EXERCISE 30–1, page 181

a. Last June my cousin Albert swam the length of the lake in forty minutes.

b. The police officer asked, "How did you know that your partner had gone to Trinidad?"

c. The team of engineers watched in horror as the newly built dam burst and flooded the small valley.

d. Correct

e. Correct

## EXERCISE 31–1, page 185

a. The pediatrician gave my daughter an injection for her allergy.

b. They skate swiftly, waving and dodging as they drive the pucks down the ice in the direction of the opposing team's goal.

c. Chris didn't know about Marlo's death because he never listens. He is always talking.

d. Though the meals are free, donations are accepted to help pay operational costs.

e. Correct

## EXERCISE 32–1, page 190

a. He pushed the car beyond the toll gate and dashed a bucket of water on the smoking hood.

b. The man at the next table complained loudly, and the waiter stomped off in disgust.

c. Correct

d. After I won the hundred-yard dash, I found a bench in the park and collapsed.

e. Knowing what she knows about the way nurses are treated in that hospital, she was brave to complain about Dr. Michaels.

## EXERCISE 32–2, page 193

a. She wore a black silk cape, a rhinestone collar, satin gloves, and army boots.

b. Correct

c. He was an impossible, demanding guest.
d. Juan walked through the room with casual, elegant grace.
e. Correct

## EXERCISE 32–3, page 198

a. He was a star in the circus, where six hundred people watched his triple somersault.
b. Ignoring several openings, Mary waited for a job with no overtime to become available.
c. Shakespeare's tragedy *King Lear* was given a splendid performance by the actor Laurence Olivier.
d. Correct
e. My youngest sister, who plays left wing on the team, now lives at The Sands, a beach house near Los Angeles.

## EXERCISE 32–4, page 202

a. Each morning this seventy-year-old woman cleans the barn, shovels manure, and spreads clean hay around the milking stalls.
b. Good technique does not guarantee, however, that the power you develop will be sufficient for Kyok Pa competition.
c. "The last flight," she said with a sigh, "went out five minutes before I arrived at the airport."
d. Correct
e. Correct

## EXERCISE 33–1, page 208

a. Don't sign up for Logic 101 unless you are prepared to change the way you think.
b. At last he was able to move his speakers, stereo, video cassette recorder, cameras, screens, and all the rest of his equipment into his own studio.
c. The man who escaped was the one we wanted.
d. Correct
e. He went out into the cold and hailed a cab.

## EXERCISE 34–1, page 212

a. The noise—the bass guitarist upstairs, the disco music downstairs, the wailing car alarm on the street, the garbage truck in the alley—was deafening; it's said that such noise raises the heart rate and the blood pressure.
b. Fashion advertising is big business; millions are spent every year in this country just on magazine ads.
c. Among the TV movies to choose from tonight are a spy thriller with Charles Bronson, who has a photographic memory; a screwball comedy with Clark Gable and Claudette Colbert, featuring the classic hitchhiking scene; and a sci-fi picture, dubbed from Japanese into English, with an oversized lizard and a giant gorilla.
d. We were very angry with the cousins for not telling us they were coming;

moreover, they stayed two weeks and never even helped with the dishes.
e.   We brought her the lumber scraps left over from the bookcase; we couldn't understand why she wanted them.

## EXERCISE 35–1, page 216

a.   Among the canceled classes were calculus, physics, advanced biology, and English 101.
b.   I entered this class feeling jittery and incapable; I leave feeling poised and confident.
c.   Correct, or: Veterans exposed to Agent Orange went to court to demand justice: justice for their wives, who suffered with the veterans in their illnesses; and justice for their children, who suffered damaging illnesses of their own.
d.   The second and most memorable week of survival school consisted of five stages: orientation, long treks, POW camp, escape and evasion, and return to civilization.
e.   In the introduction to his wife's book on gardening, E. B. White describes her writing process: "The editor in her fought the writer every inch of the way; the struggle was felt all through the house. She would write eight or ten words, then draw her gun and shoot them down."

## EXERCISE 36–1, page 220

a.   In a democracy anyone's vote counts as much as mine.
b.   Correct
c.   The puppy's favorite activity was chasing its tail.
d.   Correct
e.   A crocodile's life span is about thirteen years.

## EXERCISE 37–1, page 224

a.   "Fire and Ice" is one of Robert Frost's most famous poems.
b.   As Emerson said back in 1849, "I hate quotations. Tell me what you know."
c.   Joggers have to run up the hills and then back down, but bicyclers, once they reach the top of a hill, get a free ride back down.
d.   Joan was a self-proclaimed rabid Celtics fan; she went to every home game and even flew to L.A. for the play-offs.
e.   Despite our earlier argument, Debbie approached me after work and said, "How about a game of Ms. Pac-Man, John?"

## EXERCISE 39–1, page 231

a.   Of the three basic schools of detective fiction—the tea-and-crumpet, the hard-boiled detective, and the police procedural—I find the quaint, civilized quality of the tea-and-crumpet school the most appealing.
b.   The professional pool player needs to contend not only with abstract theories of math and physics but also with concrete details like the nap of the felt (usually running lengthwise) and the resiliency of the rails.
c.   Vin, an accomplished Eagle Scout, packed carefully for his camping trip,

remembering his sleeping bag, tent, mess kit, insect repellent—and custom-made marshmallow toaster.
d. *InfoWorld* reports that "customers without any particular aptitude for computers can easily learn to use it [the Bay Area Teleguide] through simple, three-step instructions located at the booth."
e. Pat helped Geoff put the tail on his kite, which was made of scraps from old dresses, and off they went to the park.

## EXERCISE 40–1, page 239

a. Marlon Mansard, a reporter for CBS, received a congressional citation for his work in Lebanon.
b. My grandmother told me that of all the subjects she studied, she found political science the most challenging.
c. Rev. Martin Luther King, Sr., spoke eloquently about his son's work against segregation in the South.
d. Julius Caesar was born in 100 B.C. and died in 44 B.C.
e. When she arrived in Poughkeepsie to work at IBM, Pauline was overwhelmed by the sophistication and variety of product prototypes.

## EXERCISE 41–1, page 241

a. The president of Forti Motor Company announced that all shifts would report back to work at the Augusta plant on Monday, June 6.
b. I didn't really notice any change in my life when I turned twenty-one.
c. The score was tied at 5 to 5 when the momentum shifted and carried the Standards to a swift and decisive 12 to 5 win.
d. Between 1970 and 1980 there was a 58% increase in the number of U.S. households headed by single mothers.
e. In 1984, only 1% of all male high school students planned to make a career of teaching.

## EXERCISE 42–1, page 245

a. I find it impossible to remember the second *l* in *llama*.
b. Howard Hughes commissioned the *Spruce Goose*, a beautifully built but thoroughly impractical wooden aircraft.
c. Coach Jones shouted, "Give us your best try and we'll go the distance!"
d. Bernard watched as Eileen stood transfixed in front of Vermeer's *Head of a Young Girl*.
e. I will never forget the way he whispered the word *finished*.

## EXERCISE 44–1, page 256

a. Correct
b. Many states are adopting laws that limit property taxes for homeowners.
c. Zola's first readers were scandalized by his slice-of-life novels.
d. Two-thirds of the House voted for the amendment.
e. Correct

## EXERCISE 45–1, page 261

a. District Attorney Johnson was disgusted when the jurors turned in a not guilty verdict after only one hour of deliberation.
b. *The World According to Garp* is a strange novel and an even stranger film.
c. Correct
d. Refugees from Central America are finding it more and more difficult to cross the Rio Grande into the United States.
e. I want to take Environmental Biology 103, one other biology course, and one English course.

## EXERCISE 47–1, page 267

a. Cat, gloves, mice; b. Repetition, lie, truth; c. flower, concrete (noun/adjective), cloverleaf; d. censorship, flick, dial; e. Figures, liars

## EXERCISE 47–2, page 270

a. your (pronoun/adjective), them; b. Nothing; c. I, some (pronoun/adjective), that, I, myself; d. who, his (pronoun/adjective); e. This (pronoun/adjective)

## EXERCISE 47–3, page 273

a. have been; b. can be savored; c. are, is; d. flock; e. Do scald

## EXERCISE 47–4, page 275

a. Adjectives: useless, necessary; b. Adjectives: The (article), American, tolerant; adverb: wonderfully; c. Adverbs: too, historically; d. Noun/adjective: work; e. Adjective: the (article); adverb: faster

## EXERCISE 48–1, page 281

a. Complete subject: A spoiled child; simple subject: child; b. Complete subject: all facts; simple subject: facts; c. (You); d. Complete subject: nothing; e. Complete subject: hope

## EXERCISE 48–2, page 284

a. is (linking); b. pounded (intransitive), responded (intransitive); c. can see (transitive); d. was reading (intransitive); e. is thriving (intransitive), looks (linking)

## EXERCISE 48–3, page 287

a. Direct object: a hundred fathers; subject complement: an orphan; b. Direct object: another; c. Direct objects: your door, your neighbors; object complement: honest; d. Direct object: Jack; object complement: a dull boy; e. Indirect object: her father; direct object: forty whacks

## EXERCISE 49–1, page 290

a. with no side effects (adjective phrase modifying *tranquilizer*); b. in three days (adverbial phrase modifying *smell*); c. of clear language (adjective phrase modifying *enemy*); d. in a graveyard (adverbial phrase modifying *begins*), in a river (adverbial phrase modifying *ends*); e. with words (adverbial phrase modifying *can stroke*)

## EXERCISE 49–2, page 293

a. Though you live near a forest (adverb clause modifying *do waste*)
b. who is praised by everyone (adjective clause modifying *person*)
c. What is whispered (noun clause used as subject of the sentence)
d. that trots (adjective clause modifying *dog*)
e. unless it is practiced on clever persons (adverb clause modifying *is*)

## EXERCISE 49–3, page 297

a. being sixteen (gerund phrase used as subject complement)
b. made in storms (participial phrase modifying *Vows*)
c. To help a friend (infinitive phrase used as subject of the sentence), to give ourselves pleasure (infinitive phrase used as subject complement)
d. bearing gifts (participial phrase modifying *Greeks*)
e. being dead (gerund phrase used as object of the preposition *by*)

## EXERCISE 50–1, page 301

a. complex; who always speaks the truth (adjective clause); b. compound; c. simple; d. complex; If you don't go to other people's funerals (adverb clause); e. complex; who sleep like a baby (adjective clause)

## EXERCISE 52–1, page 389

a. circular reasoning; b. false analogy; c. oversimplification; d. *post hoc*; e. hasty generalization

# *Index*

## CORRECTION SYMBOLS

*Boldface numbers refer to sections of the handbook.*

| | |
|---|---|
| abbr | faulty abbreviation **40** |
| ad | misuse of adverb or adjective **26** |
| agr | faulty agreement **21, 22** |
| appr | inappropriate language **17** |
| awk | awkward |
| cap | capital letter **45** |
| case | error in case **24, 25** |
| coh | coherence **7** |
| coord | faulty coordination **8b** |
| cs | comma splice **20** |
| dev | inadequate development **2b, 6a** |
| dm | dangling modifier **12c** |
| -ed | error in -ed ending **29** |
| exact | inexact language **18** |
| frag | sentence fragment **19** |
| fs | fused sentence **20** |
| gl/us | see glossary of usage |
| gr | grammar **47–50** |
| hyph | error in use of hyphen **44** |
| inc | incomplete construction **10** |
| irreg | error in irregular verb **30** |
| ital | italics (underlining) **42** |
| lc | use lowercase letter **45** |
| log | faulty logic **52** |
| mixed | mixed construction **11** |
| mm | misplaced modifier **12a–b** |
| mood | error in mood **27d–e** |
| ms | error in manuscript form **46** |
| nonst | nonstandard usage **28–31** |
| num | error in use of numbers **41** |
| om | omitted word **10, 31a** |

| | | |
|---|---|---|
| p | | error in punctuation |
| | ⌃ | comma **32** |
| | no , | no comma **33** |
| | ; | semicolon **34** |
| | : | colon **35** |
| | ⌄ | apostrophe **36** |
| | " " | quotation marks **37** |
| | . ? ! | period, question mark, exclamation point **38** |
| | – ( ) | dash, parentheses, |
| | [ ] . . . | brackets, ellipsis **39** |
| par, ¶ | | new paragraph **5–7** |
| pass | | ineffective passive **27f** |
| plan | | faulty planning **1** |
| ref | | error in pronoun reference **23** |
| rev | | revise **3, 4** |
| -s | | error in -s ending **28, 31b** |
| sep | | awkward separation of words **13** |
| shift | | distracting shift **14** |
| sp | | misspelled word **43** |
| sub | | faulty subordination **8c–d** |
| t | | error in verb tense **27a–c, 47c** |
| trans | | transition needed **7c** |
| v | | voice **27f** |
| var | | lack of variety in sentence structure **15** |
| vb | | error in verb form **27, 47c, 48b** |
| w | | wordy **16** |
| // | | faulty parallelism **9** |
| ⌃ | | insert |
| X | | obvious error |
| # | | insert space |
| ⌣ | | close up space |